Metamorphoses of the Werewolf

Also of Interest

Guillaume de Palerne: An English Translation of the 12th Century French Verse Romance,
translated and edited by Leslie A. Sconduto (McFarland, 2004)

Metamorphoses of the Werewolf

A Literary Study from Antiquity through the Renaissance

Leslie A. Sconduto

McFarland & Company, Inc., Publishers
Jefferson, North Carolina, and London

LIBRARY OF CONGRESS CATALOGUING-IN-PUBLICATION DATA

Sconduto, Leslie A., 1950–
Metamorphoses of the werewolf : a literary study from antiquity through the Renaissance / Leslie A. Sconduto.
p. cm.
Includes bibliographical references and index.

ISBN 978-0-7864-3559-3
softcover : 50# alkaline paper 

1. Werewolves in literature. 2. Werewolves — Religious aspects — Catholic Church. I. Title.
PN56.W45S36 2008
398.24'54 — dc22 2008032727

British Library cataloguing data are available

Manufactured in the United States of America

McFarland & Company, Inc., Publishers
Box 611, Jefferson, North Carolina 28640
www.mcfarlandpub.com

For Eugene,
who will always be my romance hero

Contents

Introduction 1

ONE The Werewolf in Antiquity 7

TWO The Church's Response to the Werewolf 15

THREE The Werewolves of Ossory and Other Medieval Wonder Tales and Marvels 26

FOUR *Bisclavret* or a Lesson in Loyalty 39

FIVE *Melion* or a Lesson About Pride 57

SIX *Arthur and Gorlagon* or a Lesson for an Adulteress 76

SEVEN *Guillaume de Palerne* or a Lesson in Noble Sacrifice 90

EIGHT A New Renaissance for the Wicked Werewolf 127

NINE Explanations or "Que cele beste senefie" 180

Notes 201

Bibliography 211

Index 217

Introduction

Lurking at the edges of our imagination, in the darkened corners of our childish nightmares and in the shadowy forests that border our towns and villages, the figure of the werewolf in popular culture still conjures up frightening images of violence and bestiality. The Oxford English Dictionary defines a werewolf as "a person who (according to mediaeval superstition) was transformed or was capable of transforming himself at times into a wolf." The first known use of "werewolf," a word of Anglo-Saxon origin, appeared in the Ecclesiastical Ordinances of King Cnut, c. A.D. 1000, as a synonym for the Devil.[1] In spite of what the Oxford English Dictionary suggests, belief in werewolves was not a new phenomenon in the Middle Ages; a reference to a werewolf can be found in the *Epic of Gilgamesh*, which was written approximately seventeen hundred years before the birth of Christ. The Greeks had their own term; they called a werewolf a "vrykolakas," while the Romans used the term "versipellis," which literally meant "turn-skin." During the first century of the Christian era, numerous legends and stories of the metamorphosis of men into wolves circulated, providing evidence of an early and persistent belief in werewolves. With few exceptions, these tales consistently portray the werewolf as a savage beast that lurks in the dark and preys on the helpless. Over the next one thousand years, references to werewolves appear primarily in patristic writings that attack these legends and consider them evidence of credence in pagan superstitions. It is only in the latter half of the twelfth century that literary accounts of the werewolf reappear. But the twelfth-century werewolf is not the "same old" werewolf from antiquity, the one we're supposed to fear — medieval literature suddenly depicts the creature sympathetically as a victim and a hero, rather than as the perpetrator of violent and bloodthirsty deeds. This change in the image of the werewolf corresponds to a growing interest in the man-beast, what Caroline Walker Bynum calls "the werewolf renaissance of the twelfth century" (94). This interest is reflected in the reappearance of literary narratives that involve a werewolf. How do we account for this "renaissance" and how can we explain this radical departure from the traditional portrayal of the werewolf? The sixteenth century, on the other hand, will experience an entirely different kind of renaissance from the one with which it is normally associated, a renaissance that will not manifest itself in a rebirth of culture but rather in a revival of the traditional werewolf of antiquity. Unlike his twelfth-century ancestor, this werewolf that has been reincarnated from antiquity will make his appearance, not in courtly literature, but in court as a real person, for the most part a rough, dirty, peasant who steps forward and claims to be a werewolf that has committed the foulest of deeds. How do we account for these two very different "renaissances"? How can we explain the radical departure from the traditional portrayal of the werewolf in the twelfth century and then the revival of the traditional werewolf in the sixteenth? To solve these mysteries and to understand the different metamorphoses of the werewolf across time, we must first understand the tradition in which they participate. And so our study will need to go back to the beginnings, to those first stories.

Chapter One, "The Werewolf in Antiquity," looks at the first reference to a werewolf that appears in *The Epic of Gilgamesh* and then introduces and analyzes some of the oldest tales of werewolves. Written from about 37 B.C. to A.D. 116 these short narratives include Virgil's story of Moeris who transforms himself into a wolf, Ovid's tale of King Lycaon who is transformed into a wolf by Zeus, Petronius' anecdote of the metamorphosis of a soldier into a wolf, and Pliny the Elder's accounts of Greek legends about werewolves. Together they create the literary context from which emerges the popular image of the werewolf feared by so many. Chapter One also reviews the process of metamorphosis itself and discusses the usefulness and difficulty of categorizing werewolves.

Chapter Two, "The Church's Response to the Werewolf," examines how the Church reacts to the popular representation of the werewolf. Seen as remnants of pagan beliefs and practices, the legends inherited from antiquity threaten Christian notions of divinity, creation, and salvation. As a result they prompt a new interpretation of the general phenomenon of metamorphosis. The chapter begins by discussing briefly the writings of the Christian convert Tertullian (c. A.D. 155–220), as well as those of Saint Ambrose (A.D. 339–397). Both men write that it is impossible for human souls to enter the bodies of animals. The chapter then continues with an analysis of the fifth-century apologetic writings of Saint Augustine, who offers a theological interpretation of the metamorphosis of human beings into wolves and other animals that directly opposes popular opinion. While popular accounts stress the reality of the werewolf, he insists on its illusory nature. According to Augustine, only God can change matter; the Devil merely deceives man's senses. The chapter concludes with an overview of the writings of medieval theologians such as Regino, Burchard of Worms, William of Malmesbury, Guillaume d'Auvergne, and Saint Thomas Aquinas, who either support Augustine's theory of metamorphosis or condemn those who believe in werewolves as infidels.

Chapter Three, "The Werewolves of Ossory and Other Medieval Wonder Tales and Marvels," begins by analyzing a historical anecdote related by Gerald of Wales in *Topographia Hibernica* (*Topography of Ireland*), a twelfth-century treatise on the geography and folklore of Ireland. In Gerald's tale, a priest encounters a werewolf who asks him to administer last rites to his wife, who is also a werewolf. Unique for its talking werewolf and for its revelation of a human body beneath the skin of the wolf, this tale also incorporates Gerald's discussion of the theological implications of the event. Although he insists on the veracity of his account, Gerald also argues that the tale remains faithful to the teachings of the Church because it illustrates one type of divine metamorphosis. The chapter then looks at other accounts of Irish werewolves, one appearing in *Konungs Skuggsjá* (*King's Mirror*), a thirteenth-century Norse work, as well as several versions of another account in Latin and in Irish. The chapter also reviews two accounts of French werewolves that appear in Gervase of Tilbury's *Otia Imperialia* (*Recreation for an Emperor*). The popular and clerical views of metamorphosis are equally represented in all the wonder tales and marvels examined in this chapter, thus demonstrating that both traditions from which the medieval werewolf literary narratives will emerge are continuing to thrive.

Chapter Four, "*Bisclavret* or a Lesson in Loyalty," Chapter Five, "*Melion* or a Lesson About Pride," and Chapter Six, "*Arthur and Gorlagon* or a Lesson for an Adulteress," consider three short narratives of the twelfth and thirteenth centuries which scholars have said make up the corpus of *The Werewolf's Tale*. Radically transforming the traditional image of the werewolf, all three texts portray the creature sympathetically as a victim and as a hero. Written against the popular image of the werewolf, they reflect the Christian interpretation of metamorphosis with their insistence on the opposition between appearance and reality. *Bisclavret* relates the story of a knight who becomes a werewolf three days every week. He is trapped in his wolf form after his wife learns about her husband's "second" nature, steals his clothes, and then marries the knight who helps her betray her husband. *Melion* tells of another husband who is betrayed by his wife. He transforms himself into a werewolf to kill a stag for his wife to eat, but while he is doing so, she runs away, taking with her his squire and the magic ring that would allow him to become a man again. *Arthur and Gorlagon*, a frame story whose narrator is none other than the werewolf who has recovered his human identity, recounts the tale of how he, too, is betrayed by his wife; this time the agent of transformation is a magic sapling. Philippe Ménard has identified three motifs that these narratives have in common: the gentleness of the werewolf; the treacherous woman, and the beast's inability to regain his human form (222). Chapters Four, Five, and Six will analyze four additional motifs that are shared by all three texts: the noble werewolf who is both hero and victim, the submission scene, the king-protector who discerns the humanity of the beast, and the werewolf's sudden violent behavior that prompts inquiries into his true nature and identity. In spite of their similarities, each tale is unique; close readings of all three reveal the subtle differences between each version of *The Werewolf's Tale.* Each narrative varies in the manner in which it plays with the tension between the human and bestial sides of the werewolf. In addition, each author uses the figure of the werewolf to convey a different message.

Chapter Seven, "*Guillaume de Palerne* or a Lesson in Noble Sacrifice," studies the werewolf motif in a remarkable adventure romance of the late twelfth century. *Guillaume de Palerne* tells the story of a young prince of Sicily who is kidnapped by a werewolf at the age of four. Woven into the story of the eponymous hero is the parallel story of Alphonse, the Spanish prince who was transformed into a werewolf by his stepmother while still a toddler. It is my contention that *Guillaume de Palerne* belongs to the corpus of *The Werewolf's Tale*, but has been overlooked, primarily because of over-reliance on the work of scholars who have either studied the romance too hastily or have defined their motifs too narrowly. Critics studying *The Werewolf's Tale* are understandably reluctant to deal with a narrative of *Guillaume de Palerne*'s length: 9667 verses as opposed to 318 in *Bisclavret* and 219 in *Melion*. Nevertheless, the romance not only participates in the same tradition as other versions of *The Werewolf's Tale*, but also provides its fullest treatment and represents an important reworking of the traditional motifs. Indeed, with Alphonse we see that the werewolf has undergone a total metamorphosis; no vestige remains of the bloodthirsty beast. He has been replaced by a self-sacrificing chivalrous hero.

Chapter Eight, "A New Renaissance for the Wicked Werewolf," analyzes eight sixteenth-century texts that either offer theoretical positions regarding the issue of the werewolf or discuss actual werewolf court cases. Because the history of werewolves in the sixteenth century is intertwined with that of witches, most of the texts deal primarily with sorcery. Whereas the writings of medieval theologians condemn as infidels those who believe in werewolves, the majority of sixteenth-century writings on sorcery and lycanthropy stress the reality of witches and metamorphosis and label as heretics those who do not believe that they exist. The texts analyzed include Heinrich Kramer's *Malleus maleficarum* (*The Witches Hammer*), Johann Weyer's *De Praestigiis Daemonum* (*Witches, Devils, and Doctors*), Jean Bodin's *De la démonomanie des sorciers* (*Demonomania of Witches*), Reginald Scot's *The Discoverie of Witchcraft*, Claude Prieur's *Dialogue de la Lycanthropie* (*Dialogue of Lycanthropy*), King James I's *Daemonologie*, Beauvoys de Chauvincourt's *Discours de la lycantropie* [sic] (*Treatise on Lycanthropy*), Henri Boguet's *Discours des sorciers* (*An Examen of Witches*), and Pierre de Lancre's *Tableau de l'inconstance des mauvais anges et demons* (*On the Inconstancy of Witches*). The chapter concludes with a brief review of the sixteenth-century prose versions of *Guillaume de Palerne*.

Chapter Nine, "Explanations or 'Que cele beste senefie,'" argues that there is not just one explanation for the werewolf "renaissance" of the twelfth century and the new portrayal of the creature, but rather a combination of factors: the twelfth century's fascination with the constancy and changeability of identity, the Church's doctrine of metamorphosis as an illusion, as well as its insistence on the rational nature of human beings, the appropriation of the marvelous in courtly romance, the usefulness of the werewolf as an ironic metaphor to warn against facile interpretation, and finally the cultural trauma resulting from an incident of cannibalism during the First Crusade. Similarly, the chapter proposes that several factors or conditions came together to create the new renaissance of the traditional werewolf in the sixteenth century: the persecution of witches combined with the belief in the reality of witches and their ability to transform themselves, the wars of religion and related violence, economic conditions in France, which led to some cases of cannibalism, and a renewed focus on the Eucharist.

So, why another book on werewolves? This is the first academic study to trace the literary history of werewolves from antiquity through the sixteenth century that includes *Guillaume de Palerne*, which is perhaps the most important werewolf text of the Middle Ages. Furthermore, this is also the only study that includes a full literary analysis of each of the four major werewolf narratives, *Bisclavret, Melion, Arthur and Gorlagon,* and *Guillaume de Palerne*. It is also the only academic study that includes a systematic analysis of all the major texts of the sixteenth century. To my knowledge, it is also the only one that includes an analysis of Claude Prieur's *Dialogue de la Lycanthropie* (*Dialogue of Lycanthropy*). Quotations from texts have been provided in English[2] and in the original language, when available, in order that serious scholars will have access to both. Since appearances can be unreliable and clues can be missed, it is only through the technique of close reading and careful interpretation that a good understanding of each text can be reached.

Chapter One

The Werewolf in Antiquity

Through the mists of time, we catch fleeting glimpses of the first werewolves, as if they were illuminated only momentarily by the light of a full moon partially obscured by clouds on a carefully constructed Hollywood sound stage. It is of course not the purpose of this study to trace the history of the werewolf through its metamorphoses in modern films. Indeed, we need to look backward rather than forward, for the monster that comes to mind when most people hear the word "werewolf" calls up old fears and images that originated almost four thousand years ago. The earliest reference to a man being transformed into a wolf appeared in the Akkadian *Epic of Gilgamesh*, a collection of mythic tales which circulated in the region of southern Mesopotamia. They were recorded by the poet Sin-leqe-unninni on clay tablets approximately seventeen hundred years before the birth of Christ.[1] In one of the tales, Ishtar, the goddess of love, is attempting to seduce King Gilgamesh. Spurning her offer, Gilgamesh replies with a long list of her former lovers and the fate they received at her hands, including the shepherd that she transformed into a wolf:

> You loved a shepherd, a herdsman,
> who endlessly put up cakes for you,
> and every day slaughtered kids for you.
> You struck him, turned him into a wolf.
> His own boys drove him away,
> and his dogs tore his hide to bits.[2]

In Greek mythology, Actaeon is killed by his own dogs after he is turned into a stag by the goddess Diana because he has seen her naked. Ishtar's unfortunate shepherd, now a wolf, suffers the same fate. But Sin-leqe-unninni does not linger on him; the shepherd is just one among Ishtar's many discarded and ill-treated lovers. So we do not learn whether the shepherd retains awareness of his humanity after his metamorphosis, as does the hapless Actaeon:

> The once heroic son of Autonoe
> Ran as he wondered by what miracle
> He had become so swift with terror — but when
> He saw himself, his face, his branching antlers
> In a stream he longed to say, "O miser-
> Able me!" but had no words, nothing but
> Animal cries while tears ran down his changed,
> Bewildered face. Only his mind remained
> What it had been [Ovid, 90–91].

In Ovid's retelling of the Greek myth in *The Metamorphoses*, his focus and purpose are of course different, as evidenced by the title of his work; in each instance, he calls the reader's attention to the metamorphosis itself and its affect on the person transformed, whereas in *Gilgamesh*, the transformation is just one minor detail in the narration of the story. Nevertheless, the similarities between the two tales cause us to speculate: was Ovid's story of Actaeon inspired by Ishtar's unnamed shepherd and did the latter also know what was happening to him? We will never know the answer to either question. What we can say with certainty, however, is that the shepherd in *Gilgamesh* is not merely the first literary werewolf, he is also the first to become a werewolf as the victim of a wicked woman. Here perhaps we find the tantalizing origin of a motif that will not reappear for almost three thousand years.

We get our next brief glimpse of a werewolf in Virgil's eighth *eclogue*, which he wrote in about 37 B.C. In this pastoral poem, a shepherd sings of Amaryllis using magical charms to bring back her lover Daphnis:

> These herbs and these poisons, culled in Pontus, Moeris himself gave me — they grow plenteously in Pontus. By their aid I have oft seen Moeris turn wolf and hide in the woods, oft call spirits from the depth of the grave, and charm sown corn away to other fields.[3]

Moeris is a powerful magician who draws on his knowledge of herbs and poisons to summon ghosts from the grave. Since he is able to transport corn we can imagine whole cornfields suddenly disappearing and reappearing in another location or even flying through the air. But Moeris is not only a magician, he is also a werewolf. Unlike Ishtar's shepherd, however, Moeris chooses to transform himself into a wolf with his herbs and poisons and the change is only temporary. In Virgil's poem he seems remarkably harmless as a werewolf, especially compared to his portrayal as a magician. Since hiding in the woods is such benign, passive behavior, certainly not the behavior one normally expects from a ferocious wolf, and since this behavior contrasts strikingly with the activity of Moeris the magician, the reader might wonder why

Moeris deliberately transforms himself into a wolf, if it is simply to hide in the forest. Adam Douglas has pointed out that because Moeris "merely hides in the woods" and uses his magical powers to help others, he is a sympathetic character within this poem (70). I would argue instead, however, that Virgil uses the werewolf's passive behavior to accentuate his double nature, not to show how nice he is. Thus in this poem Virgil has created the first werewolf with a dual personality, although surprisingly it is Moeris the magician and not Moeris the werewolf who should be feared. Yes, Moeris the magician might help his friends, but there is a vortex of violence around him, absent in Virgil's depiction of the werewolf, that could eventually pull even his friends in. The negative words "poisons," "spirits," and "grave" reinforce the sense of dread that one feels reading this portion of the *eclogue*. Moeris the "sympathetic" werewolf is inextricably linked to Moeris the magician; although he may have done no wrong as a werewolf, the overall impression that Moeris the magician/werewolf leaves is unsettling. He is therefore important in creating the context from which the traditional werewolf will emerge.

Forty-five years later, just before being banished from Rome for the rest of his life by Emperor Augustus in A.D. 8, Ovid finished *The Metamorphoses*. At the beginning of Book I, Ovid describes the creation of the world and its different ages. During the age of gold, people live in peace with one another, but during each succeeding age they become increasingly warlike and corrupt. It is during the age of iron, when men stop fearing Zeus,[4] that Ovid situates his first metamorphosis. King Lycaon of Arcadia doubts Zeus' divinity and serves him human flesh in an attempt to prove that the god is mortal.[5] According to Leonard Barkan, Lycaon's offering is an act of defiance that deliberately blurs the distinction between sacrifice and cannibalism (27). As Zeus tells his council of lesser gods:

> "The proof was simple. When I had feasted
> (So he had planned) and heavily asleep,
> Lifted to bed, he hoped to murder me.
> Nor was this scheme enough; he took a Northern
> Hostage from a cell, slit the poor devilish
> Monster's throat and tossed his warm and bleeding
> Vitals in a pot; the rest he roasted.
> This was the dinner that he put before me" [37].

If Zeus truly had been a mere mortal, he would have eaten the meal served to him by Lycaon and would have unwittingly participated in cannibalism. But of course he is saved from it by his divinity and he punishes Lycaon immediately. In the following passage we find perhaps the fullest physical description of a werewolf and the moment of his metamorphosis available, outside of those found in modern literature:

> "My thunderbolt struck the king's house to ruins,
> And he, wild master, ran like beast to field
> Crying his terror which cannot utter words
> But howls in fear, his foaming lips and jaws,
> Quick with the thought of blood, harry the sheep.
> His cloak turned into bristling hair, his arms
> Were forelegs of a wolf, yet he resembled
> Himself, what he had been — the violent
> Grey hair, face, eyes, the ceaseless, restless stare
> Of drunken tyranny and hopeless hate" [37].

Here we can almost see Lycaon. Moreover, we can almost see his transformation into a wolf as Ovid depicts the actual process, the becoming, of metamorphosis.[6] As Barkan points out in his close reading of the original Latin text, Ovid emphasizes the continuity of Lycaon's character. Lycaon was "intrinsically rabid and wolflike from the start" and he remains so when he is truly a wolf (25). Thus, the change that Ovid describes is not temporary, but represents instead a final evolution, a deepening of what already was, since Lycaon's appearance now matches his true character, "...yet he resembled / Himself, what he had been." He has become what he really was all along. As Simone Viarre notes in her study of Ovid's *Metamorphoses*:

> Le châtiment ovidien contraint l'être à devenir intensément ce qu'il est, à réaliser complètement et pour toujours une tendance qui s'est manifestée partiellement dans son existence humaine. Devenu loup, Lycaon n'est plus que haine et cruauté [360].
>
> Ovidien punishment constrains the being to become intensely what he is, to fulfill completely and forever a tendency which manifested itself partially in his human existence. After becoming a wolf, there is nothing left in Lycaon except hatred and cruelty.

Lycaon has crossed the boundary between the human and animal kingdoms, never to return. He is now a wolf. Lycaon will have to hunt down and eat animals or even human beings in order to survive; in either case he has been condemned to the same cannibalism he tried to inflict on Zeus. Yet in Lycaon's last moment of human consciousness, when he tries to speak but cannot, another Lycaon briefly appears, not the cruel tyrant, but a frightened victim "crying his terror," someone for whom we can almost feel some measure of compassion. His offense is so great and his character is so disturbing, however, that any compassion the reader might feel is only fleeting. As with all Ovidian metamorphoses, Lycaon's metamorphosis is permanent, leaving him no possibility for redemption. With Ovid's tale, we are now much closer to the traditional image of the werewolf as a blood-thirsty beast.

Sometime between A.D. 54 and 68 during the reign of Nero, Petronius, proconsul of Bithynia and Nero's Arbiter of Elegance, wrote the *Satyricon*, a loosely structured satirical novel that alternates between sophisticated displays of rhetoric and obscenities.[7] In one of its largest and most famous fragments, Trimalchio's dinner party, Petronius includes the account of a werewolf.[8] Niceros, one of the guests at the banquet, states that while still a slave he had witnessed the metamorphosis of a soldier into a wolf. According to the freedman, he was on his way to visit his lady friend one moonlit night when the soldier who had been accompanying him went into the cemetery, removed his clothing, urinated around them, then turned into a wolf and ran off howling into the woods. When Niceros tried to pick up the fellow's clothes, he discovered that they had been turned into stone. His lady friend later told him that one of the slaves had stabbed the throat of a wolf after it had attacked their sheep. Upon his return home the following morning, Niceros found the soldier in bed with a neck wound. This injury, which shows continuity between the bestial and human life and permits the identification of the werewolf, is an important motif in folklore.[9] Even though Niceros had actually seen the soldier transform himself into a wolf, it is only when he finds the soldier in bed being treated by a doctor for his neck wound that he is convinced: "I realized that he was a werewolf, and I could never sit down to a meal with him afterwards, not if you had killed me first" (139; sec. 62). Throughout his tale, Niceros emphasizes his fear. When he sees the soldier remove his clothing and urinate around them, he says that "[his] heart was in [his] mouth" and that "[he] stood like a dead man" (137; sec. 62). But Niceros' fear becomes much more pronounced with his reaction to the soldier's metamorphosis: "No one could be nearer dead with terror than I was. But I drew my sword and went slaying shadows all the way till I came to my love's house. I went in — a mere ghost and nearly bubbled out my life; the sweat ran down my legs, my eyes were dull, I could hardly be revived" (137; sec.62). Although he is almost frightened to death, Niceros insists on the veracity of his account. When he relates how the soldier turned into a wolf, he stops for a moment to interject this comment: "Please do not think I am joking; I would not lie about this for any fortune in the world." At the end of his story, he tells Trimalchio and his guests: "Other people may think what they like about this; but may all your guardian angels punish me if I am lying" (139; sec. 62). Rather than laugh at him or accuse him of lying, as he had expected, everyone believes him and is frightened by the story. Within the context of the banquet in which one outrageous event follows another, however, and considering the comic-satirical nature of the *Satyricon*, it is difficult for the modern reader to take Nicero's report seriously. Nevertheless, the inclusion of the werewolf tale in this popular literary text demonstrates the interest of the public in the motif. Moreover, Niceros' tale is important because it not only presents the first literary portrayal of a bloodthirsty werewolf, but also offers the first literary representation of an eyewitness account of the metamorphosis of a werewolf and that person's fearful response to the phenomenon. It thus adds an essential component to our understanding of the creation of the tradition.

Pliny the Elder (A.D. 23–79), a contemporary of Petronius, presents a more scholarly approach to werewolves in his *Historia Naturalis*. Interestingly, he does not describe at length the physical characteristics of the wolf, as he does with other species, but devotes all but one sentence of his article to a discussion of werewolf superstitions and legends. He precedes these stories with an announcement that they are untrue:

> We are bound to pronounce with confidence that the story of men being turned into wolves and restored to themselves again is false — or else we must believe all the tales that the experience of so many centuries has taught us to be fabulous; nevertheless we will indicate the origin of the popular belief, which is so firmly rooted that it classes werewolves among persons under a curse [59; VIII.34.80].

According to one of the legends, which he tells us was originally recorded by the Greek writer Evanthes, a member of the Anthus clan in Arcadia would be chosen by lots to become a werewolf. After removing his clothes and swimming across a marsh, the man would be transformed into a wolf and would remain in that condition for nine years. If he abstained from eating human flesh during that time, then he would swim back across the marsh and recover his human form. He would, however, look nine years older. Pliny not only does not believe the account, but uses it to reveal his opinion of the Greeks: "It is astounding to what lengths Greek credulity will go; there is no lie so shameless as to lack a supporter" (61; VIII.34.82). He follows that comment with the story of another werewolf, one that was recorded by Apollas, the author of *Olympic Victors*. According to Apollas, Daemenetus of Parrhasia turned into a wolf after tasting the entrails of a boy that had been sacrificed to the Lykaian Zeus. Ten years later he changed back into his human form, trained as a boxer, and won at the Olympics.[10] The cannibalism taboo common to these two tales is significant, bringing to mind Ovid's tale of King Lycaon. Men who break the taboo are either transformed into a werewolf or are forced to remain a werewolf as punishment. All three tales also provide evidence of a strong belief in werewolves in Arcadia, as Douglas has noted (59).[11] Pliny makes no further comments about werewolves, but instead concludes his discussion by listing popular beliefs about wolves.[12]

As we have seen thus far, many authors provide few or no details about how a man becomes a werewolf. Where details are provided, there are almost as many similarities as there are differences: clothes are removed, magic and charms are used, a body of water must be crossed or not. In the Middle Ages, this list will grow longer. We have also seen that there are basically two types of werewolves: those who are werewolves by choice—what Kirby Smith termed the "voluntary" or "constitutional" werewolf (5)—and those whose metamorphosis is imposed on them by someone else or by some outside force—what Smith called the "involuntary" werewolf (5). Lycaon and Ishtar's unfortunate shepherd fall into this second group, as neither of them choose to transform themselves into wolves, whereas Moeris and the soldier who accompanied Niceros belong to the first, since they are able to freely transform themselves into werewolves and then regain their human forms at any time. The term "constitutional" is troublesome, however, since it implies that the werewolf condition is inherent in the physical makeup of these werewolves, yet Moeris resorts to magic and herbs in order to bring about his metamorphosis. Philippe Ménard elaborated on Smith's distinction between voluntary and involuntary werewolves, noting that false werewolves, victims of an enchantment and subject to a single metamorphosis, retain some measure of their humanity; authentic or cyclical werewolves voluntarily subject themselves to repeated transformations in order to satisfy their bestial instincts. But these early werewolves, as well as their medieval successors, resist our attempts to classify them, for it is truly impossible to determine whether or not the soldier in Niceros' story is compelled somehow to transform into a werewolf or whether it is his desire to do so. As Francis Dubost notes, "on ne peut savoir si [la métamorphose] est volontaire ou non car on n'a jamais accès aux pensées du soldat" 'we can never know if the metamorphosis is voluntary or not for we never have access to the soldier's thoughts' (541). We could say the same thing about any of the later so-called "authentic" (541) werewolves.[13] To complicate matters, Bisclavret, one of the medieval werewolves that we will study in a later chapter, should be considered an "authentic" werewolf according to Ménard's classification, since he subjects himself to cyclical metamorphoses. However, like the false werewolves, Bisclavret also retains some human qualities while he is in his werewolf form. One could even argue that Lycaon is a voluntary werewolf, since his involuntary metamorphosis merely reveals his true character. According to Ménard, the metamorphosis itself is more important than anything else that happens:

> Pour dresser une typologie des récits de loup-garou, il faut se fonder essentiellement sur les causes et les conditions de la métamorphose. C'est, en effet, ce moment capital qui donne tout son sens à l'histoire, car le reste est secondaire et intéresse moins les auteurs [213].
>
> A typology of werewolf stories must be based mainly on the causes and conditions of the metamorphosis. It is, indeed, this important moment which

> gives the story its meaning, for all the rest is secondary and interests the authors less.

It is safe to say that Ménard finds "the rest of the story" uninteresting; whether or not the authors themselves did or not is harder to determine. Although the details of each transformation do add interest to their stories, most do not really tell us anything about the werewolf.[14] Moreover, the real usefulness of any typology itself is debatable. Of greater concern are the character and the activity of the man-beast after he has undergone his metamorphosis, whether it is cyclical or unique. Throughout this study, then, we will be focusing instead on the werewolf's humanity, which is expressed through his behavior.[15]

Chapter Two

The Church's Response to the Werewolf

Seen as remnants of pagan beliefs and practices, the werewolf legends inherited from antiquity threatened Christian notions of divinity, creation, and salvation. As a result they prompted a new interpretation of the general phenomenon of metamorphosis that directly opposes popular opinion. Less than a century after Pliny wrote *Historia Naturalis*, Quintus Septimius Florens Tertullianus (c. A.D. 155–220) was born in Carthage, the son of a Roman centurion. Although his family adhered to the polytheistic pagan religion of the Roman state, Tertullian later converted to Christianity while in Rome. After his return to Carthage, he became an apologist for the Church, using his classical education and writing skills to attack pagans, heretics, and defend the Christian faith that was still being severely persecuted. In his treatise *On the Soul* (*De anima*),[1] Tertullian systematically argues against the possibly that some men become animals during the process of reincarnation. He begins by stating that "it is impossible for the human soul to pass into beasts, even though the philosophers may hold that both are made up of the same substantial elements" (253). After discussing the characteristics and needs of different animals, as well as those of the human soul, Tertullian reasons that the "soul is clearly incapable of adapting itself to the bodies of animals and their natural characteristics" (255) and that if the soul changes and becomes something totally different, "this so-called metensomatosis [reincarnation] is nonsense" (255). Finally, after noting that he is "still looking for some good reason for this alleged transformation" (255), Tertullian declares that a substance cannot be equated with its nature. The nature of a substance is not necessarily unique; for example, rocks and iron are both hard. They share the same nature, that of hardness. But their substances are different. Tertullian concludes with the following example:

> So, though we may call a man a wild beast or a harmless one, we don't mean that he has the soul of a beast. Similarity of nature is clearest when there is the greatest dissimilarity of substance. By the very fact that you consider a man to be like a beast you admit that the souls are different; note that you say "similar" and not "identical" [256].

So, men can be *like* beasts but they cannot *be* beasts because their substances, their souls, are different. As the first Latin apologist for the Church, Tertullian doesn't mince words and his argument is very clear and methodical. Souls cannot change and metamorphosis is impossible.

Approximately one hundred and fifty years later, Saint Ambrose (A.D. 339–397), bishop of Milan and moral theologian and writer, comes to a similar conclusion. In A.D. 375 his beloved brother Uranius Satyrus died. Seven days after his funeral, Ambrose gave a second funeral oration in commemoration of his death. In this oration, he addresses the issue of what happens to the soul after death and the possibility of metamorphosis. Like Tertullian, he declares that it is impossible for our souls to enter the bodies of animals:

> But can we accept the opinion of those who say that our souls, after they have departed from our bodies, enter the bodies of wild beasts and various other kinds of animals? The philosophers themselves, at any rate, usually explain that these are the ridiculous creations of poets, such as might be produced by the deceitful potions of Circe. They observe further that not so much they, who supposedly underwent such things, as the senses of those who invented these stories were turned by Circe's cup, as it were, into various beasts and monsters [Ambrose, 256].

Ambrose thus dismisses transmigration of souls between humans and animals as nonsense; moreover they are only the products of the imagination of poets whose senses have been deceived. Again like Tertullian, Ambrose continues his argument by noting the great gulf separating the nature of beasts and the nature of man:

> How much more truly marvelous would it be that the soul which governs man should be able to assume the nature of beasts, so opposed to that of mankind, and, though capable of reason, pass into an irrational animal, than that the forms of bodies might have been changed! [Ambrose, 256].

According to Ambrose, the poets write their stories "in sport" and are correctly taken as fiction by the philosophers, who condemn them. However, the philosophers also believe these same stories when they are considering the question of the soul. Ambrose interprets these stories as an attempt to mock those who actually believe that the same soul who can normally control his anger through his own determination can "now be inflamed with the mad violence of a lion, and, with ungovernable anger and unbridled rage, can thirst for blood and seek for slaughter," or that the same soul who can normally lead his people and "calm them with the voice of reason, can now endure to howl in pathless and desert places in the manner of wolves" (Ambrose, 256–57). Declaring that these pagan beliefs are "incredible" and "disgusting," Ambrose concludes:

> What is more excellent than to be convinced that the work of God does not perish and that those made after the likeness of and image of God cannot be changed into the forms of beasts! It is the soul, of course, and not the body, which is according to the image and likeness of God [Ambrose, 257–258].

Metamorphosis is therefore unthinkable according to Saint Ambrose because it denies the power of God: not only does it imply that God's work is not everlasting but it also ridicules the notion that man's soul is the image of God.

During the barbarian invasions of Rome in the first part of the fifth century, Saint Augustine, mystic and bishop of Hippo, began to write *The City of* God (A.D. 413–423), an apologetic work that Thomas Merton describes as the "autobiography" of the Church by the "most Catholic of her great saints."[2] In the first ten books of *The City of God*, Augustine deals with the pagan religions of Rome, in the last twelve he discusses the "two cities." According to the bishop of Hippo, the first city is built on greed and selfishness, the second on love for one another and for God. Book XVIII, "A parallel history of the earthly and heavenly cities from the time of Abraham to the end of the world," is of particular interest to our study, since it is here that Augustine develops his theological interpretation of the metamorphosis of human beings into wolves and other animals. This interpretation will remain influential for over a thousand years. Augustine begins his discussion by briefly relating several accounts of metamorphosis, noting that they were reported to him by Varro.[3] Among them is a reference to Circe who changed Ulysses' men into animals, the legend of the Arcadian men who were chosen by lot to become werewolves, and the tale of Demaenetus, the former werewolf who became an Olympic boxer (623; XVIII.17).[4] Augustine also mentions that while traveling in Italy he heard tales of landladies who transformed men into pack animals by giving them cheese to eat that had been altered with some magical or poisonous substance. In response to these stories, Augustine declares that although the men's bodies changed, their minds did not, and compares their situation to that of Apuleius in *The Golden Ass*. He explains, however, that these metamorphoses are "demonic trickery"; they are not real, but are only illusion:

> These things are either false, or so extraordinary as to be with good reason disbelieved. But it is to be most firmly believed that Almighty God can do

> whatever He pleases, whether in punishing or favouring, and that the demons can accomplish nothing by their natural power (for their created being is itself angelic, although made malign by their own fault), except what He may permit, whose judgments are often hidden, but never unrighteous. And indeed the demons, if they really do such things as these on which this discussion turns, do not create real substances, but only change the appearance of things created by the true God so as to make them seem to be what they are not [624; XVIII.18].

Obviously, he would have had no reason to attack these superstitions if they were not accepted by the populace as real and if they did not conflict with the Christian belief that God alone can create and transform matter.[5] Augustine does not reject the phenomenon of metamorphosis, since God's power is unlimited, but he denies that it can be accomplished through any other agent. Indeed, the Bible actually includes an account of metamorphosis: God changed Nebuchadnezzar into a wild animal for seven years because the Babylonian king did not acknowledge His authority: "he was driven from men, and did eat grass as oxen, and his body was wet with the dew of heaven, till his hairs were grown like eagles' feathers, and his nails like birds' claws" (*Holy Bible, King James Version*, Dan. 4.33). Belief in metamorphosis is therefore not entirely out of the question for Christians, but it is allowed only within certain parameters. As Leonard Barkan points out,

> Augustine expounds a religion not only filled with stories of magic but also having an act of transformation at its very center; furthermore, his religion postulates an omnipotent god whose power extends eternally in both past and future directions. Is it, therefore, quite safe to rule out the possibility of metamorphosis, even as understood by pagans? [98].

The "act of transformation" to which Barkan is referring is, of course, transubstantiation, a central tenet of the Catholic faith, the belief that the consecrated bread and wine are converted into the body and blood of Christ during the sacrament of the Eucharist. Stressing the power of God and minimizing that of Satan and his followers, Augustine states that only God can change matter; the Devil merely deceives man's senses. Acceptance of these pagan superstitions challenges the supreme authority of God as the only creator. Although the participants in this kind of "demonic trickery" affirm that such a transformation has actually occurred, Augustine insists that neither the body nor the mind has been altered. Along with other medieval theologians, he distinguishes between man's psychic and physical being; *homo interior*—man's spiritual being—is made in the image of God,[6] whereas traces of God can be perceived in *homo exterior*—man's material existence.[7] The two components of *homo duplex*—*homo interior* and *homo exterior*—are thought to be in harmony with one another, but man's interior is invisible; it can only be inferred from what he does, how he looks, and what he says (Friedman 106). As the image of God, *homo interior* is located in that part of man that sets him apart from beasts: his soul, his mind, his intelligence. How then could man, made in the likeness of God, become an animal? Such an idea is unthinkable for all believers. Moreover, this idea threatens the very notion of the hierarchy that extends from the animal kingdom to the divine.[8] In order to rationalize the tales of werewolves and other metamorphoses, Augustine thus introduces the notion of the *phantasticum* "phantasm":

> I cannot therefore believe that even the body, much less the mind, can really be changed into bestial forms and lineaments by any reason, art, or power of the demons; but the phantasm of a man, which even in thought or dreams goes through innumerable changes, may, when the man's senses are laid asleep or overpowered, be presented to the senses of others in a corporal form, in some indescribable way unknown to me, so that men's bodies themselves may lie somewhere, alive, indeed, yet with their senses locked up much more heavily and firmly than by sleep, while that phantasm, as it were embodied in the shape of some animal, may appear to the senses of others, and may even seem to the man himself to be changed, just as he may seem to himself in sleep to be so changed, and to bear burdens; and these burdens, if they are real substances, are borne by the demons, that men may be deceived by beholding at the same time the real substance of the burdens and the simulated bodies of the beasts of burden [264; XVIIII.18].

Augustine then offers the following examples: that of Praestantius, who is transformed into a packhorse and travels to Rhoetia with the soldiers of the Rhoetian legion after eating poisoned cheese, and that of a philosopher who comes to a man's house and explains some Platonic philosophy to him. In the first example, Praestantius never left his bed for days; in the second, the philosopher explains that he did not come to the man's house but only dreamed that he did. Augustine declares that it was the phantasm at work in both cases. He also states that if the stories related by Varro were true, they could have happened the same way.[9] Both the victim and the witnesses were deluded; they perceived only an illusion of reality. The body and soul of the man were unaffected. Augustine is thus able to explain the phenomenon without jeopardizing the founding principles of Christian faith.

As we shall see, theologians continue to accept Augustine's theory of metamorphosis throughout the Middle Ages.[10] Early in the tenth century, around the year 906, Regino, the former Abbot of Prüm, compiled Church documents into a book entitled *De synodalibus causis et disciplinis ecclesiasticis*, which he wrote for Radbod, the Archbishop of Trier, to assist bishops as they visited their dioceses. Included in his book was the *Canon Episcopi*, a Germanic penitential.[11] Medieval penitentials, which first appeared in Ireland in the seventh century before spreading all over Europe, listed sins, along with their corresponding penance (Russell, 60). This penitential, the *Canon Episcopi*, is of particular interest to us because its condemnation of sorcery incorporates Augustine's concept of the phantasm. Noting that some women believe that they ride on beasts at night with the pagan goddess Diana and travel great distances with her, doing as she commands, the author of the penitential declares:

> Wherefore the priests throughout their churches should preach with all insistence to the people that they may know this to be in every way false and that such phantasms are imposed on the minds of infidels and not by the divine but by the malignant spirit. Thus Satan himself, who transfigures himself into an angel of light, when he has captured the mind of a miserable woman and so subjugated her to himself by infidelity and incredulity, immediately transforms himself into the species and similitudes of different personages and deluding the mind which he holds captive and exhibiting things, joyful or mournful, and persons, known or unknown, leads it through devious ways, and while the spirit alone endures this, the faithless mind thinks these things happen not in the spirit but in the body. Who is there that is not led out of himself in dreams and nocturnal visions, and sees much when sleeping which he had never seen waking? Who is so stupid and foolish as to think that all these things which are only done in spirit happen in the body?[12]

Thus, the *Canon Episcopi* rationalizes sorcery, while at the same time condemning belief in it, by explaining that witchcraft, like metamorphosis, is not real but only illusion and the result of demonic trickery. Like the men in Augustine's anecdotes, these women are only dreaming and they too are dupes of Satan. Moreover, the *Canon Episcopi* also explicitly denounces as heretics those who believe that the Devil — or anyone else — has the power to actually transform substances:

> Whoever therefore believes that anything can be made, or that any creature can be changed to better or to worse or be transformed into another species or similitude, except by the Creator himself who made everything and through whom all things were made, is beyond doubt an infidel.[13]

Although the penitential does not specifically mention werewolves or Saint Augustine, it reinforces his doctrine of metamorphosis, which will contribute to the unique nature of the literary werewolf narratives of the twelfth century.

The Canon Episcopi was such an important document that not only was it cited and referred to throughout the Middle Ages almost as often as Augustine's writings, but Burchard, archbishop of Worms, reproduced it twice, first in *Corrector*, a late tenth-century penitential, and a second time in *Decretum Libri XX* (*Decretum*), a compilation of canon law, which includes the *Correc-*

tor (c. 1008–1012). Interestingly, the *Corrector* condemns belief in pagan practices rather than condemning the actual practices. One of the specific beliefs condemned is the belief in werewolves:

> Have you believed what some are accustomed to believe, that those women who are popularly called Fates either exist or can do what people believe: namely, when a man is born, they can designate him for whatever they want; and as a result, whenever that man wishes, he can be transformed into a wolf, called in German a Werewolf, or into some other form? If you have believed that this can happen or that the divine image can be turned by someone into another form or species — except by all-powerful God — you are to do ten days penance on bread and water.[14]

As Montague Summers has pointed out, what is at stake here is not whether or not werewolves exist, or whether or not the parishioner being questioned by the priest believes that werewolves exist, but rather whether or not the parishioner believes that someone — indeed, the "powers of evil" — might be as powerful as God Himself (5). Nevertheless, Burchard remains faithful to the teachings of Augustine. More important, the existence of his penitential — this "corrector" — attests to the power of the public's continued fascination and belief in pagan superstitions and werewolf legends.

In 1125, William of Malmesbury, a Benedictine monk and chronicler, completed the *Gesta regum Anglorum*. Among the many anecdotes included in his history of the English kings is one in which he relates a story similar to one mentioned by Saint Augustine. In William's account, a young acrobat is changed into a donkey by two old women living near Rome who are "filled with one spirit of witchcraft" (293; ii, 171, 1). Although the donkey could not speak, he had not "lost a man's intelligence" (293; ii, 171, 2). The women sell the donkey to a wealthy man, telling him that the donkey will continue to entertain him with its tricks, provided that it is kept away from water. One day, however, the donkey escapes, rolls in the water, and recovers his human form. When he is tracked down by his former master's keeper, he tells the keeper the whole story, who repeats it to the wealthy man, who then repeats it to Pope Leo. The inclusion of this anecdote in William's history provides us with further evidence of the interest of the public in metamorphosis during the early twelfth century. It does not, however, indicate that William believed such tales. Indeed, he is careful to include commentary that sheds doubt on the story and reveals his opinion.[15] For example, in the anecdote we just examined, William tells us that "[t]he pope had his doubts, but was encouraged by Peter Damiani, a great scholar, to think it not surprising if these things can happen; by citing the example of Simon Magus, who caused Faustinianus to appear in Simon's shape and frighten his children, he made the pope more knowledgeable about such things for the future" (293; ii, 171,

3). William's allusion to Simon Magus, the first century magician who offered money to the Apostles Peter and John if they would give him the Holy Spirit, is very enlightening.[16] First, simony — the buying or selling of church offices and ecclesiastical pardons — was named after Simon Magus, who is considered the first heretic of the Christian Church. Second, the Bible depicts Simon Magus engaged in sorcery and deception:

> 9 But there was a certain man, called Simon, which beforetime in the same city used sorcery, and bewitched the people of Sa-má-ri-a, giving out that himself was some great one: 10 To whom they all gave heed, from the least to the greatest, saying, This man is the great power of God. 11 And to him they had regard, because that of long time he had bewitched them with sorceries [Bible, King James Version, Acts 8. 9–11].

In alluding to Simon Magus, William has drawn a parallel between him and the two old crones who "transformed" the acrobat into a donkey, it was nothing but illusion; just like the scoundrel Simon Magus who used sorcery for monetary gain and hoped to make more with the help of the Holy Spirit, the two old ladies were selling their illusions in order to purchase food and liquor. William has thus demonstrated that he concurs with Saint Augustine's theory of metamorphosis: it is indeed only illusion and the result of demonic trickery.

About a century later, Guillaume d'Auvergne, professor of theology at the University of Paris and reluctant bishop of Paris until his death in 1249, wrote *De Universo,* an ambitious work dealing with the world of creatures. Buried deep within it we find a short anecdote that is, according to Dubost, one of the most orthodox texts depicting metamorphosis (545). It is certainly one of the most straight-forward and complete accounts that we have yet seen:

> Un homme était possédé. Certains jours un esprit malin s'emparait de lui et lui faisait perdre la raison au point qu'il s'imaginait être un loup: durant ces périodes de possession, un démon le jetait dans un lieu écarté et l'y abandonnait, comme mort. Pendant ce temps le démon s'introduisait dans un loup ou revêtait lui-même l'apparence d'un loup, se montrait à tous et se livrait à des massacres terrifiants d'hommes et de bêtes: tous fuyaient à sa vue, craignant d'être dévorés. Le bruit courait que c'était cet homme qui se transformait en loup certains jours, et l'homme lui-même le croyait. Il était en outre persuadé d'être le loup responsable des massacres. Mais un saint homme, apprenant l'histoire, se rendit sur les lieux et expliqua aux gens qu'ils avaient tort de croire à la métamorphose en loup de cet homme. Il les conduit à l'endroit où il gisait, comme mort, le montra aux spectateurs, l'éveilla devant eux, le libéra de sa possession, lui montra, ainsi qu'aux autres, le loup avec lequel il croyait ne faire qu'un, ainsi qu'il le confessa publiquement.[17]

> A man was possessed. Some days an evil spirit would take hold of him and would make him lose his reason to the point that he imagined that he was a wolf: during these periods of possession, a demon threw him in a deserted place and abandoned him there, as if he were dead. Meanwhile, the demon entered a wolf or assumed the appearance of a wolf, showed himself to all and engaged in terrifying massacres of men and beasts: everyone fled at his sight, afraid of being devoured. The rumor spread that it was this man who was transforming himself into a wolf on certain days, and the man himself believed it. He was persuaded as well that he was the wolf responsible for these massacres. But a holy man, learning about the story, went to the village and explained to the people that they were wrong to believe in the metamorphosis of the man into a wolf. He took them to the place where he was lying, as if he were dead, showed him to the spectators, woke him up in front of them, freed him from his possession, showed him, as well as the others, the wolf that he thought he had turned into, and heard his confession publicly.

This tale incorporates all the elements of Augustine's theory of metamorphosis: illusion, demonic trickery, and the phantasm. Guillaume tells his readers that the man is possessed by a demon and that he imagines that he becomes a wolf. When the holy man takes the villagers to see the man who is asleep "as if he were dead," awakens him, and actually produces the wolf, proving to everyone that the wolf and the man are not one and the same, they witness a concrete demonstration of Augustine's phantasm. Guillaume also reiterates the *Corrector's* condemnation of the belief in werewolves when he has the holy man tell the villagers that they are wrong to believe "in the metamorphosis of the man into a wolf." Guillaume's anecdote thus provides a very important reminder of Christian doctrine and canon law regarding metamorphosis.

Finally, in *The Summa Theologica* (1266–73) of Saint Thomas Aquinas, the great thirteenth-century theologian, writer, and philosopher, we find no deviation from the Augustinian theory of metamorphosis. Instead, what we find there is a veritable recycling of Augustine's ideas. Aquinas frequently quotes from Augustine's *City of God in* order to support his own discussion regarding the power of demons to deceive man through "real miracles":

> Objection 1. It would seem that the demons cannot lead men astray by means of real miracles. For the activity of the demons will show itself especially in the works of Antichrist. But as the Apostle says (2 Thess. ii. 9), *his coming is according to the working of Satan, in all power, and signs, and lying wonders.* Much more therefore at other times do the demons perform lying wonders.
>
> Obj. 2. Further, true miracles are wrought by some corporeal change. But demons are unable to change the nature of a body; for Augustine says (*De Civ. Dei xviii.18*): *I cannot believe that the human body can receive the limbs of a beast by means of a demon's art or power.* Therefore the demons cannot work real miracles [557–558; Pt. 1, Q. 114, Art. 4].

In other words, according to Aquinas, and Augustine as well, any "miracles" performed by a demon can only be illusions; they are not real. He does, however, go on to expand the definition of miracle:

> But sometimes miracle may be taken in a wide sense, for whatever exceeds the human power and experience. And thus demons can work miracles, that is, things which rouse man's astonishment, by reason of their being beyond his power and outside his sphere of knowledge. For even a man by doing what is beyond the power and knowledge of another, leads him to marvel at what he has done, so that in a way he seems to that man to have worked a miracle [558; Pt. 1, Q. 114, Art. 4].

Nevertheless, demons may cause men to marvel and they may astonish men with what they have done because they do have exceptional powers:

> It is to be noted, however, that although these works of demons which appear marvelous to us are not real miracles, they are sometimes nevertheless something real. Thus the magicians of Pharaoh by the demons' power produced real serpents and frogs.[18] And *when fire came down from heaven and at one blow consumed Job's servants and sheep; when the storm struck down his house and with it his children*[19]*— these were the work of Satan, not phantoms; as Augustine says (De Civ. Dei xx. 19)* [558; Pt. 1, Q. 114, Art. 4].

According to Augustine and Aquinas, Satan uses these powers to mislead men. Quoting again from *The City of God*, Aquinas introduces the phantasm, the "phantom," into his discussion:

> Reply Obj. 1. As Augustine says in the same place, the works of Antichrist may be called lying wonders, *either because he will deceive men's senses by means of phantoms, so that he will not really do what he will seem to do; or because, if he work real prodigies, they will lead those into falsehood those who believe in him* [558; Pt. 1, Q. 114, Art. 4].

Aquinas attempts to rationalize the "miracle" of the frogs and serpents mentioned above by explaining that demons are able to transform corporeal matter if there is some natural process that would allow this to happen, such as putrefaction. If no such process exists in nature, however, then any transformation performed by a demon is just illusion:

> [T]hose transformations which cannot be produced by the power of nature, cannot in reality be effected by the operation of the demons; for instance, that the human body be changed into the body of a beast, or that the body of a dead man return to life. And if at times something of this sort seems to be effected by the operation of demons, it is not real but a mere semblance of reality.
>
> Now this may happen in two ways. Firstly, from within; in this way a demon can work on man's imagination and even on his corporeal senses, so that something seems otherwise than it is, as explained above (Q. 111, AA.

> 3, 4). It is said indeed that this can be done sometimes by the power of certain bodies. Secondly, from without: for just as he can from the air form a body of any form and shape, and assume it so as to appear in it visibly: so in the same way he can clothe any corporeal thing with any corporeal form, so as to appear therein. This is what Augustine says (*De Civ Dei xviii. loc. cit.): Man's imagination, which whether thinking or dreaming, takes the forms of an innumerable number of things, appears to other men's senses, as it were embodied in the semblance of some animal.* This is not to be understood as though the imagination itself or the images formed therein were identified with that which appears embodied to the senses of another man: but that the demon, who forms an image in a man's imagination, can offer the same picture to another man's senses [558; Pt. 1, Q. 114, Art. 4].

Interpreting and clarifying Augustine's notion of the phantasm, Aquinas emphasizes the illusory quality of creatures such as the werewolf. Moreover, in his final quotation from Augustine, he leaves no doubt in the mind of his thirteenth-century readers that to believe in the possibility of the transformation of man into beast by demons is to set themselves apart from God:

> Reply Obj. 3. As Augustine says (*QQ. 83, qu. 79) When magicians do what holy men do, they do it for a different end and by a different right. The former do it for their own glory; the latter, for the glory of God: the former, by certain private compacts; the latter by the evident assistance and command of God, to Whom every creature is subject* [558; Pt. 1, Q. 114, Art. 4].

Augustine's comment calls to mind the magician Simon Magus, who wanted to do what holy men did; he offered money for the Holy Spirit so that he too might have the power of laying hands on men and baptizing them with the Holy Spirit. Like the magicians that Augustine refers to, he did not want this power for the glory of God but for his own glory. Equating metamorphosis with "lying wonders," Aquinas warns his readers about the powers of demons and also cautions them about the dangers of being deceived by them.

As we shall see, Augustine's concept of the *phantasticum* will have literary consequences. Since the act of metamorphosis cannot occur without the help of the phantasm, and the phantasm, as Barkan has pointed out, exists materially "only in the immaterial world of dreams or the imagination" (101), Augustine established a direct link between metamorphosis and the imagination, whether he meant to or not. Moreover, since Christian writers must deny the truth — the "facts" — of the pagan tales of metamorphosis, they will also be compelled to search for what these stories might mean or represent. Metamorphosis thus becomes metaphor.[20] As we saw in Chapter One, popular accounts stress the reality of the werewolf. Clerical writings, however, insist on its illusory nature. It is from within these two very different traditions that medieval werewolf narratives will emerge.

Chapter Three

The Werewolves of Ossory and Other Medieval Wonder Tales and Marvels

Despite the warnings of the Church Fathers, public fascination with stories of werewolves continued into the Middle Ages, as their inclusion in collections of medieval wonder tales and marvels attests. During the latter part of the twelfth century (1185–1186), Gerald of Wales, who was also known as Giraud de Barri and Giraldus Cambrensis, accompanied the future King John of England on an expedition to Ireland. Archdeacon of Brecknock in Brecknockshire, with the ambition of following in his uncle's footsteps and becoming bishop of St. David's in Pembrokeshire, Gerald was also a historian and writer.[1] Previous to his appointment as archdeacon in 1175, Gerald had spent many years in Paris, where he had studied philosophy, canon law, and theology. Two years after his expedition with John to Ireland, he wrote *Topographia Hibernica*, a treatise on the country's geography and folklore.[2] In it Gerald relates an encounter between a priest and a werewolf, which he presents as a historical anecdote, rather than as a legend. Late one night, while traveling from Ulster to Meath unaccompanied except for a boy, an unnamed priest is approached in the woods by a wolf who tells him not to be afraid and then speaks to him of God. Terrified and begging the wolf not to harm him, the priest asks him "what creature it was that in the shape of a beast uttered human words" (57). The werewolf responds in the following manner:

> "There are two of us, a man and a woman, natives of Ossory, who, through the curse of one Natalis, saint and abbot, are compelled every seven years to put off the human form, and depart from the dwellings of men. Quitting entirely the human form, we assume that of wolves. At the end of the seven years, if they chance to survive, two others being substituted in their places, they return to their country and their former shape. And now, she

> who is my partner in this visitation lies dangerously sick not far from hence, and, as she is at the point of death, I beseech you, inspired by divine charity, to give her the consolations of your priestly office" [Otten, 57].

Of course the priest is not only very frightened, but also extremely reluctant to administer every last rite to the werewolf's female companion:

> [T]he priest followed the wolf trembling, as he led the way to a tree at no great distance, in the hollow of which he beheld a she-wolf, who under that shape was pouring forth human sighs and groans. On seeing the priest, having saluted him with human courtesy, she gave thanks to God, who in this extremity had vouchsafed to visit her with such consolation. She then received from the priest all the rites of the church duly performed, as far as the last communion. This also she importunately demanded, earnestly supplicating him to complete his good offices by giving her the viaticum[3] [Otten, 57–58].

In order to reassure the terrified priest that he will not be committing blasphemy by giving her the viaticum, the werewolf pulls down the wolf skin of the female and reveals her human form:

> He then intreated him not to deny them the gift of God, and the aid destined for them by Divine Providence; and, to remove all doubt, using his claw for a hand, he tore off the skin of the she-wolf, from the head down to the navel, folding it back. Thus she immediately presented the form of an old woman. The priest, seeing this, and compelled by his fear more than his reason, gave the communion; the recipient having earnestly implored it, and devoutly partaking of it. Immediately afterwards, the he-wolf rolled back the skin, and fitted it to its original form [Otten, 58].

The following morning, after leading the priest and his companion out of the woods, the male werewolf thanks him and prophesies about the future of Ireland and the fortunes of the English in that land. We hear nothing more of the werewolves, but we do learn that Gerald has been asked to attend a synod convened by the bishop of Meath in which the fate of the priest is to be decided. Although he is unable to attend, after the bishop's clerks provide Gerald with details "which [he] had heard before from other persons," Gerald advises the bishop in writing that the matter should be decided by the pope (Otten, 59). The bishop and synod follow Gerald's advice and order "the priest to appear before the pope with letters from them, setting forth what had occurred, with the priest's confession, to which instruments the bishops and abbots who [are] present at the synod [affix] their seals" Otten, 59). These last details relating to Gerald not only lend additional credibility to the account, but also testify to his standing in the ecclesiastical community of the world that he has created.[4]

The account of the Ossory werewolves is remarkable for many reasons.

First of all, the tale is unique because it is the only one in which a werewolf talks, as Jeanne-Marie Boivin has noted (53). This ability immediately reveals the beast's humanity and points to the disparity between his appearance and his true nature. However, according to Boivin, instead of making the werewolf seem less monstrous, speech reinforces his dual nature and therefore actually dramatically amplifies the horror felt by the priest (53). Second, no other werewolf account depicts a human body hidden beneath the skin of the wolf.[5] Boivin observes:

> On peut voir dans cet épisode la traduction visuelle, l'illustration la plus saisissante et le développement dans ses extrêmes limites d'un trait distinctif des histoires de loups-garous au Moyen-Age: l'opposition entre l'extérieur — l'apparence animale — et l'intérieur — l'intelligence humaine conservée. (56) We can see in this episode the visual translation, the most striking illustration of a distinctive trait in the stories of werewolves in the Middle Ages that has been developed to its farthest limits: the opposition between the exterior — the animal appearance — and the interior — the human intelligence that has been conserved.

Contemporary werewolf accounts only hint at this inner reality; Gerald's story, however, leaves no doubt. Boivin declares that this scene negates metamorphosis and reduces lycanthropy to disguise or trickery (56).[6] But she fails to take into account the fact that the Ossory werewolves are unable to fully remove their wolf skin "disguises." In addition, if there were no metamorphosis in this account, if it were just disguise or trickery, then what we would have here would be equivalent to the diabolical illusion described by Augustine, although in this case it would be divine, since it was caused by an agent of God; thus Boivin would be equating divine power with demonic power. John Carey notes:

> It is suddenly as if a werewolf is not a human being transformed, as Gerald himself assumes elsewhere in his discussion, but simply one disguised with a wolf's skin. This can be paralleled in werewolf stories outside Ireland, and in Irish tales of magical skins or garments which are used to effect transformation into birds or seals [63].

The werewolf story outside Ireland involving a wolf skin that immediately comes to mind can be found in the Norse Volsung Saga, in which a father and his son find two wolf shirts or skins. After putting them on, they become wolves for nine days, cannot remove the skins, and behave as wolves would. On the tenth day, they are able to remove the shirts and burn them.[7] But these are no ordinary disguises. While they are wearing the skins, which they are unable to remove until the end of a specified term, they are compelled to behave as a wolf would. As long as the Ossory werewolves have the outward appearance of wolves, which function as an imposed disguise that they have no ability to remove, they must live as exiles in the world of wolves. What makes the werewolves in Gerald's account different is the Christian interpretation that has influenced almost every aspect of the tale. Although the Ossory werewolves are not constitutional werewolves, they are what Ménard calls false werewolves, since they are victims of a curse and are subject to a single metamorphosis.[8] They have indeed undergone a true metamorphosis, one that falls within the parameters of Christian doctrine; that is, as people created in the image of God, they have not become animals, but have merely acquired the appearance of animals and have retained that quality which sets them apart, their reasoning or their intelligence. When the male wolf peels down his female companion's wolf skin to reveal "the form of an old woman," he does so only to prove that she is still a human being. The male wolf has the miraculous ability to peel down her wolf skin, for the same reason that he has the miraculous ability to speak: so that he might convince the priest to give his companion the last rites of the Church. As a Christian woman, the female werewolf, knowing that she is about to die, asks for the viaticum and receives it piously. Once the Eucharist has been given to her, however, her human appearance disappears: "the he-wolf rolled back the skin, and fitted it to its original form" (Otten, 58). According to Dubost, "la peau est métaphore du paraître" "the skin is a metaphor for appearance" (546). I would argue instead that the form of the old woman that is revealed when the wolf skin is pulled down is a metaphor for her humanity that has remained unchanged. Finally, Gerald's account is also unique for its Christian setting in which it presents a pair of werewolves whose metamorphosis has been inflicted on them as expiation for communal sin. The saintly origin of the curse, the miraculous abilities of the male wolf, the piousness of the female wolf, the involvement of the priest, and the viaticum episode all reinforce the Christian nature of the tale.

After Gerald relates the encounter, he discusses its theological implications. This is not surprising, considering his religious background. Gerald interprets this particular metamorphosis as a miracle, drawing a comparison between it and the incarnation of Christ:

> It cannot be disputed, but must be believed with the most assured faith, that the divine nature assumed human nature for the salvation of the world; while in the present case, by no less a miracle, we find that at God's bidding, to exhibit his power and righteous judgment, human nature assumed that of a wolf. But is such an animal to be called a brute or a man? [Otten, 59].

Although Gerald is comparing the metamorphosis of the Ossory werewolves to the incarnation of Christ here, he is not equating the werewolves to Christ; he is simply saying that both are examples of the miraculous and unlimited power of God, who can transform himself into man and, if he chooses, transform men into beasts.[9] Furthermore, he notes that God is using metamorphosis to carry out his divine vengeance — his judgment — on the inhabitants of Ossory and to make visible his authority over mankind. Although Gerald also raises the issue of the nature of the transformed creature, he is at first reluctant to make a decision, suggesting that divine miracles should be admired, not debated. After briefly mentioning Augustine's discussion of monsters, however, Gerald answers his question by citing the bishop of Hippo:

> "We must think the same of them as we do of those monstrous births in the human species of which we often hear, and true reason declares that whatever answers to the definition of man, as a rational and mortal animal, whatever be its form, is to be considered a man" [Otten, 60].

Therefore, according to Gerald, the Ossory werewolves should be considered human beings, regardless of their appearance. Referring to the werewolf legends related in *The City of God*, Gerald reiterates Augustine's theory of metamorphosis:

> We agree, then, with Augustine, that neither demons nor wicked men can either create or really change their natures; but those whom God has created can, to outward appearance, by his permission, become transformed, so that they appear to be what they are not; the senses of men being deceived and laid asleep by a strange allusion, so that things are not seen as they really exist, but are strangely drawn by the power of some phantom or magical incantation to rest their eyes on unreal and fictitious forms [Otten, 60].

With God's permission, the man and woman from Ossory were transformed into werewolves, but it is only their outward appearance that has been changed so that they "appear to be what they are not." They have not become animals but have only acquired the appearance of animals; inside they are still human beings. The priest is allowed to see this truth when the old woman is dying and wants to receive the last rites of the Church.

Gerald concludes his discussion of metamorphosis by giving examples of divine transformations and by referring to the mystery of the Eucharist:

> It is, however, believed as an undoubted truth, that the Almighty God, who is the Creator of natures, can, when he pleases, change one into another, either for vindicating his judgments, or exhibiting his divine power; as in the case of Lot's wife, who, looking back contrary to her lord's command, was turned into a pillar of salt; and as the water was changed into wine; or that, the nature within remaining the same, he can transform the exterior only, as is plain from the examples before given.
>
> Of that apparent change of the bread into the body of Christ (which I ought not to call apparent only, but with more truth transubstantial, because, while the outward appearance remains the same, the substance only is

> changed), I have thought it safest not to treat; its comprehension being far beyond the powers of the human intellect [Otten, 61].

Boivin finds Gerald's interpretation of the werewolf encounter contradictory, since the cleric affirms that the metamorphosis is a divine miracle, yet denies its reality with the wolf skin episode (62). Implying that the transformation must be total to be real, Boivin once again seems to be confusing demonic metamorphosis with the sacred. Gerald, however, is postulating two different kinds of divine metamorphosis: God may actually change one substance into another, as he did when he turned Lot's wife into a pillar of salt and the water into wine at the wedding at Cana, or he may merely transform or disguise the outward form, as he did with the two werewolves. In Gerald's account, this exterior transformation is not presented as mere illusion. Yes, the wolf skin episode shows the human body intact beneath the animal disguise and, as Boivin suggests, reveals that the metamorphosis has affected only the appearance of the woman. Nevertheless, by depicting the act of pulling back the skin of the wolf, the narrator provides tangible evidence that some sort of external transformation took place and demonstrates the power of God, which is not limited, but infinite. The man and the woman are unable to remove their disguise; it is imposed on them by divine will. Boivin also criticizes Gerald for not being able to clearly distinguish between real and illusory metamorphosis, as well as between divine and demonic metamorphosis (63). In each of the examples provided by Gerald, however, he emphasizes how those who were transformed remained "human and rational," how they did not become "bestial," how they did not "devour human flesh" as wolves normally would, and how their forms were "counterfeit," etc. (Otten, 60). Only their outward appearance is changed. Gerald is very careful to show how these transformations conform to the Augustinian theory of metamorphosis, which states that "demons can accomplish nothing by their natural power ... except what [God] may permit.... And indeed the demons ... do not create real substances, but only change the appearance of things created by the true God so as to make them seem to be what they are not" (624; XVIII.18). Since according to Church doctrine, demons cannot act without divine permission, werewolf accounts inevitably resist our attempts to classify them. It is not surprising, then, if Gerald might have had difficulty distinguishing between the divine and the diabolic. Finally, while Boivin considers the juxtaposition of lycanthropy and the mystery of transubstantiation "curious" (63), Caroline Walker Bynum offers this critique of his conclusion:

> Gerald ends, somewhat awkwardly, with an incoherent although orthodox statement that the Eucharist is transformation in which the metamorphosis occurs at the level of substance or nature while the appearance endures.

> Aware perhaps that he has failed to find a satisfactory classification for the werewolf with whom he began, Gerald concludes with the warning that it is safest not to treat the Eucharist at all [17–18].

Although Gerald actually refuses to draw a parallel between metamorphosis and the mystery of the Eucharist, this juxtaposition is significant and perhaps deliberate. It is possible that he has recognized the chiastic relationship between transubstantiation and Christian metamorphosis: they act as mirrors reflecting their opposites.[10] More important, Gerald's reference to bread chang ing "into the body of Christ" reminds us that he began his analysis of the theological implications of the account of the Ossory werewolves by noting how "divine nature assumed human nature for the salvation of the world." Gerald thus uses the ultimate example of divine metamorphosis to frame his discussion.

This account of the werewolves of Ossory in *Topographia Hibernica*, then, is significant in several ways. First, it portrays a twelfth-century theologian explaining the existence of a pair of werewolves in terms of Christianity and its doctrine. We therefore have a clearer indication of the clerical attitudes toward metamorphosis immediately prior to the time that the medieval literary texts that we will be looking at will have been written. Second, the narrative stresses the humanity of the werewolves and with it the opposition between outer appearance and inner reality, which are important themes in all of the medieval werewolf tales. Third, it presents the werewolf form as both transformation and a disguise that one is obliged to wear as a means of atonement for communal sin. Finally, it formulates the ontological questions that the werewolf tales and the romance *Guillaume de Palerne* attempt to answer: is this creature man or beast?

Gerald's account, however, is not the only one that deals with Irish werewolves. Another version can be found in the *Konungs Skuggsjá* (*King's Mirror*), a thirteenth-century Norse work belonging to the *miroir des princes* genre.[11] As in *Topographia Hibernica,* divine vengeance for wickedness is given as the explanation for the transformation, but there are several differences between the two accounts. The most obvious difference of course, is the absence of any encounter between the werewolves and a priest. Second, there is no mention of Ossory in this version of the tale. Third, it is Saint Patrick, not Natalis who has cursed the Irish, causing them to become werewolves. John Carey believes that it is possible that the place name was left out and the name of the saint was changed to Patrick because neither Ossory nor Natalis would be recognizable to a Norse audience (51). In addition, details are given about the specific reason for this punishment:

> It is told that when the holy Patricius preached Christianity in that country, there was one clan which opposed him more stubbornly than any other

> people in the land; and these people strove to do insult in many ways both to God and to the holy man. And when he was preaching the faith to them as to others and came to confer with them where they held their assemblies, they adopted the plan of howling at him like wolves [*Kings Mirror*, 115].

According to Carey, "[the] role of howling in the anecdote ... recalls indications in the early literature that the characteristic utterances of groups perceived to be antagonistic to the Church were equated with the barking or howling of dogs.[12] This particular detail consequently augments the historic credibility of the account. Furthermore, the type of punishment that Saint Patrick metes out on them is somewhat different than that inflicted on the people of Ossory by Natalis:

> When he saw that he could do very little to promote his mission among these people, he grew very wroth and prayed God to send some form of affliction upon them to be shared by their posterity as a constant reminder of their disobedience. Later these clansmen did suffer a fitting and severe though very marvelous punishment, for it is told that all the members of that clan are changed into wolves for a period and roam through the woods feeding upon the same food as wolves; but they are worse than wolves, for in all their wiles they have the wit of men, though they are as eager to devour men as to destroy other creatures. It is reported that to some this affliction comes every seventh winter, while in the intervening years they are men; others suffer it continuously for seven winters all told and are never stricken again [*Kings Mirror*, 115–116].

Although the Ossory werewolves are transformed one couple at a time for seven years to atone for the sins of their community, here an entire family and all their descendants are being punished simultaneously. Moreover, while some undergo repeated cyclical metamorphoses every seven years, others are werewolves for seven years in a row and then never undergo the metamorphosis again. Finally, even though the werewolves described in the *Konungs Skuggsjá*, like the werewolves of Ossory, retain their human intelligence, they also have the savage hunger of wolves for human flesh. Thus, the victims of this metamorphosis also victimize their own community, unlike the Ossory werewolves who function as scapegoats and suffer for their community. All told, what we have here is a werewolf account whose Christian content has been greatly diluted. Nevertheless, the *Konungs Skuggsjá* tale is an important one in that it obviously participates in the same oral tradition as that of the Ossory werewolves and adds to our understanding of Gerald's account.

Another account of Irish werewolves appears in a Latin poem *De Mirabilibus Hibernie* (*On the Marvels of Ireland*) written by Bishop Patrick of Dublin sometime before his death in 1084.[13] Similar accounts can be found in the Middle Irish *De Ingantaib Érenn* (*On the Wonders of Ireland*)[14] and in a thirteenth-century Latin poem called *De hominibus qui se vertunt in lupos* (*Men Who Change Themselves Into Wolves*).[15] An Irish version of the latter is also included in Nennius of Bangor's *Historia Britonum* (*History of the Britons*). All these accounts tell of men who have the ability to change themselves at will into wolves; when they transform themselves, they leave their human bodies behind and tell their friends and family not to move their bodies. If they are injured while in their lupine form, their human bodies will show the same marks or wounds of injury; in their mouths will be seen pieces of the raw meat from the animals that they have been eating. No attempt has been made to provide any Christian explanation for these metamorphoses; there is no curse or divine vengeance at work here. Because of this, Carey attributes the idea that the werewolves leave their bodies behind not to Augustinian influence but rather to the belief attested to in folklore that souls can leave the body and travel but cannot return to the body if it is disturbed (55–6).[16] At the very least, we certainly do not seem to be dealing here with what has been termed the false or sympathetic werewolf; rather, these are authentic constitutional werewolves.[17] *De Ingantaib Érenn* (*On the Wonders of Ireland*) adds one important detail lacking in the others: it identifies the werewolves as the "descendents of Laigne[ch] Faelad in Ossory" (54). This detail is significant for two reasons. First, it gives the account an important point in common with Gerald's account. According to Carey,

> Both Gerald and *De Ingantaib Érenn* state that the werewolves belong specifically to Ossory. Of our four main sources, these are the two which differ from one another the most. This renders it likely that the link with Ossory was present in the tradition from which all four derive, but was omitted by the author of *Konungs Skuggsjá* and by Bishop Patrick as having no interest for their Norse and (probably) English audiences [56–57].

Therefore, all of the accounts of Irish werewolves probably draw from the same oral tradition, which also probably originally specified Ossory as its location. Second, as brother of the sixth-century King Feradach mac Duach of Ossory, Laignech Faelad was the ancestor of its future kings.[18] Thus, *De Ingantaib Érenn* (*On the Wonders of Ireland*) sets up a parallel between the werewolves of Ossory and its ruling family. The implied comparison is not all flattering. As Carey observes, "[s]uch a story is unlikely to have arisen in Ossory itself. It may be significant that Natalis' church of Kilmanagh is situated only a couple of miles from the Tipperary border" (57). Comparing the various accounts of Irish werewolves, Carey also notes "the incongruity of the account in *Konungs Skuggsjá,* where the werewolves are on the one hand the victims of St Patrick's curse, but on the other a scourge to their innocent neighbours" (63). As we saw above, the Christian content of this particular werewolf account is somewhat diluted. Perhaps, instead, the account is closer to its oral source. Using the information we have obtained from *De Ingantaib Érenn* (*On the Wonders of Ireland*), I would suggest that this "incongruity" in *Konungs Skuggsjá* reflects the poet's attempt to use the werewolf motif as metaphor to depict a ruling family that is terrorizing its neighbors while he tries at the same time to contain this metaphor within the bounds of Christian doctrine.

French werewolves also make their appearance in wonder tales at about the same time as the Irish werewolves. After having spent time in England as a young man at the court of Henry II and after having served at the court of King William II in Sicily, Gervase of Tilbury lived in Arles, where he had been appointed judge of Provence. Sometime between 1209 and 1214, he wrote *Otia Imperialia* (*Recreation for an Emperor*) for the amusement and education of Emperor Otto IV. In this encyclopedic description of the world and collection of marvels, he included anecdotes regarding two werewolves from Auvergne. Before looking at those accounts, let us first consider the context he establishes to prepare his readers. Early in Book I, in his chapter "The Opening of the Eyes after Sin," Gervase offers a comment that makes his attitude toward the possibility of metamorphosis clear:

> This allegation that women change into serpents is remarkable, but not to be repudiated. For in England we have often seen men change into wolves according to the phases of the moon. The Gauls call men of this kind *gerulfi,* while the English name for them is *werewolves, were* being the English equivalent of *wir* (man) [87–89; I.15].

What is important here is that Gervase presents the werewolves of England as unequivocal fact, something that he infers he has been an eyewitness to, saying "*we have seen* men change into wolves," not just once, but "often." Nevertheless, he does not offer any specific examples of these English werewolves to support his statement. Gervase also clearly accepts the transformation of women into serpents; although this particular belief could have a misogynistic basis. His stance becomes uncertain, however, when he speaks of metamorphoses that others have told him about:

> It has also, so they say, been a regular practice of the women of Greece and Jerusalem to turn men who spurn their desire into asses. They put a strange sort of spell on them so that they have to bear toil and burdens in the form of an ass until the enchantresses themselves take pity on them and remit their punishment. I do not know whether to attribute all this to an optical trick by which witnesses are deceived, or whether it is a result of there being demons at large in the world which suddenly reconstitute the elements of the things we are talking about (which is what Augustine says happened in the case of the rods which the magicians changed into serpents) [89; I.15].

In the case of these men who have been turned into asses, Gervase is not so clear. Although he studied canon law and he does refer to Augustine's theory of demonic illusion and trickery, Gervase says nothing that would suggest outright acceptance of Augustinian doctrine. He leaves his reader wondering, with him, whether or not these men were really transformed into animals. In addition, he says nothing about the state of their minds. When relating the tale of Italian landladies who turned travelers into beasts of burden, Saint Augustine is careful to stress that the men who have been transformed retain their human intelligence.[19] Gervase continues his discussion by briefly summarizing the Melusine legend, in which a knight marries a beautiful woman after promising that he would never see her naked. One day, however, he peeks at her while she is bathing; she then turns into a serpent and disappears forever.[20] Gervase prefaces this highly improbably tale by saying, "For my part, I know of a happening of which I was once given a reliable account" (89; I.15). He thus presents this legend — like the English werewolves who transform themselves "according to the phases of the moon" — as something to be believed.

Gervase begins his chapter "Human Beings Who Turn into Wolves" with a statement that the educated men of his time were undecided as to whether or not Nebuchadnezzar "was really changed into an ox for the period of divine penitence imposed on him" or whether he had simply "adopted the lifestyle of a beast," since "it is surely easier to make a creature by transformation than to create one out of nothing" (813; III.120). Again, as we saw with the tale of the women in Greece and Jerusalem who supposedly turned men into asses, Gervase does not weigh in on the matter. This might seem particularly surprising, as the source of this tale of metamorphosis is not a folk tale or oral tradition, but rather the Bible. Yet, as he pointed out, many theologians were also undecided about Nebuchadnezzar's status.[21] Gervase proceeds in his discussion by once again boldly proclaiming his belief in werewolves as he reprises his earlier statement about the influence of the moon: "One thing I know to be of daily occurrence among the people of our country: the course of human destiny is such that certain men change into wolves according to the cycles of the moon" (813; III.120). Gervase then relates the story of Raimbaud de Pouget, a knight in the diocese of Clermont in Auvergne who had been disinherited by his lord. After wandering alone in the forest "like a wild beast" and "deranged by extreme fear" he lost his mind and "turned into a wolf," attacking the old and eating the young, until a woodcutter chopped off one of his paws and he recovered his human form. "Thereupon he confessed in public that he welcomed the loss of his foot, because when it was cut off he was freed from that wretched, wicked condition which would have brought his damnation" (815; III.120). This particular account is remarkable because it offers the perspective of someone who has been a werewolf. With its description of Raimbaud's gradual descent into madness and bestiality, it recalls the metamorphosis of Lycaon in Ovid, but there is nothing in Gervase's account to suggest that Raimbaud's transformation into a beast is a final evolution, a deepening of what he has always been. Moreover, this metamorphosis is only temporary. When Raimbaud recovers his human form, he expresses relief and a negative attitude about his werewolf condition that is in line with Christian doctrine.

Gervase's second anecdote, although briefer still, is even more remarkable, for all the information regarding this werewolf is provided by Chaucevaire, the werewolf himself. He lives in the town of Luc and he becomes a werewolf through the influence of the moon, specifically during the phase known as the new moon:

> He says that when the time has come he parts company from all his friends, lays his clothes under a bush or a secluded rock, and then rolls naked in the sand for a long time until he takes on the shape and voracity of a wolf, gaping for prey with wide-open mouth and yawning jaws.[22] He asserts that the reason why a wolf runs with its mouth open is that it can only unlock its jaw with a great effort and with the help of its paws, and it is unable to do so when it is overtaken by hunters. It is then therefore rendered unable to catch anything and is easily caught itself [815; III.121].

Chaucevaire, like the soldier in Petronius' *Satyricon*, removes his clothing before his metamorphosis, although he hides his, instead of turning them into stone. One motif frequently appearing in werewolf literature is that a werewolf cannot recover his human form if his clothing is stolen or lost. This particular motif is used to explain why the soldier in the *Satyricon* urinates around his clothing, thus turning them into stone and making it impossible for Niceros to take them.[23] We will also see this motif in *Bisclavret*.[24] Since Chaucevaire states that his metamorphosis is caused by the new moon, it is not clear that his clothing would be required in order for him to recover his human form. It seems just as likely that all that is needed is a change in the phase of the moon and that he hides his clothing so that he will be able to conceal his nakedness once he has recovered his human form. Although Gervase introduces the passage with the remark that "Chaucevaire is tormented by having to suffer the same fate" (815; III.121), what is most striking about the anecdote is Chaucevaire's matter-of-fact attitude toward his cyclical werewolf condition, as well as his emotional detachment. Unlike Raimbaud, he feels no remorse for what he becomes. As a result, we find no suggestion of Christian doctrine anywhere in this account. According to Francis Dubost:

> Avec l'inquiétant Chaucevaire, on se trouve en présence d'une authentique image d'autrefois, qui trouble et qui dérange parce qu'elle échappe aux explications élaborées par la pensée officielle [549].

> With the unsettling Chaucevaire, we find ourselves in the presence of an authentic image from the past, one which is upsetting and disturbing because it eludes the official explanations that have been developed.

Although Raimbaud and Chaucevaire seem at first glance to be very similar, they are actually almost at opposite ends of the werewolf spectrum. Thus Gervase seems to be caught between his own beliefs and those of the Church, never quite able to give up one side for the other. Dennis Kratz notes that "Gervase admits that the weight of learned opinion is not on the side of his own credulity" (60) and Laurence Harf-Lancner points out that:

> Les Otia Imperialia attestent donc l'existence d'un conflit, dans la conscience d'un clerc du XIIIe siècle, entre une conception "populaire" et une conception cléricale de la métamorphose ["Métamorphose illusoire, 218].
>
> *Otia Imperialia* therefore attests to the existence of a conflict, in the mind of a thirteenth-century cleric, between a popular and clerical conception of metamorphosis.

As we have seen, the same can be said of all the medieval collections of wonder tales and marvels that we have examined. The popular and clerical views of metamorphosis are equally represented in them, thus demonstrating that both traditions from which the medieval werewolf literary narratives will emerge are continuing to thrive.

Chapter Four

Bisclavret or a Lesson in Loyalty

Sometime between 1160 and 1178, a woman living at the English court wrote twelve *lais* (lays) — short narrative poems in octosyllabic couplets — that were originally intended to be read or recited aloud.[1] In one of these *lais*, *Guigemar*, she identifies herself simply as Marie. Other than the fact that Marie dedicates her *lais* to a noble king, possibly Henry II, very little is really known about her.[2] Scholars also attribute two other works to her: the *Espurgatoire seint Patriz* (*The Purgatory of Saint Patrick*), which was signed by a Marie, as well as a French translation of *Aesop's Fables*. In the prologue to the translation of fables, the poet states that her name is Marie and that she is from France: "Marie ai nom, si sui de France."[3] Because of this verse, the sixteenth-century literary historian Claude Fauchet named her Marie de France. Two hundred years later, when the collection of *lais* was discovered in a thirteenth-century Anglo-Norman manuscript,[4] scholars agreed that the Marie who had translated the fables was probably also the author of these *lais*. Since that time, she has been referred to by the name Marie de France.[5]

Included in Marie's *lais* is one called *Bisclavret*.[6] This remarkable poem is of interest to us because in it we find the first literary treatment of the noble werewolf. Marie begins this particular *lai* with a brief vocabulary lesson:

> Quant des lais faire m'entremet,
> Ne voil ublier *Bisclavret;*
> *Bisclavret* ad nun en bretan,
> Garwaf l'apelent li Norman [1–4].

> Since I have taken it upon myself to write lays,
> I do not want to forget *Bisclavret;*
> *Bisclavret* is its name in Breton,
> The Normans call it *Garwaf.*

Garwaf is the Norman equivalent of the French term *garou*, which means werewolf. The exact meaning of *bisclavret*, however, has been the subject of debate for over one hundred years, with scholars proposing various possibilities: "speaking wolf," "wearing short pants," "dear little speaking wolf," "rational wolf," and "wolf-sick" or "leprous wolf."[7] Although scholars have not been able to reach any conclusion about the origin or meaning of this word, indeed Joseph Loth referred to it as "énigmatique," "enigmatic" (300), in reading the first four verses of the *lai* at least it is clear that Marie uses the term "bisclavret" as a synonym for "werewolf."

Before beginning her story, Marie offers her listeners a look at the popular image of the werewolf as a bloodthirsty beast. It is against this tradition that she will construct her *lai:*

> Jadis le poeit hum oïr
> E sovent suleit avenir,
> Hume plusur garval devindrent
> E es boscages meisun tindrent.
> Garvalf, ceo est beste salvage;
> Tant cum il est en cele rage,
> Hummes devure, grant mal fait,
> Es granz forez converse et vait.
> Cest afere les ore ester:
> Del Bisclavret vus voil cunter [5–14].

> Long ago you could hear about it
> And it often used to happen,
> That many men became werewolves
> And lived in the woods.
> The werewolf is a savage beast;
> As long as he is overcome by this rage,
> He devours men, he does much harm,
> Deep in the forest he lives and wanders.
> Now let us leave that situation alone:
> I want to tell you about the Bisclavret.

Marie presents these werewolves as legends of old, emphasizing this idea with her use of past tenses in verses five through eight and by saying that these stories were told "jadis" (long ago). In verse nine, however, she switches to the present tense, indicating that these metamorphoses, with all their resultant savagery, are perhaps still occurring. This ambiguity has the unsettling effect of making her listeners a bit anxious as to what might follow. It is significant that Marie states in verses thirteen and fourteen that she does not want to talk about those werewolves anymore, because she wants to tell us about *the* Bisclavret. First, her statement implies that he is unlike the violent werewolves that she has just described; second, her use of the definite article combined with the fact that Bisclavret is capitalized also implies that he is unique, that he is perhaps the only Bisclavret. Finally it is also noteworthy that Marie uses the term "garwalf" when describing the traditional werewolf. She thus once again distinguishes it from Bisclavret, whose tale she is about to tell.

After the poem's prologue, Marie introduces her protagonist, telling us of a nobleman who lived in Brittany with his wife. She describes him as a handsome and good knight who behaved nobly, was a close friend of his lord, and was liked by all his neighbors (17–20). In other words, he appears to be the ideal knight. We also learn that he has a beautiful wife and that they love each other: "Il amot li et ele lui" (23), "He loved her and she loved him." Although everything seems perfect in their world, this is not the case: his wife is troubled by the fact that three days each week he disappeared and no one, not even his men, knew what happened to him or where he went (24–28). Like Marie's original intended audience, we have privileged information that the knight's wife does not have. Because we have read Marie's prologue, we have a good idea why this noble knight might be disappearing for three days every week, even though there are certainly other possible explanations. He would not be the first husband to be off dallying with another woman and this is exactly what his wife suspects. One day, he returns "joius et liez," "joyous and cheerful" (30) after another three-day disappearance, apparently delighted to be once again at home with his wife. But things will never be the same for the couple, as the knight finds out when first she accuses him of having a mistress—"Mun escïent que vus amez," "I believe that you love someone else" (51)—and then begins to interrogate him. He is reluctant to answer all of his wife's questions, telling her that terrible things will happen if he reveals his secret:

> "—Dame," fet il, "pur Deu merci!
> Mal m'en vendra si jol vus di,
> Kar de m'amur vus partirai
> E mei meïsmes en perdrai" [53–56].
>
> "My lady," he said, "in the name of God, have pity!
> Harm will befall me if I tell you,
> For you will no longer love me
> And I will lose my very self."

His comment about losing his self, his identity, is one that we will return to later. As we shall soon see, this knight is either a prophet or knows his wife very well. Of course his response does not allay her suspicions, but only arouses her curiosity and makes her more persistent. Nevertheless, worn down by all her coaxing and begging, he finally tells her:

> "Dame, je devienc bisclavret.
> En cele grant forest me met,

Al plus espés de la gaudine,
S'i vif de preie e de ravine" [63–66].

"My lady, I become a werewolf.
I go deep into the forest,
Into the thickest part of the woods,
And I live off prey and plunder."

Two things are worthy of our attention here. First, the knight says that he becomes a "bisclavret," not a "garwaf" or "garwalf." Second, although the *garwalf* is described by Marie as causing great harm and devouring men (11), the knight describes himself only as living "off prey and plunder" (66); he says nothing about killing or eating men. The concern he expressed earlier about losing his wife's love reinforces this distinction. A different picture of the werewolf is beginning to emerge here. At the same time, through Marie's narrative the character of the wife is starting to coming into focus. What follows after the knight reveals that he is a werewolf is particularly astonishing: instead of reacting with fear or surprise, the wife does not react at all, but continues her interrogation. Appearing to be devoid of emotion, she asks him if he undresses or keeps his clothes on (69). We have seen this same kind of matter-of-fact attitude toward metamorphosis before, this same emotional detachment, but we saw it in Chaucevaire, the cyclical werewolf described by Gervase of Tilbury in *Otia Imperialia*.[8] Here, on the other hand, we see it in a wife whose husband has just revealed to her that he is a werewolf. Although the wife seems to be emotionally detached from what her husband has just told her, she does appear to have a great deal of interest in the details of his transformation. Even after he tells her that he goes stark naked, she isn't satisfied with what he has told her but wants to know what he does with his clothes. Her persistence at continuing her interrogation of him, along with her lack of affect, is starting to get suspicious; perhaps she is just as familiar with Petronius' tale of the werewolf and the legends of the Arcadian werewolves as we are and knows how necessary the werewolves' clothes are for the recuperation of their human state.[9] The knight, alarmed at her question, refuses to answer:

"— Dame, ceo ne dirai jeo pas,
Kar si jes eüsse perduz
E de ceo feusse aparceüz,
Bisclavret sereie a tuz jurs.
Ja nen avreie mes sucurs
De si k'il me fussent rendu.
Pur ceo ne voil k'il seit seü [72–78].

"My lady, that I will not say,
For if I lost them

And this were known,
I would be a werewolf forever.
I would not have any remedy
Until they were returned to me.
That is why I do not want anyone to know."

Although Marie told us how much the handsome knight and his beautiful wife loved each other—"Il amot li et ele lui" (23), "He loved her and she loved him"—their marital relationship seems to be unraveling. Or perhaps things never were what they seemed to be all along. After having revealed his darkest secret, the knight is obviously reluctant to trust her any further. But the wife is even more insistent. She begins by proclaiming her love for him: "—Sire ... [j]eo vus eim plus que tut le mund!" (79–80), "My lord ... I love you more than the entire world!" After telling him twice that he should not fear her, she asks him what harm she has done to him that he should conceal something from her. Finally, using what Michelle Freeman has called "emotional blackmail" (293), Bisclavret's wife wears him down: "Tant l'anguissa, tant le suzprist, / Ne pout el faire, si li dist" (87–88), "She harassed him so much and mislead him so much / That he could not do anything else, and so he told her."[10] He has revealed his last secret.

Now Marie's focus switches to the wife. It is only after Bisclavret tells his wife about how he leaves his clothing in a hollow stone under a bush near an old chapel that Marie finally reveals the wife's true feelings:

La dame oï cele merveille,
De poür fu tute vermeille.
De l'aventure s'esfrea.
En maint endreit se purpensa
Cum ele s'en puïst partir:
Ne voleit mes lez lui gisir [97–102].

The lady heard this marvel,
And was scarlet all over from fear.
The whole adventure terrified her.
She plotted for a long time
How she might separate from him:
She never wanted to lie down next to him again.

The wife's fear is a normal reaction; who wouldn't be horrified to learn that their spouse was a shape-shifter? One could even argue that her lack of affect earlier was due to shock. What is uncertain at this point is which character Marie wants us to sympathize with, the husband or the wife. As the tale continues, however, her allegiance will lose its ambiguity. The wife now has the upper hand, thanks to the weapon that her husband has given her, the knowledge of what he does with his clothing. Unfortunately, unlike the werewolf in Petronius' *Satyricon,* he did not turn his clothing into stone; the only thing protecting it is secrecy. Once he reveals its hiding place to his wife, his fate is sealed. All that remains is for her to find a way to make use of this knowledge. One part of his "prophecy" has already come true; as the knight told his wife, if he divulged his secret to her, she would no longer love him (55). Recalling that there is a knight in the region who has loved her for a long time, she sends a messenger to him and tells him that she will finally grant him her love and her body. After he arrives, she reveals everything and sends him to get her husband's clothing. At this point Marie interjects a comment: "Issi fu Bisclavret trahiz / E par sa femme maubailiz" (125–126), "Thus Bisclavret was betrayed / And destroyed by his wife." Marie's allegiance is no longer in doubt. Moreover, with this act of treachery, the second part of the knight's prophecy has come true; he has lost himself, he is no longer knight or husband but is now only Bisclavret, doomed to wander in the forest.[11] Because his men are accustomed to his disappearances, after some time, people accept that he has gone away for good and his wife marries the other knight "[q]ue lungement aveit amee" (134), "who had loved her such a long time." This could be the end of Marie's tale, but of course it is not.

One year passes in silence, marked only by Marie's brief comment "[i]ssi remest un an entier" (135), "thus an entire year passed." This silence echoes the silence that Marie established at the beginning of the *lai* regarding Bisclavret's three-day absences. Now we hear nothing of the wife and her new husband, nor do we hear anything of Bisclavret's activities. This silence, filled as it must be with the unspoken sadness of the werewolf who has had his life and his identity stolen from him, who has lost his wife and no longer enjoys a happy homecoming, stands in stark contrast to the presumed happiness of the knight who at long last has finally married the woman he loves. One day, however, the king is hunting in the forest when his dogs and hunters come upon Bisclavret. After chasing him all day, they are about to kill him. This scene recalls the one in *Gilgamesh*, in which the shepherd, Ishtar's former lover, is torn into pieces by his own dogs after she transforms him into a wolf, as well as Ovid's legend of Actaeon, who is also killed by his own dogs after Diana transforms him into a stag because she has seen him naked.[12] In both instances, the metamorphoses are used by powerful females, indeed, by goddesses, as acts of vengeance. Bisclavret's case, of course, is different. His wife is not a goddess; she gains power over him only through his own misplaced trust and she supposedly uses this power only because she is frightened of him. Moreover, before the *lai* begins, Bisclavret is already a werewolf— what Smith termed a constitutional werewolf and Ménard describes as a cyclical werewolf— but now he is trapped in his lupine form by his wife, whereas the shepherd and Actaeon are false werewolves because they are victims of a unique metamorphosis brought about through magic or a curse.[13] Finally, Bisclavret's situation is also unlike theirs because he is not torn to shreds by the king's dogs; instead, he runs over to the king and begs for mercy:

> Des que il [li bisclavret] ad le rei choisi,
> Vers lui curut quere merci.
> Il l'aveit pris par sun estrié,
> La jambe li baise e le pié [145–148[.
>
> As soon as he [the werewolf] saw the king,
> He ran toward him to ask for mercy.
> He took hold of him by his spur,
> He kisses his leg and his foot.

According to Ménard, the abandonment of clothing marks symbolically the rejection of civilization, humanity, and reason.[14] But what we have just seen in this passage speaks to the contrary. In spite of the fact that Bisclavret took off his clothing prior to his metamorphosis and is now in lupine form, he is not behaving like a wolf. He certainly has not rejected civilization or humanity; with his comportment he demonstrates that he has retained his reason. Indeed, Marie never speaks of any savage acts that Bisclavret commits as a wolf. She does, however, describe his human and courtly demeanor when he encounters the king hunting in the forest. In this particular act of supplication, we find a transformation of the feudal ceremony of homage, which Marc Bloch describes as follows:

> Imagine two men face to face; one wishing to serve, the other willing or anxious to be served. The former puts his hands together and places them, thus joined, between the hands of the other man — a plain symbol of submission, the significance of which was sometimes further emphasized by a kneeling posture. At the same time, the person proffering his hands utters a few words — a very short declaration — by which he acknowledges himself to be the "man" of the person facing him. Then chief and subordinate kiss each other on the mouth, symbolizing accord and friendship [Feudal Society, 145–146].

The modifications of the submission scene in *Bisclavret* are, of course, necessitated by the situation of the man-beast, who is unable to place his hands in the hands of his lord, unable to speak, and smart enough not to attempt to kiss the king on the mouth! As we shall see, in spite of his physical limitations, the werewolf enacts enough of the ceremony to make it recognizable to the king.

Reflecting Augustine's theory of metamorphosis, which insists that the humanity of the "transformed" creature is untouched, Marie emphasizes the incongruity between Bisclavret's appearance and his behavior. Although he appears to be a wild animal, he is still a man. The king marvels at his display of human intelligence and courtly manners:

"Seignurs, fet il, avant venez!
Ceste merveillë esgardez,
Cum ceste beste s'humilie!
Ele ad sen d'hume, merci crie.
Chaciez mei tuz ces chiens ariere,
Si gardez que hum ne la fiere!
Ceste beste ad entente e sen" [151–57, emphasis added].

My lords, he said, come forward!
Look at this marvel,
And how this beast is paying homage!
It has the intelligence of a man, it is begging for mercy.
Chase all these dogs away,
Do not let any man strike it!
This beast has understanding and intelligence.

Recognizing that this is no ordinary wolf, the king puts Bisclavret under his protection. Marie reinforces the gentle, human image of the werewolf with her comment about his conduct at court:

N'i ad celui ke nel'ad chier,
Tant esteit francs et deboneire;
Unques ne volt a rien mesfeire [178–180].

There was no one who did not like him,
He was so noble and gentle
He never wanted to do anything wrong.

Using the words "francs" (noble) and "debonaire" (gentle), which are usually used to describe knights and other noblemen, Marie emphasizes the disparity between Bisclavret's lupine appearance and his inner reality for the benefit of her courtly audience. Bisclavret is able to reveal his nobility — his humanity — to those around him by behaving chivalrously. Thus, in spite of his lupine appearance, Bisclavret is well-liked by everyone at court. As for Bisclavret himself, he is especially fond of the king:

U ke li reis deüst errer,
Il n'out cure de desevrer;
Ensemble od lui tuz jurs alout:
Bien s'aparceit que il l'amout [181–184].

Wherever the king might go,
He had no desire to leave him.
He always went everywhere with him:
It was very apparent that he loved the king.

Bisclavret has obviously resumed the relationship he enjoyed with the king when he was still a knight: "De sun seignur esteit privez" (19) "He and his lord were close friends." The poet also makes it very easy for her courtly audience to sympathize with this man-beast, who seems to have taken on the mannerisms of a faithful dog. Even though Bisclavret himself had acknowledged to his wife that he lives off prey and plunder when he becomes a werewolf—"Dame, jeo devienc bisclavret / ... S'i vif de preie et de ravine" (63, 66), "My lady, I become a werewolf ... / And I live off prey and plunder"—any violent acts that he may have engaged in are never actually depicted by Marie. As Ménard notes in his study of Marie de France's work,

> [P]our faire du protagoniste un personnage sympathique — ce qui est paradoxal dans les histoires de loups-garous — Marie nous cèle la vie sauvage du loup. Elle passe sous silence toute la face nocturne de son être. Sinon, nous aurions éprouvé plus d'horreur que de pitié. Quand elle le présente, elle en fait un animal doux et bienveillant, une sorte de chien-loup qui baise le pied du roi, couche aux pieds de son lit et lui porte une évidente affection [*Les Lais*, 177].

> To make the protagonist a sympathetic character — this situation is a paradox in werewolf stories — Marie conceals from us the savage life of the wolf. She is silent about the entire nocturnal side of its existence. If she weren't, we would have felt more horror than pity. When she presents him, she makes him a gentle and benevolent animal, a kind of dog-wolf that kisses the king's foot, sleeps at the foot of his bed and obviously feels affection toward him.

As we shall discover, in the twelfth century, all literary werewolves are portrayed to varying degrees in a sympathetic light. In another article, Ménard declares that we suspect that there is a hidden cruelty in Bisclavret, an irresistible need to hurt and kill innocent victims.[15] As to just how savage this particular werewolf actually is, we'll never know, but it seems unlikely that such a horrifying bloodthirsty beast would have run to the king for help and begged for mercy instead of turning and attacking those who were chasing him. It is much more plausible that all that Marie has concealed is a hungry man-beast hunting for his dinner. Marie also makes her protagonist a sympathetic character by introducing him first as a noble knight and as a husband who loves his wife and is happy to be home after a three day absence. In doing so, she establishes that he is no ordinary werewolf.

Bisclavret's courtly behavior continues and in fact becomes the norm. One day, however, the king holds a plenary court that is attended by all of his barons, including the knight who had married Bisclavret's wife. As soon as the werewolf sees his rival, his behavior undergoes a spectacular metamorphosis:

> Si tost cum il vint al paleis
> E li bisclavret l'aparceut,
> De plain esleis vers lui curut:
> As denz le prist, vers lui le trait.

Ja li eüst mut grant leid fait,
Ne fust li reis ki l'apela,
D'une verge le manaça.
Deus feiz le vout mordre le jur! [196–203].

As soon as he [the knight] arrived at the palace
Bisclavret saw him,
And ran toward him at full speed:
He took him in his teeth, and dragged the knight toward him.
He would have really done great harm to him
If the king had not called him back
And if he had not threatened him with a stick.
Twice that same day he tried to bite him!

At first glance, it would seem that Marie has finally revealed the ferocious beast for what he really is. Carefully reading, however, tells a different story. Bisclavret does not kill the knight nor does he really injure him. Like a trained dog who responds to his master's commands, or a knight who obeys the orders of his lord, he restrains his violent outburst. Moreover, his behavior is deemed extraordinary by those who witness it:

Mut s'esmerveillent li plusur,
Kar unkes tel semblant ne fist
Vers nul hume ke il veïst.
Ceo dient tuit par la meisun
K'il nel fet mie sanz reisun:
Mesfait li ad, coment que seit,
Kar volentiers se vengereit [204–210, emphasis added].

Almost everyone is astonished,
For he has never acted this way
Toward any man that he has seen.
Everyone in the household says
That he would not do it without a reason:
The knight must have wronged him somehow,
For Bisclavret wanted to avenge himself.

Not only is Bisclavret's behavior labeled unusual, behavior that would normally be considered ordinary for a wolf, but his behavior is justified by the knights, who assume that the other knight must have harmed the beast in some way. What exactly is Bisclavret's real motivation? We can only conjecture, but it is certainly possible that after finding his clothing missing the werewolf returned home and saw the knight with his wife. Certainly Marie's courtly audience and we, as privileged readers of this text, understand why Bisclavret attacked the knight. It is significant that in this passage Marie introduces the notion of combat and chivalric justice in this passage with her choice of the word "vengereit" (210). The knights in the kings' household are thus starting to think of the werewolf as if he were another knight who must retaliate for some mistreatment done to him, as vengeance is not the deed of an animal. It is also noteworthy that instead of siding with the knight, who is, after all, like them, the king's knights back the werewolf. Their opinion of him as merely the king's pet that they have been ordered to protect seems to be changing, for indeed they could have cared for the werewolf without speaking in his defense, just as they could have shielded the knight from harm without criticizing him.

Marie continues to play with the disparity between Bisclavret's inner and outer realities as she tells his *aventure* (adventure). One day not long after Bisclavret attacked the knight, the king goes hunting in the same forest where he had found the werewolf. As usual, Bisclavret accompanies him. The following morning, Bisclavret's wife, hearing that the king is staying in a lodge nearby, brings the king a gift. Using the diction of combat and chivalric justice, Marie prepares her listeners for the final encounter between Bisclavret and his spouse:

> Quant Bisclavret la veit venir,
> Nuls hum nel poeit retenir:
> Vers li curut cum enragiez.
> *Oiez cum il est bien vengiez:*
> Le neis li esracha del vis!
> Que li peüst il faire pis? [231–236, emphasis added].
>
> When Bisclavret sees her coming,
> No one can hold him back:
> He ran toward her enraged.
> *Hear how he avenged himself:*
> He ripped her nose off her face!
> What could he have done to her that would have been worse?

Obviously, instead of merely duplicating, this scene actually amplifies Bisclavret's first violent episode, when he attacked the knight. Now he appears to be acting as a wolf should act. This time he is neither restrained nor called back in time and he succeeds at exacting his revenge on his wife. She will bear the mark forever of her treachery. But because of what he has done, Bisclavret is about to be torn to pieces, until a wise man advises the king to intervene:

> "Unke mes humme ne tucha
> *Ne felunie ne mustra,*
> Fors a la dame qu'ici vei.
> *Par cele fei ke jeo vus dei,*
> Aukun curuz ad il vers li,
> E vers sun seignur autresi.
> Ceo est la femme al chevalier

Que taunt sulïez aveir chier,
Ki lung tens ad esté perduz,
Ne seümes qu'est devenuz" [245–254].

"Never has he touched anyone
Or committed any act of treachery,
Except against this lady.
By the faith that I owe you,
He has some animosity toward her
And toward her lord as well.
She is the wife of the knight
Whom you used to love so much,
The one who has been missing for a long time;
We do not know what happened to him."

The king's advisor correctly links the woman attacked by Bisclavret to the knight who had disappeared that the king loved so much. As he reads and interprets the text that Bisclavret has been acting out, the wise man thus begins to solve the mystery of the werewolf for the king. Although Bisclavret is unable to speak, his actions once again reveal that that there is more to him than meets the eye. Marie's feudal diction in this passage is also worth mentioning. First, the wise man introduces his conclusion regarding Bisclavret's actions by stating "Par cele fei ke jeo vus dei" (248), "By the faith that I owe you." The wise man's declaration is an allusion to the ceremony of homage, in which a vassal promises that he will be his lord's man and gives his word that he will "porter fei" or "foi" or "feid," depending on the dialect, which means that he will remain faithful to his lord. The sage uses this statement to indicate that what he is about to say he believes to be the truth, for he would not lie to his lord. This particular verse also gives more importance to an earlier verse in which the wise man notes that never has the beast " felunie ne mustra" (246), "committed any act of treachery." An act of treachery, of course, is not something that an animal would do, but it is something that a knight would do who has betrayed his oath to his lord. By the same token, it is something that husbands or wives would do who have betrayed their marriage vows. Marie thus accentuates the theme of loyalty, while at the same time reinforcing the growing recognition of Bisclavret's status as a knight. With the werewolf's mutilation of his wife, Marie reminds the audience of his bestial side. But in providing motivation for his actions, she transforms his wolflike behavior into the deeds of a knight. Neither the rightness of Bisclavret's action nor the sympathy of the narrator is left in doubt. Although he is unable to return to his human condition, Bisclavret is still a knight entitled to seek revenge and punish his treacherous wife.

Paradoxically, it is Bisclavret's wolf-like behavior, which contrasts with his normal gentle demeanor at court, that will lead to the eventual discovery of his dual nature and the recovery of his human form. One piece is still missing from the puzzle that this man-beast has become, along with his inexplicable violence; no one has yet recognized that Bisclavret and the missing knight are one and the same. It becomes obvious that more information is needed and that the best source is the wife of the missing knight, the woman that Bisclavret has just attacked. Interestingly, although this man-beast is protected from harm and justifications for his actions are sought at every step, no such courtesy is extended to the wife. Outcries of misogyny might be warranted, if Marie had not written other *lais* in which women are portrayed in a very sympathetic light as the victims of their jealous husbands.[16] There is no misogyny here; instead, what we find is evidence of the loyalty felt by the members of a group to another member.[17] Bisclavret belongs to the king's household; the knight's wife does not. Moreover, the situation also provides evidence that suspicion has been cast in the woman's direction; based on Bisclavret's attack, the assumption has been made that she cannot be trusted. Thus, to find out what she knows, the wise man does not simply suggest asking her what she knows, but instead proposes that she be tortured. The king followed the sage's advice and had the lady tortured. She then reveals Bisclavret's secret and her treachery:

Tant par destresce e par poür
Tut li cunta de sun seignur:
Coment ele l'aveit trahi
E sa despoille li toli,
L'aventure qu'il li cunta,
E que devint e u ala;
Puis que ses dras li ot toluz,
Ne fud en sun païs veüz.
Tres bien quidot e bien creeit
Que la beste Bisclavret seit [265–274].

Because of the torture and because of her fear
She told him everything about her lord:
How she had betrayed him
And had taken his clothing,
About the adventure that he had told her,
And what happened to him and where he went:
Since she had taken his clothing,
He had not been seen on his lands.
She truly thought and believed
That Bisclavret was this beast.

Once again, in this passage Marie's feudal diction calls attention to the *lai*'s theme of loyalty. The wife tells the king everything about "sun seigneur" (266), "her lord / husband" and admits that she betrayed him (267). More important, of course, the wife provides the vital clue to Bisclavret's human identity and the key to its recovery. This scene also parallels the scene at the beginning of the *lai* in which Bisclavret reluctantly reveals his secret to his wife. Like the wife who is devoid of emotion when she learns that her husband is a werewolf, the king and his court express no surprise when they discover that this beast is not merely a remarkably courtly wolf, but is actually a werewolf and the knight whom the king loved so much. Instead of reacting emotionally, the king simply forces the wife to bring Bisclavret's clothing back and has them given to him. When Bisclavret pays no attention to the clothes, the king just sends for the wise man, who advises him as follows:

> "Sire, ne fetes mie bien!
> Cist nel fereit pur nule rien,
> Que devant vus ses dras reveste
> Ne mut la semblance de beste.
> Ne savez mie que ceo munte:
> Mut durement en ad grant hunte!" [283–288].

> "My lord, you are not doing the right thing!
> For nothing in the world will he
> Put his clothes back on in front of you
> And transform his bestial appearance in front of you.
> You do not understand how important this is:
> He is very ashamed about it!"

This passage is very significant because it is the only one that gives us any insight into Bisclavret's attitude toward his werewolf "condition." At this point, however, we cannot determine the accuracy of the wise man's statement. But the king follows his advice, has Bisclavret taken to his chambers, along with his clothing, and leaves him there for awhile. When the king returns to the room later with two of his barons, Bisclavret has transformed himself and is asleep on the king's bed. Since he does undergo his metamorphosis once he is in the private space of the king's chambers, we can safely assume that the wise man's interpretation of the werewolf's reluctance and shame is accurate. His comment is therefore especially important because Bisclavret never talks after he recovers his human form. As a result Bisclavret never speaks of his wife's betrayal or of his act of vengeance. Marie's courtly audience and the modern reader, like the king, his knights, and wise man, are forced to interpret the text that Bisclavret creates; just as Christian writers are compelled by Augustine's theory to search for the meanings of the pagan tales of metamorphosis. Although we are privy to different amounts of information, we are all obliged to look beyond his appearance to determine what his acts mean. For inside this beast, there is still a man with human feelings.

Bisclavret's duality is evidently of no consequence to the king, whose only reaction when the werewolf recovers his human form is to celebrate the knight's return: "Le reis le curut enbracier; / Plus de cent feiz l'acole e beise" (300–301), "The king runs to embrace him / More than one hundred times he hugs and kisses him." The king's reaction to finding the human form of Bisclavret asleep in his bed stands in stark contrast to that of Bisclavret's wife, who betrayed her husband because she was horrified at what she had discovered about him and "[n]e voleit mes lez lui gisir" (102), "never wanted to lie down next to him again." Judith Rothschild has pointed out that "the king has assumed the role that Bisclavret's wife refused" (134).[18] But it is more complicated than that; there is a difference in their situations. The king has had the benefit of seeing and living with Bisclavret in his werewolf form, the form that Bisclavret's wife was so terrified of that she ended up betraying him. She refused the *garwaf*, the traditional monstrous and bloodthirsty werewolf that Marie depicts in the prologue to this *lai*; the king, however, accepted the *bisclavret,* the werewolf who remains a human inside and conforms to Christian doctrine. Although Marie tells us that the king returns Bisclavret's domain to him and gives him even more than she can say, we hear no more about whether or not he ever becomes a werewolf again. According to Ernest Hoepffner, it is not important that Marie does not tell us if Bisclavret has been cured of his malady, for his lycanthropy, his werewolf condition, is really only a secondary aspect of the tale; its true subject is love (148). Freeman notes that Bisclavret's wife is the "real werewolf" because she has "devoured the human being who was her husband, having made him, as well as her lover, prey to her own ambitions and pride" (294).[19] She then suggests that perhaps we are not told if Bisclavret becomes a werewolf again because it is "no longer relevant" and that this is Marie's way of recreating the silence that she had established at the beginning of the *lai* (298). Rothschild thinks Bisclavret won't become a werewolf again because he has finally received the tenderness and "understanding of his true nature" that he needed that his wife could not or would not give him (131),[20] whereas François Suard declares that Bisclavret has been cured of his lycanthropy through the process of substitution after his wife takes his place as a werewolf (274). Matilda Tomaryn Bruckner, on the other hand, speculates that perhaps Bisclavret is afraid of his dual nature and that after his wife betrays him he "discovers his ability to control the beast with his human ... understanding and good sense" (259).[21] I would argue, however, that if Bisclavret's werewolf status at the end of the *lai* is irrelevant, it is because *Bisclavret* is essentially a story of loyalty.

If it is not already clear that Marie's *lai* is not a tale about love, but rather a tale about fidelity, it becomes even more apparent in the denouement, where we learn that the king has banished Bisclavret's wife from his realm, along with the knight "*[p]ur ki sun seignur ot trahi*" (308), "*for whom she had betrayed her lord.*" We also learn that some of her children bear their mother's mark of infidelity:

> Enfanz en ad asez eü;
> Puis unt esté bien cuneü
> E del semblant e del visage:
> Plusurs des femmes del lignage,
> C'est veritez, senz nes sunt neies
> E sovent ierent esnasees [309–314].
>
> She had quite a few children;
> Who were then well known
> For their appearance and their face:
> Several of the women of her lineage,
> It is true, were born without noses
> And often were noseless.

Just as she did earlier, Marie emphasizes loyalty, or the lack of loyalty, in this passage, with her choice of words: "Pur ki sun seignur ot trahi" (308) /, "For whom she had betrayed her lord." Bisclavret's wife has taken the place of her husband; noseless, she now looks like a wolf. Her appearance thus accurately reflects her monstrous nature. Just as her husband had to explain his disappearances, she will now have to explain her missing nose. Moreover, her secret identity, like Bisclavret's, is now out in the open; everyone knows that she betrayed her husband.[22] Like Cain, she is marked forever because of her treachery and exiled from her country.[23] But God marked Cain as a sign of his protection so that men would know not to kill him (Gen. 4.15). The missing nose on Bisclavret's wife's face functions as an altogether different kind of sign, as we've already seen.[24] According to several critics, cutting off someone's nose was a common punishment for adultery.[25] Hoepffner offers the possibility that Marie might have written the *lai* in order to explain why some women were born noseless:

> Ce detail bizarre, et d'un gout quelque peu douteux, n'est pas dans la manière de Marie. Ce n'est pas elle qui a dû l'inventer. Elle a dû le trouver dans la tradition du conte. On nous permettra de risquer une supposition. Je pense que ce detail physiologique doit être le veritable point de depart du conte du *Bisclavret.* Un défaut physique, une tare caractéristique dans certaine famille noble, que Marie a eu la discretion de ne pas nommer, appelait une explication [148].
>
> This bizarre detail, of somewhat questionable taste, is not Marie's style. She could not have invented it. She must have found it somewhere in the tradition of the tale. Allow me to venture a guess. I think that this physiological detail must be the real point of departure for the tale of the *Bisclavret.* A physical fault, a characteristic flaw in a certain noble family that Marie was discreet enough to not name, required an explanation.

This hypothesis is intriguing, but if it were true, Marie would probably have devoted more of the *lai* to the wife than she did. Like Hoepffner, Bruckner also raises the question of whether or not the *lai* is "simply a tale invented to explain a line of noseless females" (252). She correctly notes, however, that Marie makes it clear in her epilogue that Bisclavret is the subject of her tale:

> L'aventure k'avez oïe
> Veraie fu, n'en dutez mie.
> De Bisclavret fu fez li lais
> Pur remembrance a tuz dis mais [315–318].
>
> The adventure that you have heard
> Was true, do not doubt it.
> The *lai* was made about Bisclavret
> To remember him forever.

Marie thus brings her story full circle, opening it with a comment about not forgetting (1–2) and ending it with a comment that the *lai* was written in order that Bisclavret would be remembered. In her article, "The Naked Beast: Clothing and Humanity in *Bisclavret*," Edith Benkov notes the originality of Marie's handling of the werewolf motif:

> Marie breaks with the preceding thematic narrative tradition through the creation of Bisclavret and transforms the werewolf into a creature whose subversiveness will not be directed against society. Rather, through a series of ironic thematic twists, Bisclavret is not only changed into an ill-treated and betrayed husband, but into a sympathetic character whose "beastliness" will both serve justice and restore a certain order, albeit one which is different from that at the outset of the tale [28].

The justice that Bisclavret serves is loyalty to one's vows, for neither marriage nor feudal society can survive if these vows are not respected. Marie de France did not, of course, invent this story nor did she create Bisclavret, as Benkov implies; the poet is retelling in verse form one of the old Breton *lais* that she heard sung. Although Marie's characterization of Bisclavret is in direct opposition to the traditional image of the werewolf in folklore that she presents at the beginning of the *lai* (5–12), we have no way of knowing how faithful she is to her source. The fact remains, however, that Marie presents a non-traditional werewolf in her *lai*; more precisely, she presents one that conforms to the Augustinian theory of metamorphosis, for this werewolf retains his humanity. In addition, Bisclavret is not merely a "sympathetic character"; he is the hero of the narrative. The moral transformation of the werewolf from villain into noble hero is a stunning development, one that will be duplicated and amplified in the medieval werewolf narratives that follow it. Marie does not end her *lai* with an explicit moral; this is consistent with her elliptic style throughout *Bisclavret*. As Sophie Quénet notes, "Marie de France excelle dans le non-dit" (159), "Marie de France excels in what is not said." In the Prologue to her *lais*, Marie herself speaks of the ancients who wrote obscurely so that those who studied them might "gloser la lettre / [e] de lur sen le surplus mettre" (15–16), "comment on the text / and add their own knowledge to it." And so it is up to us, her readers, to carefully read each *lai* and determine its message. As for *Bisclavret*, it seems clear that this heroic werewolf was intended to teach Marie's courtly audience a lesson about loyalty.

Chapter Five

Melion or a Lesson About Pride

Written shortly after Marie de France's *Bisclavret,* the anonymous Arthurian *Lai de Melion* (c. 1190–1204) presents a different version of the tale of the noble werewolf.[1] We know nothing about the author, except that he was probably a *jongleur* or wandering minstrel and that he was probably from the Picard region in northern France, since the *lai* is written in that dialect. Although the *lai* shares many plot elements with *Bisclavret, Melion* begins in an altogether different manner. Indeed, we will be almost one-third through the *lai* before we hear anything at all about werewolves. Instead, the poet tells us of a "bacheler" (noble young man) at King Arthur's court who was called Melion:

> [M]olt par estoit cortois e prous,
> e amer se faisoit a tos;
> molt ert de grant chevalerie
> e de cortoise compaignie [7–10].
>
> He was very courtly and brave
> and loved by everyone;
> he showed great prowess
> and he was always courteous to those around him.

In short, like Bisclavret, Melion possesses all the qualities of the ideal knight. It is no wonder that he is loved by everyone. We immediately learn, however, that one day each knight makes a vow and that Melion's is particularly surprising:

> Cil Melïons .I. en voa
> que a grant mal li atorna.
> Il dist: "Ja n'ameroit pucele
> que tant seroit gentil ne bele,

que nul autre home eüst amé,
ne que de nul eüst parlé" [17–22].

This Melion made a vow
that turned out very badly for him.
He said: "I would never love a maiden
no matter how nice or beautiful she is
that has loved another man,
or has spoken of another man."

Obviously, Melion has set himself a difficult task. Although he might find a maiden who has never loved another man, he has placed his standards impossibly high by also requiring that she will never have spoken of another man. According to Alexandre Micha, Melion is the masculine counterpart to the woman who is very proud about love, the woman who is disdainful or difficult regarding her choice of a husband.[2] There is, however, another possibility. The poet describes Melion as "bacheler," a "young man." Unlike Bisclavret, who is already married, Melion is perhaps not much more than an adolescent. Naïveté and youth often go hand in hand. So do, of course, pride and youth. We will need to keep both options in mind as we continue our analysis. At any rate, from what the narrator tells us, *we* do know that Melion's vow will cause him major difficulties.

Melion's life undergoes its first drastic change after the maidens at King Arthur's court learn of his vow and take offense: "qant les puceles l'oïrent / molt durement l'en enhaïrent" (27–28), "when the maidens hear about it / they feel a strong hatred for him." With his vow he has criticized and rejected them and has also implied that he is better than they are. The knight who was loved by everyone is now hated, at least by the women. Moreover, the maidens also take action against him. More than one hundred hold a meeting about it and make their own group vow:

[D]ïent jamais ne l'ameront,
n'encontre lui ne parleront,
dame nel voloit regarder,
ne pucelë a lui parler [33–36].

They said that never will they love him,
never will they speak to him,
not one woman wanted to look at him,
not one maiden wanted to speak to him.

Insinuating that no "ordinary" woman is good enough for him, Melion has now become the target of their collective scorn. While Melion's vow was directed generally at women who might not fulfill his conditions for his future bride, the vow of the women at King Arthur's court zeroes in specifically on Melion; they will never love him. Moreover, they will never look at him or speak to him. He has effectively been shunned by the maidens who are using his vow as justification for excluding him from their company. Alexandre Micha notes that the Melion poet was influenced by another of Marie de France's *lais* called *Guigemar*.[3] But *Guigemar* is the story of a knight who has no interest in love at all. We might think the same thing of Melion if it were not for his reaction once the women begin to ignore him:

> Qant Melïon ice oï,
> molt durement s'en asopli;
> ne voloit mais querre aventure,
> ne d'armes porter n'avoit cure;
> molt fu dolans, molt asopli;
> e de son pris alques perdi [37–42].
>
> When Melion heard this,
> he was extremely despondent;
> he no longer wanted to seek adventure,
> and he was no longer interested in bearing arms;
> he was very mournful and sad;
> and his reputation suffered because of it.

This is definitely not the reaction of a knight like Guigemar "[k]e unc de nule amur n'out cure," "who was never interested in love."[4] Melion wants to find a woman to love and he wants to get married. He is just extremely and perhaps unreasonably choosy about who that woman will be. Unfortunately, his high standards are consequently used as a weapon against him. Noticing Melion's despondency, King Arthur asks him: "tes grans sens qu'est il devenus, / ton pris et ta chevalerie?" (46–47), "what has become of your great intelligence, / your reputation and your prowess?" The king then offers the knight a castle surrounded by woods, rivers and forests "que molt as chiere" (58), "that is so dear to you." Melion accepts this gift and in effect goes in to self-imposed exile, although he is accompanied by one hundred knights. After his arrival in his new fiefdom, the poet repeats his innocuous comment twice about how much Melion likes the forest, all within the space of five verses:

> Li païs bien li conteça
> e *la forest que molt ama.*
> Qant il i ot .I. an esté,
> molt a le pais enamé,
> *car ja deduit ne demandast*
> *que en la forest ne trovast* [65–70].
>
> The land pleased him well
> and *the forest that he liked so much.*
> When he had been there a year,
> he was very attached to the land,

for there was no pleasure that he sought
that he did not find in the forest.

This type of repetition is usually significant and since we already know that *Melion* is the tale of a werewolf, our suspicions are aroused as to what the eponymous hero is up to in the forest. Exactly what kind of pleasure is he seeking there? Nevertheless, these suspicions are immediately quelled by the next few verses:

Un jor estoit alé chacier
Melïon et si forestier.
Od lui furent si venëor
ki l'amerent de bone amor,
car ce estoit lor liges sire,
totes honors en lui remire.
Tost orent .I. grant cerf trové
tost l'orent pris e descoplé [71–78].

One day Melion went hunting
with his forester.
With him were his hunters
who had great love for him,
for he was their liege lord,
all honor can be seen in him.
Quickly they found a large stag,
quickly they captured it and released it.

Werewolves are not accompanied by their forester and their hunters; they are solitary creatures that roam the woods in search of unsuspecting prey. As a result, what we have learned, then, is that Melion probably loves the woods so much because he likes to hunt. Moreover, he does not kill the stag, but instead captures it and releases it. This is the act of a gentle heart. Melion is probably not, at least not yet, engaging in the activities of a werewolf. We have also learned in this passage that he has recovered the status that he had lost earlier: he is loved by his men.

But Melion's masculine world is about to invaded and his life is about to change again because of the vow he made a year ago at King Arthur's court. While stopped in the woods to listen to the baying of his hounds, Melion sees a beautiful young woman riding toward him. After greeting her, Melion asks her where she was born and what has brought her there. The maiden states that she will not lie to him and that she is of high birth and noble lineage. She then makes this surprising declaration:

"D'Yrlande sui a vos venue,
sachiés que je sui molt vo drue.
Onques home fors vos n'amai,

ne jamais plus n'en amerai.
Forment vos ai oï loer,
onques ne voloie altre amer
fors vos tot seul; ne jamais jor
vers nul autre n'avrai amor" [109–116].

"From Ireland I have come to you,
know that I am totally your sweetheart.
I have never loved any man except you,
never will I love another.
I have heard you praised highly,
never have I wanted to love another
except for you alone; never
will I feel love for another."

For Melion, the maiden is literally a dream-come-true. His vow has been fulfilled, but not because he has gone on a quest for a bride; his bride has come in search of him. This is first of all a testament to Melion's reputation. It is also, however, an indication of his character; whether he was fearful of rejection or simply content to wait and see what happens, he seems to be playing what is normally considered the woman's role here. This scene calls to mind the poem by the twelfth-century troubadour Jaufré Rudel, in which he sings of his love for a woman that he has never seen:

Lanquan li jorn son lonc en may
M'es belhs dous chans d'auzelhs de lonh,
E quan mi suy partitz de lay
Remembra m d'un'amor de lonh...
Iratz e gauzens m'en partray,
S'ieu je la vey, l'amor de lonh:
Mas non sai quoras la veyrai,
Car trop son nostras terras lonh [1–4, 22–25].

When the days are long in May
The sweet distant songs of the birds are pleasing to me,
And when I have left that place
I remember a love faraway...
Sad and happy I will leave,
If I ever see my faraway love,
But I do not know when I will see her,
For our lands are so far apart.[5]

Rudel's poem, whether it was based on fact or was the simply the result of artistic invention, generated the legend of the "princesse lointaine" (the distant princess), an unattainable ideal of courtly love. Here in the *Lai de Melion*, however, we see the maiden living this legend. She is not content to love from afar; she goes after her knight and gets him. And so she does. They marry and have two sons, and as the poet says, ".III. ans le tint en grant chierté" (130), "for three years he cherished her."

Once again, Melion's life is about to change. And once again, it will be because of his vow. This time, it will be his undoing. One day, he goes hunting again, this time with "sa chiere feme" (134), "his dear wife." After spotting an enormous stag, he points it out to his wife. She then suddenly declares that she will never eat again if she doesn't eat some of that stag and then she falls off her horse in a swoon. Unable to comfort his wife, a tearful Melion reassures her, telling her not to cry and to look at a ring that he is wearing:

> ".II. pieres a ens el caston,
> onques si faites ne vit on,
> l'une est blance, l'autre vermeille,
> oïr en poés grant merveille:
> de la blance me toucerés
> e sor mon chief le meterés,
> qant jo serai despoilliés nus,
> leus devenrai, grans e corsus.
> Por vostre amor le cerf prendrai
> e del lart vos aporterai.
> Por Deu vos pri, ci m'atendés
> e ma despoille me gardés.
> Je vos lais ma vie e ma mort;
> il n'i auroit nul reconfort
> se de l'autre touciés n'estoie;
> jamais nul jor hom ne seroie" [157–172].

> "It has two stones in its setting,
> no one has ever seen any made like them,
> one is white, the other scarlet,
> hear a great marvel about them:
> touch me with the white
> and put it on my head,
> when I am undressed and naked,
> I will become a large and powerful wolf.
> For love of you I will catch the stag
> and I will bring you some of its flesh.
> In the name of God I beg of you, wait for me here
> and watch my clothing.
> I leave you in charge of my life and my death;
> there would be no solace
> if I were not touched by the other stone;
> never again would I be a man."

Unlike Bisclavret, Melion does not hesitate but reveals his secret immediately to his wife; he trusts her implicitly and places her happiness and welfare above his own. He also clearly states that he is doing this because he loves her. But the revelation of his secret power seems almost unnecessary; after all, Melion the knight should be able to catch the stag for his wife without the help of Melion the werewolf. Unless, of course, Melion the knight, this man with the gentle heart, finds it impossible to actually kill any of the animals he hunts. Unlike Bisclavret, who becomes a werewolf three days every week, Melion seems at first glance to have total control over his transformation. According to Francis Dubost, "Melion ... se transforme en loup à son gré, grâce à un auxiliaire magique, une bague...." (557), "Melion ... transforms himself into a wolf as he likes, thanks to a magic helper, a ring." Sophie Quénet makes a similar observation: "Mélion peut se transformer quand il le désire; ainsi, par le biais d'un objet magique, Mélion reste maître de son pouvoir et de son temps" (150), "Melion can transform himself when he wants; thus, by means of a magic object, Melion remains master of his power and of his time." E. Margaret Grimes goes beyond stating that Melion's metamorphosis is voluntary; she also declares that it is "a gift of which he [is] proud" (33). But Melion's power is also actually limited by the conditions attached to this ring; he cannot transform himself without the assistance of someone else, someone he can absolutely rely on to touch him with the scarlet stone so that he can recover his human form. Rather than being "proud" of this gift, he seems rather anxious about its potential negative consequences. It is consequently unlikely that Melion has ever taken advantage of the powers of his special ring before.

The *Lai de Melion* is unique among medieval literary werewolf narratives, for the poet actually gives his courtly audience, as well as the modern reader, a glimpse of Melion as he undergoes his metamorphosis. Indeed, we witness each step of the process:

> Il apela son escuier,
> si se commande a deschaucier.
> Cil vint avant, sel descaucha,
> e Melïon el bois entra.
> Ses dras osta, nus est remez,
> de son mantel s'est afublez.
> Cele l'a de l'anel touchié
> qant le vit nu e despoillié.
> Lors devint leu grant e corsus,
> en grant paine s'est enbatus [173–182].

> He called his squire,
> and ordered him to remove his chausses.
> The squire came forward, removed his chausses,
> and Melion entered the woods.
> He removed his clothing, remained naked,

> and put on his cloak.
> His wife touched him with the ring
> when she saw him naked and unclothed.
> Then he became a large and powerful wolf,
> with great difficulty he gave himself over to it.

As we see here, simply removing his clothes has no effect on Melion; nothing happens until he is touched with the ring. Philippe Ménard notes that these stones capable of changing a man into a wolf must be the creative invention of the *Melion* poet, since he is unaware of any lapidary attributing this power to any gemstone (221). It certainly is possible that the *Melion* poet invented this motif, but there is another explanation for its origin. In her introduction to the *lai*, Prudence Tobin states, in response to the criticism that *Melion* is a bad imitation of *Bisclavret*, "Que l'auteur de *Melion* ait connu le lai du *Bisclavret*, cela paraît assez sûr, mais les détails qui se trouvent dans les autres récits et non pas dans *Bisclavret* semblent indiquer que l'auteur a puisé à d'autres sources" (295), "That the author of *Melion* knew the lay of the *Bisclavret*, that seems certain enough, but the details which are found in the other tales and not in *Bisclavret* seem to indicate that the author drew from other sources." As we shall see in our study of the adventure romance *Guillaume de Palerne* in Chapter Seven, a ring that has an exceptional stone with special powers is one of the objects used to transform the werewolf Alphonse back into a man. Since *Guillaume de Palerne* was written between 1194 and 1197 and, like the *lai de Melion*, it was written in Picard, it is very possible that the *Melion* poet was familiar with the adventure romance and that it is one of the sources that he drew from. Finally, we learn in verse 182 that the passage from man to wolf is a very difficult one for Melion; the experience does not seem to be something anyone would want to repeat, much less endure on a regular basis.

The metamorphosis of Melion to werewolf is evidently a turning point in their relationship for his wife. As soon as the knight, now a wolf, takes off in pursuit of the stag, his cherished wife turns tail and rides off on her horse in the other direction. Before leaving, she makes only one comment to the squire, who she has accompany her, "Or le laissons assés chacier" (190), "Let us allow him to hunt as long as he wants." And so she returns to Ireland, where her father is the king and where, according to the poet, "des or ot ce qu'ele demande" (200), "from that moment had everything she asked for." According to Laurence Harf-Lancner, the manner in which the maiden met Melion suggests that she is a fairy.[6] The circumstances of their meeting certainly suggest at first glance that she might be a fairy, since she appears in the woods after Melion catches and releases the stag. In Melusinian and Morganian tales, however, the knight normally pursues a stag, or another animal, until he comes upon the fairy, at which point he abandons his pursuit of the animal. The sequence and timing are different in *Melion*. Harf-Lancer also cites Melion's "refus d'aimer," "refusal to love" (225) as additional evidence that his wife is a fairy. But we have already demonstrated that Melion's high standards for his future bride do not constitute a lack of interest in love; one only needs to remember his reaction when the maidens at King Arthur's court shun him to see that he has not refused love at all. Since Melion did not refuse love, there is no reason to believe that his future wife has to be someone from the supernatural realm. This maiden is not from the Otherworld, she is only from Ireland, a land that mortals may freely visit and from which they may return. At no time does she bestow any special gifts on Melior that would indicate that she is a fairy nor does she exercise any power over him other than the one he gives her when he reveals the secret of his ring and hands it over to her. Moreover, the narrator's remark that when she arrived in Ireland she received everything she wanted (200) refutes the notion that she might be a fairy, since the maiden would not need to be in her father's kingdom in order to have her wishes granted if she were indeed a fairy. Dubost notes that Melion's wife becomes "une femme perfide," "a treacherous woman / wife" in the second half of the story in an arbitrary manner after undergoing a moral metamorphosis parallel to Melion's physical metamorphosis (559). According to Tobin, the wife's sudden change in her attitude towards her husband has no obvious explanation (68, 296). Dubost also remarks on the absence of motivation in *Melion*. We have seen, however, that Marie de France's style is elliptical only in certain parts of *Bisclavret*; thus she conceals Bisclavret's life as a werewolf but reveals the motivation behind his wife's betrayal. The *Melion* poet, on the other hand, leaves almost nothing to the imagination in terms of the activity of the werewolf but conceals the wife's motivation for her abandonment of her husband. Nevertheless, he gives us clues. The narrator's comment "des or ot ce qu'ele demande" (200), "from now on she has what she asks for," is in line with the wife's bizarre statement that she must have some of the stag to eat or she will die. Taken together, they paint a picture of a very self-centered woman. The narrator's comment also implies that this princess may not always have received everything she wanted from her husband. It thus supplies one possible motive for her sudden abandonment of her husband. Moreover, the wife's reaction seems remarkably reasonable, since she has just witnessed the metamorphosis of her husband into a wolf "grant e corsus" (181), "big and strong." I would argue then that if indeed the wife does undergo a moral metamorphosis, the catalyst for her transformation is the fact that she is present while her husband becomes a werewolf. She is probably quite frightened, and reasonably so, but unlike Bisclavret's wife she does not engage in adultery. As a result, the depiction of Melion's wife is definitely less negative than what we find in Marie's *lai*. Bisclavret's wife plots against her husband and betrays him because she does not want to lie in bed with a man who, she has learned, changes himself into a werewolf three days a week. Melion's wife, on the other hand, sees her ideal literally turn into a monster right in front of her eyes and so she runs away, abandoning him and, with him, her shattered dream.

Now, Melion is about to experience the full effect of that fateful vow he took over four years ago. As we shall see, throughout what follows in the rest of the *lai* the poet emphasizes Melion's enduring humanity in spite of his lupine appearance. Melion returns as quickly as he can, carrying the meat "en sa bouche" (210), "in his mouth." "Bouche," however, is normally used only to refer to the mouth of a human being; "gole" is the appropriate word to refer to the mouth of an animal. We thus have our first reminder that Melion is still a man. Of course Melion returns to the place where he left his wife, only to discover that she is gone. Abandoned by her, the woman he loved and trusted with "[his] life and [his] death" (169), he finds himself imprisoned in his animal state. The poet points out Melion's dual status with the words *leus* (*wolf*) and *ome* (*man*), but focuses on the beast's very human reaction to his wife's betrayal:

> Molt fu dolans, ne set que face,
> qant il ne le troeve en la place.
> Mais neporqant se *leus* estoit,
> *sens e memoire d'ome* avoit [215–18, emphasis added].
>
> He was very unhappy and does not know what to do,
> When he does not find her there.
> But even though he was a *wolf*,
> he had *the intelligence and memory of a man*.

The narrator's statement that Melion has not lost his capacity to reason emphasizes the werewolf's humanity and highlights the disparity between his exterior form and his inner reality. Moreover, it creates a sympathetic bond between the creature and the poet's courtly audience. Waiting until dark, Melion takes the risk of boarding a boat that would be sailing to Ireland that evening, but as the narrator notes, "de sa vie n'avoit cure" (226), "he was not worried about his life." This, of course, is not the mentality of a beast that the poet is portraying here, but the reaction of a deeply depressed human being who has undergone a significant trauma. The next morning the boat arrives along the coast of Ireland:

> E qant il sont al port venu,
> Melïon n'a plus atendu
> ains issi fors de son cloier,
> de la nef sailli el gravier.

Li maronier l'ont escrié,
e de lor aviron geté;
li uns l'a d'un baston feru,
a poi k'il ne l'ont retenu.
Lies est qant lor fu escapés,
sor une montaigne est alés;
molt a regardé le païs
ou il savoit ses anemis [237–248].

And when they came to the port,
Melion did not wait any longer
but jumped out from his rack,
from the ship he jumped down on the shore.
The sailors shouted after him,
and struck him with their oars;
one of them with a stick,
they came close to capturing him.
He was happy when he escaped them,
he went up on a mountain
and looked out over the country
where he knew his enemies were.

This particular passage is significant for several reasons. First of all, we see that Melion still has a reckless disregard for his own life, as he leaves the boat in broad daylight and in full view of the sailors. This scene depicting Melion's escape from the boat is very reminiscent of one in *Guillaume de Palerne* that we shall study in Chapter Seven and provides further evidence that the adventure romance might have been one of the sources that the *Melion* poet drew from when composing his *lai.* In this passage, the poet also reveals the werewolf's emotional state after getting away from the sailors "Lies est qant lor fu escapés" (245), "He was happy when he escaped them." More important, the poet reveals Melion's attitude toward his wife and squire; they are his "anemis" (248), "enemies." With this choice of feudal diction the poet leaves no doubt that, although Melion is trapped in his lupine form, it is clearly the mentality of Melion the knight that dominates and controls his actions.

Unlike Marie de France, the *Melion* poet does not gloss over the werewolf's violent nature nor does he cover the man-beast's activities with silence. Instead, he fully depicts them:

En une forest est alés,
vaches e bues i a trovés;
molt en ocit e estrangla;
iluec sa guerre comencha;
plus en i a ocis de cent
a cest premier commencement [253–258].

He went into a forest,
found cows and oxen there,
killed and strangled many of them;
there he began his war;
he killed more than one hundred
to begin with.

Thus we see Melion slaughtering more than a hundred cattle. But he doesn't stop there; ten other wolves join him, doing everything he wants, "tant les blandi e losenga" (270), "he flattered and cajoled them so much." For the next year Melion and his pack of wolves devastate the country, attacking and killing both men and women (273–278).

Par le païs molt se forvoient,
homes e femes malmenoient.
Un an tot plain ont si esté,
tot le païs ont degasté,
homes e femes ocioient,
tote la terre destruioient [273–278].

They wandered throughout the country,
they brutalized men and women.
For one full year they were like this,
they ravaged the country,
killed men and women,
and destroyed the entire country.

According to Ménard, Melion attacks the cattle and causes all this damage in spite of himself; he cannot control what he does because he is werewolf.[7] Bynum also states that Melion has been "contaminated" by his wolf shape to kill people, in spite of his "intelligence and memory" (97). Robyn Holman, on the other hand, states that "Melion continues to provide for his needs by butchering livestock."[8] It is highly unlikely, however, that one wolf would have eaten one hundred cows and oxen in a short period of time. Indeed, the violence that Melion engages in does seem senseless, exactly what a werewolf would do, but the poet has already justified the werewolf's bloody deeds by saying that Melion's *anemis* (enemies) are in Ireland (248) and by labeling his actions a war: "iluec sa guerre comencha" (256), "there he began his war." As Hoepffner points out, the poet's description of the devastation caused by Melion and his band of wolves mirrors Wace's description of Arthur's violent conquest of Ireland in the twelfth-century *Roman du Brut*.[9] This intertextual allusion reinforces the idea that Melion is still a knight in search of vengeance, even though he is trapped in his lupine form. Melion is very much in control of his actions; he is waging war against the entire country of Ireland because it is his wife's home and he is convinced that she is there. Placing these events within a feudal context allows the courtly audience to identify with this unlikely hero.

The poet continues to portray Melion the werewolf and his pack of wolves as a band of knights waging war. We have already seen that Melion gained the loyalty of the ten other wolves through cajolery and flattery (270). These are strategies that are normally employed by human beings with other human beings, not with animals; obviously Melion is still a man inside who is obliged to uses the skills that he has. Although the king tries to catch them, they always manage to elude his traps. Their fortune is about to change, however, as the hunt for them continues:

> Une nuit orent molt erré,
> traveillié furent e pené;
> en .I. bois joste Duveline...
> por reposer i sont entré;
> traï seront e engané [281–83, 287–88].
>
> One night they had wandered far,
> they were tired and exhausted;
> in a woods near Dublin...
> they went in to rest;
> they will be betrayed and deceived.

What we see described here are eleven tired knights; the narrator's use of the words "traï" (betrayed) and "engané" (deceived) make this clear. There is after all nothing in this passage to remind us that they are wolves. Melion, of course, is the only one who is really a knight trapped in a wolf's body and he is merely doing what he has been trained to do; the other ten are just wolves but Melion is using them to assist him in waging his war as if they were indeed knights. The poet describes them collectively and thus presents them all to us as knights. The peasant who sees them resting, however, sees only the eleven wolves that everyone has been seeking and immediately runs to tell the king what he has found. One thousand dogs are used to find the wolves and the woods are surrounded by snares and a crowd of men carrying axes, clubs and swords. All of the wolves are "detrancié e ocis" (317), "cut into pieces and killed," with the exception of Melion, who saved himself "par engien" (322), "through [his] cleverness," by jumping over the snares. Obviously, Melion was able to put his "memoire d'ome" (218) to use; he still had his 'memory of a man' that told him to beware of the snares. Although he has escaped, he is not happy:

> Qant Melïon fu escapés,
> sor une montaigne est montés;
> molt fu dolans, molt li pesa
> de ses leus que il perdu a [331–334].

When Melion had escaped,
he climbed up on a mountain;
he was very sad, it grieved him very much
that he has lost his wolves.

Melion is alone again, without his companions, his fellow wolf-knights. And Melion, the man with the gentle heart, mourns their loss. But, as the narrator informs his courtly audience, his situation is about to change: "ore avra socors briement" (336), "now he will soon have help." Unbeknownst to Melior, King Arthur is on his way to make peace with the Irish king and to enlist his aid in his war against the Romans (337–42). Melion spots Arthur's ship approaching the coastline of Ireland. Recognizing his shield, Melion's sadness dissipates:

L'escu le roi bien ravisa,
sachiés, de voir, grant joie en a;
molt en fu liés, molt s'esjoï,
car encor quide avoir merci [357–60].

He saw the king's shield,
Know, in truth, he had great joy about it;
he was very happy about it, he rejoiced greatly,
for he believed the king would again have pity on him.

King Arthur is his liege lord. Once before, when Melion had been shunned by all the maidens at the royal court, the king had come to his rescue. Knowing that sooner or later he will be captured by the Irish king, Melion also realizes that King Arthur is his only hope for escaping the certain death that awaits him. What is particularly interesting in this passage and the following passage is the fact that the poet reveals the thought processes of the werewolf. Marie de France emphasizes the disparity between Bisclavret's inner reality and outward appearance externally, by presenting the various reactions of the king and the members of his court to the werewolf's bestial and courtly behavior. The *Melion* poet, however, also allows his audience glimpses of the mental state and thoughts of the werewolf and thus accentuates the opposition. Clearly, there is a man hidden inside the body of the wolf. Unfortunately, Melion has no way to tell Arthur who he is and ask for his protection:

Bien set, se del roi n'a confort,
qu'en Yrlande prendra la mort;
mais il ne set comment aler,
leus est, e si ne set parler;
e nekedent tostans ira,
en aventure se metra [395–400].

Well he knows, if he has no help from the king,
That he will die in Ireland.

> But he does not know what to do;
> He is a wolf and so he cannot speak;
> and nevertheless he will still go,
> he will put his life at risk.

The narrator underscores Melion's humanity when he reminds the listeners of the difficulties that the hero faces because he is a prisoner of his lupine form and thus creates a bond between them and Melion. Any audience could certainly sympathize with Melion's frustration at his predicament. Melion's reckless disregard for his safety is now tempered and transformed by his own realistic and thoughtful consideration of his situation. Risking his life in this manner now seems like the only option remaining for him. Unable to speak or communicate except through his comportment, the werewolf runs straight to the king and, like Bisclavret, assumes a feudal posture of submission by throwing himself at the feet of the king:

> As piés le roi se lait chaïr,
> ne se voloit pas redrecier,
> Dont la veïsciés merveillier [406–08].
>
> He fell at the feet of the king
> and did not want to get up again,
> and for this everyone marveled.

This unwolfly, though courtly, behavior astonishes King Arthur, who immediately extends his protection to the beast:

> Ce dist li rois: "Merveilles voi!
> Cis leus est ci venus a moi.
> Or, sachiés bien qu'*il est privés*,
> mar ert touchiés ne adesés!" [409–12, emphasis added].
>
> The king said: "See this marvel!
> This wolf came up to me.
> Now, know well that *it is tame*,
> Woe to whoever touches it or harms it!"

The *Melion* poet adapts the submission motif in several ways. First, the scene occurs not in the forest during a hunt but in Arthur's quarters at a time when there is no immediate threat to Melion's life. Second, the werewolf's actions are reduced to the essential: he throws himself at the king's feet, but does not attempt to hold them or kiss them. Third, the king remarks that the beast is *privés* (tame), unlike the king in *Bisclavret*, who notes that the werewolf has the understanding of a man. This last modification reflects the narrative technique of the *Melion* poet, who uses the consciousness of the beast, rather than the comments of others, to establish the continued vitality of his human nature, which remains uncompromised, in spite of his appearance.

After the submission scene, however, the poet uses the behavior of the werewolf to accentuate the incongruity of his situation. Like a faithful dog, Melion accompanies the king everywhere and lies at his feet. To reinforce this image, the poet tells us repeatedly that the werewolf could not be separated from the king (443–44, 449, and 469–70). But we are also told that Melion eats the same food and drinks the same wine that is served to Arthur and his knights. Even more surprising, when King Arthur entered the castle keep of the Irish king's castle in Dublin, "li leus li tint par le giron" (476), "the wolf held on to him by his tunic or by the tail of his robe." Melion thus becomes part of what seems to be a chivalric ceremonial procession just as if he were one of Arthur's knights. From the very beginning, his comportment causes the knights to marvel:

> Lors dist Gavains: "Segnor, veés,
> *cis leus est tous desnaturés.*"
> Entr'aus dïent tot li baron
> *c'ainc si cortois leu ne vit on* [429–32, emphasis added].
>
> Then Gavain said: "My lord, see,
> *this wolf is altogether unnatural.*"
> Among them all the barons say
> *That they have never seen such a courtly wolf.*

Melion's continued gentle demeanor redefines others' expectations of him and his courtly behavior becomes the norm, just as it did with Bisclavret. His manner changes abruptly when he spots his former squire, however:

> Par l'espaule le vait saisir,
> cil ne se pot a lui tenir;
> en la sale l'a abatu,
> ja l'eüst mort e confondu.
> ne fuissent li sergant le roi
> qui la vindrent a grant desroi [491–96].
>
> He goes to seize him by the shoulder,
> and the squire is unable to hold him off.
> he knocked him down in the middle of the hall,
> and would have destroyed him and killed him
> if it weren't for the king's servants
> who came running in precipitously.

Like Bisclavret's assault on his wife, Melion's sudden attack on his former squire violates what those who know him have learned to expect of him and sends a signal to all onlookers that this event needs to be interpreted. His act becomes a text that must be read. As in *Bisclavret*, Melion's natural wolf-like deeds, which contrast with the gentle behavior he had previously exhibited as a "leus desnaturés," trigger the inquiry that ultimately leads to the discovery of the werewolf's human identity. With this narrative pattern, Marie de France and the author of *Melion* not only provide satisfactory conclusions to their *lais*, but also accentuate the instability of binary pairs such as normal / abnormal and *vilain*, "villainous" / *courtois*, "courtly," whose meanings may vary according to the context in which they are used. Accustomed to courtly behavior from Bisclavret and Melion, the bystanders are shocked by the bestiality they witness; the behavior that in other situations would be considered "normal" for a werewolf is now deemed "abnormal." The werewolf thus serves as a standard for defining courtliness, as well as a reminder of the violence that courtliness and chivalric customs were designed to contain. Now Arthur is compelled to reiterate his role as protector and warn others not to harm the beast:

> "— Mar ert touchiés, fait il, par foi!
> Sachiés que li leus est a moi" [501–02].
>
> "— Woe to whoever touches it, he says, on my word!
> Know that this wolf is mine."

Realizing that the wolf would not have tried to kill any man without good reason, Arthur forces the squire to explain the beast's actions. The king of Ireland persuades his daughter to give him the magic ring and he in turn gives it to Arthur. As soon as the werewolf sees the ring, he recognizes it and, assuming a feudal posture of submission, kneels at Arthur's feet and kisses them (535–36). The king is about to touch Melion with the ring and transform him when he is stopped by Gavain, who tells him to take the wolf to a room and do it there in privacy, "qu'il n'ait honte de la gent" (542), "so that he will not be ashamed because of the people." This motif appears to be a direct borrowing from *Bisclavret*. In Marie's *lai*, it was used to reveal Bisclavret's attitude toward his lupine condition and was reinforced by the fact that the werewolf ignored his clothing when it was brought to him, thus seeming reluctant to transform himself in public. Here in the *lai de Melion*, however, the werewolf does not ignore the ring but appears to place himself in a position so that he can be immediately transformed. At any case, Melion is taken to a private chamber by King Arthur. Once again the poet lets his courtly audience, as well as the modern reader, see Melion undergo his metamorphosis:

> L'anel li a sor le chief mis,
> d'ome li aparut le vis,
> tote sa figure mua,
> lors devint hom e si parla.
> As piés le roi se lait cheïr,
> d'un mantel le firent covrir [547–552].

He put the ring on his head,
the face of a man appeared,
his entire form changed,
then he became a man and spoke.
He dropped to the feet of the king,
they covered him with a cloak.

Although Melion's reverse metamorphosis — his passage from wolf to man — occurs in stages, it seems to be much easier than the transformation he endured from man to wolf. Interestingly, it is his head, or more specifically his face — that which individuates a human being and is used to identify him — that is transformed first. It is also noteworthy that for the third time in the *lai* Melion assumes the feudal posture of submission; doing it now as a man not only reinforces the courtly meaning of his gesture when he did it as a wolf but also directs our attention toward the king and his authority, which Melion is acknowledging with his action.

Throughout the second half of the *lai*, Melion's meting out of vengeance has been a dominating theme. Until this moment, however, none of it has been directed at the person most responsible for his situation: his wife who abandoned him and in doing so trapped him in his lupine form. Now that he has recovered his human form, Melion finally has his opportunity. After the Irish king delivers her to Arthur indicating that he can do whatever he wants with her, "voille l'ardoir, voille desfaire" (568), "whether he wants to burn her or kill her," Melion can only think of punishing her with the same fate he endured:

Meliöns dist: "Jel toucherai
de la piere, ja nel lairai."
Artus li a dit: "Non ferés!
por vos beaus enfans le lairés" [569–72].

Melion said: "I will touch her
with the stone, I will never leave her."
Arthur said to him: "No, you will not do it!
for the sake of your beautiful children, you will leave her."

Unlike Bisclavret, who never speaks again after he recovers his human form, Melion talks more than any other character from this moment on. This pattern duplicates the fact that Melion's humanity is primarily revealed by letting us see his thoughts while he is a werewolf, whereas Bisclavret's human intelligence is revealed through the reactions of others to his behavior. Now, in choosing to punish his wife by turning her into a werewolf, Melion makes abundantly clear his attitude toward being one himself. Obviously, this experience is not only one that he does not care to repeat but it is also undoubtedly one that he has never undergone before. After all of Arthur's barons beg

Melion not to touch her with the ring, he agrees to leave her in Ireland. As he departs with Arthur, however, Melion commends his wife to the devil, saying that he would never be able to love her again or take her back because of the way she mistreated him and that he didn't care if she were burned or hung. The *lai* ends with an explicit moral, also voiced by Melion:

> Melïons dist "Ja ne faldra
> que de tot sa feme kerra,
> qu'en la fin ne soit malbaillis;
> ne doit pas croire tos ses dis" [587–90].
>
> Melion said, "It will never fail
> that if you believe your wife in everything,
> that in the end you will be mistreated;
> you must not believe everything she says."

What is most interesting here is what Melion does not say; he doesn't say that you cannot believe *anything* your wife says—just that you cannot believe *everything* she says. It is, of course, impossible to know exactly which statement Melion is referring to, her declaration to him about how she had never loved another man and would never love another, or her implied promise to wait for him and guard his clothes while he was securing the meat from the stag for her. But the logical choice is the latter, especially since Melion took his "chiere feme" (134), "dear wife," on the hunt that led to his metamorphosis. If there was trouble in his personal paradise before this moment, he certainly seemed to be unaware of it. At any rate, according to the *Melion* poet, the lesson that we should take away from his tale is that women cannot always be trusted. But is this really all there is to it or are there other lessons to be learned? After hearing Melion's story, its courtly audience should have also realized the arrogant foolishness of setting such impossibly high standards for the person you plan to marry because it can leave you vulnerable to the demands of this "ideal" person once you find him or her; after all, this one in a million person may not be so perfect after all. Moreover, through Melion's thoughts and through his courtly behavior after Arthur's arrival in Ireland, the poet proves that Melion's werewolf appearance is only an illusion and that he conforms to Augustine's theory of metamorphosis, which insists that the humanity of the "transformed" creature is untouched. Finally, when Melion accedes to Arthur's request and gives up the idea of punishing his wife, he abandons his pride and acknowledges the supremacy of the king's authority and role as protector and peacemaker. Melion thus reveals the *lai*'s last message, that violence and personal desires for vengeance can only be controlled through chivalric customs and royal justice.

Chapter Six

Arthur and Gorlagon or a Lesson for an Adulteress

Arthur and Gorlagon, an anonymous Latin text of the thirteenth or fourteenth century, offers still another portrait of the noble werewolf, one that is even more violent than that seen in *Bisclavret* or *Melion*.[1] Nevertheless, as we shall see, the author emphasizes the residual humanity of the werewolf from the very beginning and thus conforms to Augustine's theory of metamorphosis. This frame story begins during a banquet at Pentecost when King Arthur exuberantly kisses his queen in front of everyone. Shocked, she asks him to explain why he has kissed her so publicly and in such a manner. In the course of their ensuing conversation, she tells him that he must think that he knows how she feels about him. Arthur then replies, "I doubt not that your heart is well disposed towards me, and I certainly think that your affection is absolutely known to me," but his wife says, "You are undoubtedly mistaken, Arthur, for you acknowledge that you have never yet fathomed either the nature or the heart of a woman" (234). Although the queen seems to be telling him that her heart is not "well disposed" toward him, Arthur appears to be totally oblivious to this admission. Instead of trying to find out exactly what his wife's sentiments are toward him, however, he initiates a quest for himself about women in general as he makes the following announcement: "I call heaven to witness that if up to now they have lain hid from me, I will exert myself, and sparing no pains, I will never taste food until by good hap I fathom them" (234).[2] As Kemp Malone notes, "[t]he domestic affairs of King Arthur were well known throughout Europe" (445). Although Arthur seems totally unaware of Guenevere's relationship with Lancelot, the tale's medieval readers certainly were not. And so, as Arthur leaves on his quest, they are most likely thinking, along with the modern reader, that he has already missed an important point and that whatever he learns will be wasted knowledge.

Seeking an explanation for the behavior of women, Arthur visits in succession three kings. He first visits Gargol, a king who is known for his wisdom. Because he arrives just as Gargol sits down to dine, Arthur is informed by Gargol that he will not tell him what he knows of the ways of women until the next day. He adds that since his is such a "weighty question" (235) and Arthur is tired, he should first dismount and have something to eat. Although Arthur has vowed not to eat anything until he has learned the nature of women, he is soon cajoled into eating. The following morning, when he asks King Gargol for the answer to his question, the king replies, "You are displaying your folly, Arthur. Until now I thought you were a wise man, as to the heart, the nature, and the ways of woman, no one ever had a conception of what they are, and I do not know that I can give you any information on the subject" (236). Telling Arthur that he has an older brother Torleil who is wiser, Gargol suggests that he speak to him. When Arthur visits his kingdom, this scenario repeats itself; Arthur is persuaded to dine with Torleil and the next day this king also admits that he knows nothing about women and sends Arthur on to his older brother King Gorlagon. After two failed attempts to learn the nature of women, however, Arthur has finally learned his lesson; he refuses Gorlagon's repeated offers of hospitality. Indeed, after beginning to tell Arthur "what happened to a certain king" (237), Gorlagon interrupts his story nine times to plead with Arthur to dismount, but Arthur remains constant and does not abandon his vow.[3] According to George Kittredge, Gorlagon's repeated invitations can be explained by the fact that it is a disgrace to have his hospitality rejected; he can not continue his banquet until Arthur agrees to join him (210). More significant, each time that Gorlagon repeats his offer, he adds "when I have told you all you will be but little the wiser."[4] It is not clear, however, whether his comment is intended to evaluate the value of his tale or the ability of Arthur to learn anything from it. This repetition serves not only as an admonition to Arthur but perhaps also to the tale's readers that little will be learned from this tale, at least about the nature of women.

Nevertheless, King Gorlagon at last relates the story of a king whom he describes as "noble, accomplished, rich, and far-famed for justice and for truth" (238). He thus possesses all the requisite qualities of the ideal sovereign. But something else also sets him apart from ordinary men, for in his garden there is a sapling that began to grow the moment he was born. If anyone cuts down this sapling and strikes the king's head with its narrow end and says "Be a wolf and have the understanding of a wolf" (238), he will be immediately transformed into a wolf. Because of the enormous power of the sapling, the king encloses the garden with a high wall and only allows a trusted servant who is also his friend to enter. Moreover, he visits the sapling several times a day and refuses to eat until he has assured himself of its safety, and thereby his own. Like Bisclavret, the king is married to a beautiful woman, "fair to look upon" (238). Unlike Bisclavret's wife, however, she does not love her husband. As Gorlagon tells Arthur, "she loved a youth, the son of a certain pagan king, and preferring his love to that of her lord, she had taken great pains to involve her husband in some danger so that the youth might be able to lawfully enjoy the embraces for which he longed" (238). The king's frequent visits to his garden immediately arouse her curiosity and "with a treacherous smile" (238) she asks him why he goes there so often. Like Bisclavret, he resists answering her questions at first and she responds, like Bisclavret's wife, by accusing him of having a mistress. She then declares that she will not eat again until he explains himself, "I call all the gods of heaven to witness that I will never eat with you henceforth until you tell me the reason" (239). Here we see that a pattern has been firmly established as the protagonists all refuse to eat until they acquire the information they are seeking. The wife's vow mimics Arthur's, but his is made in good faith, whereas hers is made in order to manipulate her husband. Although her husband makes no explicit vow, he refuses to eat each day until he has verified that the sapling is still safe. On the third day, the king begs his wife to eat and she, like Bisclavret's wife, begins to engage in emotional blackmail: "You ought to have no secrets from your wife, and you must know for certain that I would rather die than live, so long as I feel that I am so little loved by you" (239). After she promises that she will never reveal his secret and will "keep the sapling as sacred as her own life" (239), the king finally tells his wife everything. But as Gorlagon tells Arthur, "having got from him that which she had so dearly wished and prayed for, [she] began to promise him greater devotion and love, although she had already conceived in her mind a device by which she might bring about the crime she had been so long deliberating" (239). As opposed to what we saw in *Bisclavret* and *Melion*, the author of *Arthur and Gorlagon* leaves no doubt at all about the culpability of the wife; she has not only been unfaithful to her husband but has been plotting against him, long before she knew that he could be transformed into a wolf. For this wife, the only possible explanation for her behavior is her wickedness. The next day, after cutting down the sapling, she runs to embrace her husband and strikes him on the head with the magic wand, saying "Be a wolf, be a wolf" (239). In her haste, however, she also says "have the understanding of a man," instead of "have the understanding of a wolf" (239). As Gorlagon tells Arthur, "it came about as she had said; and he fled quickly to the woods with the hounds she set on him in pursuit, but his human understanding remained unimpaired" (239). This scene recalls the transformation of the shepherd in *Gilgamesh* and that of Actaeon in Ovid's *Metamorphoses*; in each a man is changed into a wolf by a wicked woman and is set upon by dogs. More important, however, twice within the space of two consecutive sentences, the author refers to the fact that the king retains his human understanding. From the very beginning, then, he underscores the enduring humanity of the werewolf and thus conforms to Christian doctrine regarding metamorphosis.

As a werewolf, the king seems even more bestial than Melion. Indeed, he is probably the most violent of the medieval werewolves, in spite of the fact that with the wife's declaration, "have the understanding of a man," the author provides the clearest statement in any tale that the wolf has retained the reasoning of a man. At times, however, he is depicted in a very sympathetic manner, whereas no redeeming qualities are attributed to his wife. But the storyteller is hardly objective; as the reader and Arthur later learn, he turns out to be none other than the transformed werewolf himself, King Gorlagon. This particular feature makes *Arthur and Gorlagon* unique, for no other medieval werewolf text has as its narrator the werewolf himself.[5] Like Marie de France and the *Melion* poet, the author/narrator of *Arthur and Gorlagon* attempts to minimize the werewolf's savagery by motivating his behavior. First, his treacherous wife immediately married her young pagan lover. After wandering alone in the forest for two years, Gorlagon then "allied himself with a wild she-wolf and begot two cubs by her" (240). As Douglas correctly notes, *Arthur and Gorlagon* is *unique* in that it is the only narrative in which a werewolf mates with a wolf (153). Douglas suggests that the tale's author "colored his accounts of the werewolf's deeds of violence" because he found it so difficult to accept the "essential goodness" of a werewolf that would mate with a "real wolf" (153). But the werewolf has his own reasons for being violent, one which has already been revealed — his wife's betrayal — and others which the narrator has not yet disclosed. Moreover, the author uses Gorlagon's relationship with his mate to demonstrate the depth to which the king has sunk in his despair, and perhaps in his moral metamorphosis, as well as to parallel the queen's unholy union with her pagan lover. As Malone observes, "what could be more monstrous, indeed, to the medieval mind, than the conduct of a lady who prefers a heathen lover to a Christian husband?" (418) The narrator's announcement of the birth of Gorlagon's wolf cubs is immediately followed by a reminder, not of his monstrosity, but of his humanity: "And remembering the wrong done him by his wife (as he was still possessed of his human understanding), he anxiously considered if he could in any way take his revenge upon her" (240). Gorlagon's violence begins when he goes into town with his mate and cubs and kills his wife's illegitimate sons as vengeance for her betrayal, he "[tore] them cruelly limb from limb" (240). But his thirst for vengeance is still not satisfied and he returns again to town with his cubs, attacks the queen's brothers "and tearing out their bowels gave them over to a frightful death" (240). The cycle of violence escalates when the queen's servants, who have been ordered to watch for the wolves, catch Gorlagon's cubs and hang them:

> The wolf, overwhelmed with very great grief for the loss of his cubs and maddened by the greatness of his sorrow, made nightly forays against the flocks and herds of that province, and attacked them with such great slaughter that all the inhabitants, placing in ambush a large pack of hounds, met together to hunt and catch him; and the wolf, unable to endure these daily vexations, made for a neighboring country and there began to carry on his usual ravages. However he was at once chased from thence by the inhabitants, and compelled to go to a third country: and now he began to vent his rage with implacable fury, not only against the beasts but also against human beings [241].

By referring to Gorlagon's emotions, the author portrays the werewolf as a grieving father and thus emphasizes the beast's humanity. Like Melion, his violence seems to be directed against an entire country, indeed against three countries in succession; unlike Melion, however, as Gorlagon's violent acts continue the narrator no longer offers any suggestion that he is acting out of revenge or waging war against the people of these countries. His grief and sorrow have turned into anger. Now Gorlagon is simply described as "vent[ing] his rage" (241) and can be compared to Raimbaud de Pouget, whose metamorphosis was akin to a descent into madness.[6] Although the author does not condone the werewolf's behavior, he does motivate it.

In the midst of his brutal portrayal of the werewolf, the author continues to remind the reader that there is a man trapped inside this wolf. Because the werewolf has caused so many to live in fear, the king of the land decides that he must be caught. Gorlagon tells Arthur how he learned of this plan,

> So one night when the wolf had gone to a neighboring village, greedy for bloodshed, and was standing under the eaves of a certain house listening intently to a conversation that was going on within, it happened that he heard the man nearest him tell how the King had proposed to seek and track him down on the following day, much being added as to the clemency and kindness of the King [241].

Although the werewolf had gone into the village "greedy for bloodshed," with the explicit intent of killing someone, or at the very least of wreaking violence, instead he "returned trembling to the recesses of the woods, deliberating what would be the best course for him to pursue" (241). This is not the reaction of a bloodthirsty, depraved monster that has totally lost touch with his humanity, but rather the reaction of a human being who sees that perhaps there is some hope for him after all. Like Bisclavret and Melion, Gorlagon decides to throw himself at the mercy of the king:

> In the morning the huntsmen and the King's retinue with an immense pack of hounds entered the woods, making the welkin ring with the blast of horns and with shouting, and the King, accompanied by two of his intimate friends, followed at a more moderate pace. The wolf concealed himself near the road where the King was to pass, and when all had gone by and he saw the King approaching (for he judged from his countenance that it was the King) he dropped his head and ran close after him, and encircling the King's right foot with his paws he would have licked him affectionately like a suppliant asking for pardon, with such groanings as he was capable of. The two noblemen who were guarding the King's person, seeing this enormous wolf (for they had never seen any of so vast a size), cried out, "Master, see here is the wolf we seek! see, here is the wolf we seek! strike him, slay him, do not let the hateful beast attack us!" The wolf, utterly fearless of their cries, followed close after the King, and kept licking him gently [241–242].

The author of *Arthur and Gorlagon* shows less originality in his handling of the submission scene and appears to depend heavily on Marie de France's treatment of the motif. Occurring as it does in the forest during a hunt, it almost duplicates the scene in *Bisclavret*, although one significant change has been made; here the king is actually hunting specifically for the werewolf. Gorlagon's actions, which mimic those of Marie's werewolf, reinforce the similarity. Furthermore, as in *Bisclavret*, the king discerns the humanity of the werewolf and offers the beast his protection:

> The King was wonderfully moved, and after looking at the wolf for some time and perceiving that there was no fierceness in him, but that he was rather like one who craved for pardon, was much astonished, and commanded that none of his men should dare to inflict any harm on him, declaring that he had detected some signs of *human understanding* in him; so putting down his right hand to caress the wolf he gently stroked his head and scratched his ears [242, emphasis added].

In *Bisclavret* and *Melion*, the werewolf enacts the feudal ceremony of homage in order to gain the king's mercy and protection. Marie de France never portrays Bisclavret engaged in any violent acts prior to the submission scene and Melion's violence is always depicted as acts of war. Here, for the first time, the werewolf seems to be asking not only for the king's mercy, but also for his pardon for the innocent victims that he has harmed who had nothing to do with his wife's betrayal. Like Melion, the werewolf behaves like a pet dog in the presence of the king, who just happens to be Gorlagon's brother Gargol. And like Bisclavret and Melion, he accompanies his master everywhere and never leaves his side. The narrator, however, weakens this image and reminds the audience of the disparity between Gorlagon's outward appearance and inner reality with his incongruous description of the werewolf dining with the king: "He daily stood at table before the King at dinner time with his forepaws erect, eating of his bread and drinking from the same cup" (242). Although a similar scene in *Melion* provokes comments from the knights that the werewolf is unnatural, in *Arthur and Gorlagon* the beast's eating habits incite no remarks at all and thus seem to be accepted by the onlookers as normal.

As in *Bisclavret* and *Melion*, the motif of the werewolf's sudden regression to violent behavior emphasizes the duality of Gorlagon's nature and eventually results in an investigation of his true identity. As Gorlagon tells Arthur, the werewolf "never showed any fierceness towards or inflicted any hurt upon anyone" (242). We shall see, however, that his docility disappears when he witnesses the adulterous behavior of his royal benefactor's wife and almost kills the queen's lover. The king announces that he will be visiting another king for ten days and asks his wife to protect his wolf and care for him while he is gone. The queen protests, claiming that she is afraid that he might attack her during the night, but we learn from the narrator that "the Queen already hated the wolf because of the great sagacity which she had detected in him (and as it so often happens that the wife hates whom the husband loves)" (243). Thus both the king and the queen have observed the werewolf's understanding and wisdom, although the queen does not admit to it. In order to calm his wife's fears, the king has a golden chain made, by which the werewolf will be fastened to the steps at their bed during the night. In spite of the king's instructions, the queen keeps the wolf chained up all day long. While her husband is gone, she visits his steward, whom she loves "with an unlawful love" (243). Then, toward the end of her husband's absence, she becomes more daring:

> So on the eighth day after the King had started, they met in the bedchamber at midday and mounted the bed together, little heeding the presence of the wolf. And when the wolf saw them rushing into each other's impious embraces he blazed forth with fury, his eyes reddening and the hair on his neck standing up, and he began to make as though he would attack them, but was held back by the chain by which he was fastened. And when he saw they had no intention of desisting from the iniquity on which they had embarked, he gnashed his teeth, and dug up the ground with his paws, and venting his rage over all his body, with awful howls he stretched the chain with such violence that it snapped in two. When loose he rushed with fury upon the sewer [steward] and threw him from the bed, and tore him so savagely that he left him half-dead. But to the Queen he did no harm at all, but only gazed upon her with venom in his eye [243–244].

This episode presents an important variation of the motif, since Gorlagon's motivation is different from that of Bisclavret and Melion. He is not seeking revenge, but is acting out of devotion to his lord, although perhaps the queen's behavior further enrages him because it recalls his own wife's infidelity. The episode thus becomes a *mise-en-abyme* of the betrayal of Gorlagon by his wife and reinforces the message that women cannot be trusted. The author also varies the motif in that the werewolf, unlike Bisclavret who rips off his wife's nose, does not harm the queen at all, although she is certainly as available and as guilty as the steward. The werewolf's behavior here suggests either that he maintains a different code of conduct toward women or, more likely, that he retains an attitude of respect toward the position occupied by the queen as wife of his benefactor, in spite of her immoral conduct. In order to conceal her own misconduct, the queen tells her servants that the werewolf had "devoured her son, and had torn the sewer [steward] as they saw while he was attempting to rescue the little one from death, and that he would have treated her in the same way had they not arrived in time to succor her" (244). She then hides her son in an underground chamber with his nurse and when her husband returns she tells him that the werewolf killed their child. This scene recalls elements of the folktale *Canis* and further develops the image of the werewolf as a faithful dog.[7] When the king arrives home, he is met by his wife, whom the narrator describes as "the deceitful woman, full of cunning ... her hair cut close, and cheeks torn, and garments splashed with blood" (244). She tells her husband how the wolf has "devoured" their son and how it almost killed the steward and would have killed her as well, and then points to the "blood of the little one splashed upon [her] garments [as] witness of the thing" (245). Just then the werewolf makes his entrance:

> Hardly had she finished speaking, when lo! the wolf hearing the King approach, sprang forth from the bedchamber, and rushed into the King's embraces as though he well deserved them, jumping about joyfully, and gambolling with greater delight than he had ever done before [245].

Anyone who has ever seen a dog greet his master after a long absence will immediately recognize this scene, which stands in stark contrast to the last one in which the werewolf appeared. More important, Gorlagon's behavior appears to contradict the testimony of the queen. Although he cannot speak while he is in his lupine form, he is still able to communicate his innocence:

> At this the King, distracted by contending emotions, was in doubt what he should do, on the one hand reflecting that his wife would not tell him an untruth, on the other that if the wolf had been guilty of so great a crime against him he would undoubtedly not have dared to meet him with such joyful bounds [245].

The king's duplicitous wife expects her husband to believe her and the evidence of the crime that she has staged; certainly she counts on the wolf being punished, perhaps even killed, although it is not clear how long she thinks she can conceal her son. But her plans did not take into account the manner in which the wolf might greet her husband and she is ultimately undone by this unforeseen event. Meanwhile, as arbiter of justice, and as husband, the king, who is still undecided about what he should do, "refuse[s] food" (245). Here we see a slight modification of the motif of refusing to eat until information has been acquired; in this case the king has received two conflicting pieces of information and needs further data in order to choose between the two. Since the wife is lying, there is nothing more she can do to prove her point. The wolf, however, has truth and knowledge on his side. Like the medieval ancestor of Lassie, he leads the king to his son:

> [T]he wolf sitting close by him touched his foot gently with his paw, and took the border of his cloak into his mouth, and by a movement of the head invited him to follow him. The King, who understood the wolf's customary signals, got up and followed him through the different bedchambers to the underground room where the boy was hidden away. And finding the door bolted the wolf knocked three or four times with his paw, as much as to ask that it might be opened to him. But as there was some delay in searching for the key — for the Queen had hidden it away — the wolf, unable to endure the delay, drew back a little, and spreading out the claws of his four paws he rushed headlong at the door, and driving it in, threw it down.... Then running forward he took the infant from its cradle in his shaggy arms, and gently held it up to the King's face for a kiss [245].

The heroic image of the wolf breaking down the door, followed by the startling and oxymoronic but tender image of the beast carefully holding the baby in his arms so that his father may kiss him, reveal that this is no ordinary wolf. Gorlagon is truly a man in "wolf's clothing," although the king has yet to learn this. But the wolf's actions do cause the king to "marvel" and say "There is something beyond this which is not clear to my comprehension." Obviously, he knows that the wolf did not kill his son; what he does not understand is why his wife has concocted such an outrageous story. Now the wolf leads the king to the dying steward and has to be restrained from attacking the man again. When the king questions him, the steward repeats the queen's story and the king replies:

> "You are evidently lying: my son lives: he was not dead and at all, and now that I have found him and have convicted both you and the Queen of treachery to me, and of forging lying tales, I am afraid that something else may be false also. I know the reason why the wolf, unable to bear his master's disgrace, attacked you savagely, contrary to his wont" [245–246].

Telling the steward that he will have him "deliver[ed] to the flames" if he doesn't tell the truth, the king finally forces him to confess. Furious, the king conducts a full investigation, after which the steward and the queen are both executed for their crime; the steward is "flayed alive and hanged" and the queen is "torn limb from limb by horses and thrown into balls of flame" (246). The king has settled the problem that he had, unbeknownst to him, with his wife, but there is still the unresolved matter of his wolf.

Although its plot is more complicated, *Arthur and Gorlagon* has essentially the same schema as the two *lais*. The wolf's violence against the steward, which is contrary to his typical behavior, as well as the queen's obvious lie about the death of her son, warns Gargol, who investigates further and with the werewolf's help discovers the truth about the queen's treachery. This change in comportment also causes the king to question Gorlagon's true nature:

> After these events the King pondered over the extraordinary *sagacity* and industry of the wolf with close attention and great persistence, and afterwards discussed the subject more fully with his wise men, asserting that the being who was clearly endued with such great *intelligence* must have the *understanding of a man*, "for no beast," he argued, "was ever found to possess such great *wisdom*, or to show such great devotion to any one as this wolf has shown to me. For he *understands* perfectly whatever we say to him: he does what he is ordered: he always stands by me, wherever I may be: *he rejoices* when I rejoice, and when I am in sorrow, *he sorrows* too. And you must know that one who has *avenged* with such severity the wrong which has been done me must undoubtedly have been a man of great *sagacity* and ability, and must have assumed the form of a wolf under some spell or incantation" [246, emphasis added].

Like Marie de France, the author of *Arthur and Gorlagon* stresses his hero's humanity with the king's comments regarding the creature's understanding, wisdom, and intelligence, as well as his very human emotions of joy and sorrow. The author's use of the diction of combat and chivalric justice—"avenged"—in this passage also points to the disparity between his lupine form and his inner reality. Unlike Marie de France and the *Melion* poet, however, the cleric who wrote *Arthur and Gorlagon* has constructed his tale in such a way that the king protector must also play the role of a detective. There is no one available who knows the truth of the werewolf's identity, other than the werewolf himself, who immediately reacts to the king's conclusion. Unable to speak, Gorlagon is once again forced to communicate his thoughts in other ways: "At these words the wolf, who was standing by the King, showed great joy, and licking his hands and feet and pressing close to his knees, showed by the expression of his countenance and the gesture of his whole body that the King had spoken the truth" (246–247). Understanding by these signals that he has come to the correct conclusion, the king has the werewolf lead them to his kingdom, with the hope that they might be able to help him recover his human form. When they arrive in the werewolf's kingdom, the king and some of his men visit one of its cities, where they learn that "all the men of that province, both high and low degree, were groaning under the intolerable tyranny of the king who had succeeded the wolf, and were with one voice lamenting their master, who by the craft and subtilty [sic] of his wife had been changed into a wolf, remembering what a kind and gentle master he was" (248). This passage is significant for two reasons. First, it verifies the king's assumption about Gorlagon's true identity and nature. Second, it add another unique characteristic to the tale; for of those that we have studied thus far, none of the others provide evidence that anyone other than the wife and accomplice had knowledge of the metamorphosis of the hero. After returning with his troops, the king attacks and captures the tyrant king and his queen, Gorlagon's wife. She is brought before "a council of the chief men of the kingdom" and the king, who tells her, "O most perfidious and wicked woman, what madness induced you to plot such great *treachery* against your *lord*!" (248, emphasis added). As in *Bisclavret,* the author of *Arthur and Gorlagon* uses feudal diction to emphasize the importance of loyalty to one's vows. The king asks her to produce the sapling that she had used to transform her husband, but she claims that it had been "broken up and burnt in the fire" (248).[8] After being tortured "daily ... and allowed ... neither food nor drink" (248), the queen finally reveals the truth and retrieves the sapling. The king takes the wand and strikes the werewolf on the head with it, saying: "Be a man and have the understanding of a man" (249). Gorlagon immediately recovers his human form, but he is not exactly as he had been prior to his original metamorphosis: "The wolf became a man as he had been before, though far more beautiful and comely, being now possessed of such grace that one could at once detect that he was a man of great nobility" (249). Now he is not only more "beautiful" and more "comely" than he had originally been, but he also seems to be more refined and noble. In other words, he has been physically and morally transformed by his experiences as a werewolf. When asked how his wife and her lover should be punished, Gorlagon condemns to death the man who had taken his place. Instead of executing his wife, however, he merely divorces her because of "his inborn clemency" (249). With Gorlagon's human form and kingdom restored to him, the king returns to his own realm.

At this point, the reader might think that the tale has been told and that Arthur can at last acquiesce to Gorlagon's request to dismount and eat. But that is not the case; instead, Arthur tells him that he will not do so until Gorlagon has answered the following question: "Who is that woman sitting opposite you of a sad countenance and holding before her in a dish a human head bespattered with blood, who has wept whenever you have smiled, and who has kissed the bloodstained head whenever you have kissed your wife during the telling of your tale?" (249). This shocking and gruesome spectacle, which had been in front of Arthur the entire time that he was listening to Gorlagon's tale, has been concealed from the reader the entire time and is now revealed at the last moment.[9] The surprise and abruptness of this revelation only heightens the horror we feel and it isn't lessened when Gorlagon at last completes his tale. After acknowledging that he was the werewolf, he reveals that it was to his own brother's kingdoms that he had traveled while trapped in his lupine form, first to the kingdom of King Torleil and then to that of King Gargol, and that it was the latter who had been so kind to him and had helped him recover his human form.[10] Finally, in response to Arthur's question, Gorlagon tells him:

> "And the bloodstained head which that woman sitting opposite me embraces in the dish she has in front of her is the head of that youth for love of whom she wrought so great a crime against me. For when I returned to my proper shape again, in sparing her life, I subjected her to this penalty only, namely, that she should always have the head of her paramour before her, and when I kissed the wife I had married in her stead she should imprint kisses on him for whose sake she had committed the crime. And I had the head embalmed to keep it free from putrefaction. For I knew that no punishment could be more grievous to her than a perpetual exhibition of her great wickedness in the sight of all the world" [250].

It is difficult for us as modern readers of this medieval tale to separate ourselves from our modern mentality. Gorlagon has indeed spared the life of his treacherous queen, but in his "clemency" he has invented what appears to be a most cruel and unusual punishment. For him, this punishment resides in the fact that her guilt is on permanent display for all to see. Yet she may be suffering a far more grievous penalty as she is continually forced to confront the loss of the man she supposedly loved in a most horrible way. The image of this sad, weeping woman kissing the bloody severed head creates a striking contrast with that of the smiling Gorlagon as he kisses his new wife and gives one pause. It would seem that his anger has finally been transformed into this last act of vengeance. As a werewolf, he is depicted as "venting his rage"; Gorlagon's final violent deed as retribution for his metamorphosis, however, appears to be the result of cold-blooded calculation. According to Mihaela Bacou, in each of the three werewolf tales that we have studied, the wife's lover is most likely the "double négatif," "negative double"; of the hero, whereas the king is his "double positif," "positive double" (42).[11] Bacou further states:

> Dans *Arthur and Gorlagon*, il [l'amant] devient même l'image humaine, par sa tyrannie, du destin du loup, de la violence animale de l'homme méta-

> morphosé. Ce qui est justifiable chez le second ne l'est pas chez le premier, mais cette similitude renforce son statut de double négatif [42–43].
>
> In *Arthur and Gorlagon,* he [the lover], because of his tyranny, even becomes the human image of the wolf's fate, of the animal violence of the transformed man. What is justifiable in the second isn't in the first, but this similarity reinforces his status as negative double.

Bacou has indeed identified a significant relationship between the male protagonists, although as we have seen, all of Gorlagon's "animal violence" is certainly not justifiable, since he is never described as waging war against the people of his brother's kingdoms and his subjects are victims of his wife and her lover, just as he is. Furthermore, Bacou notes that in all three tales, the werewolf's violence is justified "justement parce qu'il 'est' loup" (43), "just because he is a wolf." But Bisclavret never engages in violence except when he attacks his wife and her lover in order to avenge their treachery against him.[12] As for Melion, all his violence in Ireland is associated with the war that he is waging there against the homeland of his traitorous wife.[13] Gorlagon, on the other hand, initially acts violently out of sorrow and grief, but eventually is merely "venting his anger." According to Bacou, Gorlagon is different after his metamorphosis because he has evolved psychologically:

> La domestication du loup en fera un chien, non dans le sens où ce dernier est l'animal châtré, mais dans la mesure où il reconstruit son devenir en se faisant homme meilleur parmi les hommes alors que son apparence est celle d'un loup.... Le parallélisme développé en *Arthur et Gorlagon* souligne le fait que le héros, l'amant et le roi n'étaient finalement qu'une seule et même personne à des stades d'évolution différents, le loup-garou étant le seul à subir une évolution psychologique constructive" [44].
>
> The domestication of the wolf will make him a dog, not in the sense of being a castrated animal, but to the extent that he reconstructs his future by making himself a better man among men even though his appearance is that of a wolf.... The parallelism developed in *Arthur and Gorlagon* underlines the fact that the hero, the lover and the king were ultimately only one and the same person at different stages of evolution, the were-wolf being the only one to undergo a constructive psychological evolution.

The fact that Gorlagon was a king prior to his metamorphosis indicates that he was already a "better man among men." Unfortunately, while trapped in his lupine form, he allowed his anger to control his behavior. Nevertheless, Gorlagon himself tells Arthur that after he recovers his human form he is more "beautiful," more "comely" and appears more noble and refined. He certainly may have undergone some sort of "evolution," as Bacou suggests. But it is much more likely that he makes a conscious decision to "reconstruct his future," that is, to turn 180 degrees from the path he is on and to look for a way to recover his human identity, when he overhears the conversation about the king's plans to track him down. He does not domesticate himself nor is he domesticated by anyone else; instead, he behaves in a courtly manner within the constraints of his lupine form. Finally, if Bacou is correct, and Gorlagon represents the final evolution, then that would seem to posit the manner in which he punished his wife as something to emulate. But Gorlagon is, after all, still just a man with all his flaws, his anger, and his need for vengeance.

So what does Arthur learn from Gorlagon? The narrator tells us that after hearing his tale, "Arthur dismounted and ate, and on the following day returned home a nine days' journey, marveling greatly at what he had heard" (250). As we have already seen, throughout the telling of his tale, Gorlagon warns Arthur that when he has told his tale Arthur "will be but little the wiser." When he relates how his wife tried to find out why he visited his garden so often, he comments that "it is customary for a woman to wish to know everything" (238) and subsequently refers to her "obstinacy" about the matter (239). Later, when he tells him about the other queen's hatred of the werewolf, he observes that a wife frequently "hates whom the husband loves" (243). These are minor issues, however. Ultimately, Gorlagon relates the story of the infidelity of two wives who happen to be queens, but his account is set within the tale of another queen, Arthur's wife, who is also unfaithful. Has Arthur learned anything from Gorlagon's story? He should, for this frame tale with its three layers of adulterous women is set within another frame. The tale opens with Arthur being chastised by his queen for kissing her exuberantly in the presence of others; it closes with the revelation that Gorlagon has been kissing his new wife throughout the telling of his tale while his former wife has been forced to kiss the severed head of her lover. Since Arthur seemed blissfully unaware of his own wife's infidelity when he left on his quest, it is doubtful that the Arthur who leaves Gorlagon's kingdom "marveling greatly at what he had heard" has really learned anything about the "nature and heart of a woman." But when he returns to his court, it is likely that he will repeat Gorlagon's tale to his wife. Perhaps she will remember Gorlagon's first wife and that severed head; perhaps she will even think twice before she criticizes Arthur again for kissing her at a banquet. The tale of *Arthur and Gorlagon* thus serves as a cautionary tale for this adulteress and for unfaithful women everywhere.

Chapter Seven

Guillaume de Palerne or a Lesson in Noble Sacrifice

Surviving in only one manuscript from the thirteenth-century, *Guillaume de Palerne* is an anonymous *roman d'aventure* (adventure romance) written in the Picard dialect of northern France, most likely between 1194 and 1197.[1] Very little is known about the poet who wrote *Guillaume de Palerne.* Since the verse romance is written in the Picard dialect, he was probably either from that region or at least very familiar with its language. The poet does tell us that he wrote the romance for "la contesse Yolent," "Countess Yolande" (9656), at her request: "Cest livre fist diter et faire / Et de latin en roumans traire," "She had this book written and made / And translated from Latin into French" (9659–9660).[2] Yolande has been identified as the aunt of Baldwin VI, the Count of Flanders and Hainaut who became Emperor of Greece. Her second husband Hugh, the Count of Saint Pol, traveled with Philip Augustus, the King of France, from Sicily to Palestine for the Third Crusade during the winter of 1190-1191.[3] The poet who wrote *Guillaume de Palerne* may very well have been a cleric in Hugh's entourage. The knowledge of Palermo and Sicily that he demonstrates in the romance certainly suggests that he actually visited the island, perhaps while en route to the Holy Land or while returning from the Third Crusade. *Guillaume de Palerne* is of interest to our study because the romance relates the story of a young prince of Sicily who is kidnapped by a werewolf at the age of four. Woven into the story of the eponymous hero is the parallel story of Alphonse, the Spanish prince who was transformed into a werewolf by his stepmother when he was still a toddler.[4] Indeed, it is in *Guillaume de Palerne* that we find the fullest treatment of the literary treatment of the noble werewolf, as well as the most complete transformation in the depiction of the werewolf from bloodthirsty beast to chivalrous hero. Out of this romance emerges a werewolf remarkably different from those we find in the shorter tales.

As we have seen, the three medieval literary narratives that we have looked at thus far, *Bisclavret, Melion,* and *Arthur and Gorlagon,* bear striking resemblances to one another. Reflecting the Christian doctrine of metamorphosis, these tales have come a long way from the popular accounts of the bloodthirsty werewolf whose humanity totally disappears after his metamorphosis. In his edition of *Arthur and Gorlagon,* Kittredge claims that *Bisclavret, Melion,* and *Arthur and Gorlagon* are all versions of one story, *The Werewolf's Tale* (14, 19).[5] Ménard, on the other hand, disputes Kittredge's assertion, saying that there are too many differences in the details concerning the metamorphosis of the wolf, as well as in the narrative structure itself of the stories. He does note, however, a similarity between these stories and *Guillaume de Palerne*:

> On observera seulement que dans quatre textes, *Guillaume de Palerne,* le *Bisclavret, Melion, Arthur et Gorlagon,* se retrouvent trois traits communs: la méchante femme, l'impossible retour à la condition humaine et le motif du loup doux et humain.[6]
>
> We will only observe that in four texts, *Guillaume de Palerne,* the *Bisclavret, Melion, Arthur et Gorlagon,* are found three common traits: the wicked woman, the impossible return to the human condition and the motif of the gentle and human wolf.

Since Ménard's primary interest is the phenomenon of metamorphosis itself, he dismisses these motifs as insignificant. But the three short narratives share other motifs: the noble werewolf who is both hero and victim, the submission scene, the king-protector, and the unexpected and sudden violent behavior of the werewolf that leads to the discovery and recovery of his identity.[7] These similarities far outweigh the differences and are too important to be overlooked. It is obvious that the authors all draw upon the same set of motifs and participate in a common tradition.

The *Guillaume* poet also avails himself of these motifs, playing with them, adapting them, and weaving them into the strands of Guillaume's story to create the precise literary actualization that is *Guillaume de Palerne.* All the narrative elements are modified in the romance, although some only to a minor extent. Alphonse is not *the* hero of this narrative; he is one of two heroes. Like Bisclavret, Melion, and Gorlagon, he is noble and the victim of a treacherous woman. Alphonse, however, is only a child at the time of his metamorphosis; he is therefore betrayed by his wicked stepmother Brande, not by an unfaithful wife, as are the other three werewolves.[8] Since Guillaume and Alphonse are approximately the same age,[9] this modification is a natural consequence of the narrative's emphasis on the childhood and youth of the primary hero. Alphonse's age and vulnerability accentuate his innocence. Trapped in the body of the werewolf, Alphonse retains his humanity. Unlike the werewolf condition of Bisclavret, Melion, and Gorlagon, however, Alphonse's "werewolfness" is totally foreign to him. It is a true disguise: his metamorphosis is linked neither to his nature, as it is with Bisclavret, nor to his possession of an object endowed with magic properties, as it is with Melion and Gorlagon. Unlike the old man and woman in *Topographia Hibernica,* who are forced to become werewolves for seven years as communal penance, Alphonse has no wrong to atone for. Like Ishtar's shepherd and Actaeon, Alphonse is a true victim and has no personal potential for becoming a werewolf; the condition is imposed on him from the outside. His duality thus fully illustrates the Christian theory of metamorphosis as illusion. As we shall see, the *Guillaume* poet extensively modifies the motifs of the submission scene, the king-protector, and the unexpected and sudden violent behavior of the werewolf that leads to the discovery and recovery of his identity.

At the beginning of the romance, the poet carefully crafts an illusion, one which mimics the motif of the werewolf itself while at the same time playing with this very motif. Unlike what we find in *Bisclavret, Melion,* and *Arthur and Gorlagon*, Alphonse's story is not told in strict chronological order, for his story is subordinate to that of Guillaume's. Thus when he makes his first appearance in the romance he has already been transformed. Guillaume, who is only four years only, is in the park outside the palace in Palermo with his parents, King Embron and Queen Felise. Unbeknownst to them, Embron's brother is plotting with the child's nursemaids to poison the boy and King Embron so that he can inherit the throne himself. Although the narrator warns the reader that danger is at hand, it does not come from Guillaume's uncle:

Par le vergier li rois ombroie
80 Et la roïne a molt grant joie,
Mais se sevent com lor grans dex
Lor est presens devant lor ex.
L'enfant florretes va cuellant,
84 De l'une a l'autre va jouant.
Atant esgardent la ramee:
Saut uns grans leus, *goule baee,*
Afendant vient comme tempeste;
88 Tuit se destornent por la beste;
Devant le roi demainement
Son fil travers sa goule prent [79–90, emphasis added].

In the orchard the king is resting in the shade
80 And the queen is very happy,
But they do not know that their great grief
Is about to appear before their very eyes.
The child is gathering flowers;

84 From one flower to another he goes playing.
At this moment they are looking at the foliage:
A great wolf jumps out, his mouth gaping open;
He comes rushing like a tempest.
88 Everyone turns away because of the beast;
Right in front of the king himself
The wolf takes his son in his mouth.

Like a storm that shatters the tranquility of a summer day, the werewolf enters the scene. Nothing is more obvious than the opposition that the poet presents here between peace and violence and between innocence and evil. This contrast is reinforced by the vocabulary and rhythm of the passage. *Vergier* (orchard), *ombroie* (shade), *joie* (happy), *l'enfant* (the child), *florrettes* (flowers), *cuellant* (gathering), and *jouant* (playing) all present an image of well-being that is strengthened by the soothing sound of the elongated vowels and predominately soft consonants (vv. 79–84). The spell is broken in the next sequence with the combination of hard consonants, short vowels, and violent imagery offered by the poet's lexical choices: *saut* (jumps), *leus* (wolf), *goule baee* (mouth gaping open), *afendant* (rushing), *tempeste* (tempest), *destornent* (turns away), *beste* (beast), *prent* (takes) (vv. 85–90). This scene is significant for several reasons. First, it establishes the importance of the werewolf's role in the romance. From the very beginning, Guillaume's and Alphonse's lives are intertwined. Unlike the three shorter tales where the listeners are forced to wait until the narrative has progressed quite a bit before they see the werewolf, here they encounter him almost immediately. Second, in this scene the poet begins to develop the *leitmotif* of the "goule baee" (86), "mouth gaping open," which will reappear in key scenes throughout the romance.[10] Third, the scene de-emphasizes the importance of the process itself of metamorphosis. Only later do we learn how Alphonse becomes a werewolf. Finally, in keeping with the poet's announcement in his prologue that he will reveal his hidden knowledge in the romance (vv. 1–17), the scene draws attention to the narrative's theme of illusory appearance by giving everyone a false impression. Although the narrator refers to Alphonse as "uns grans leus" (86), "a great wolf," in this passage, less than one hundred verses later, while mourning for her son who has been carried off, Queen Felise grieves "Or es a leu garoul peuture" (151), "Now, you are food for a werewolf." The queen's horror is perfectly understandable, since she last saw Guillaume in the mouth of the werewolf. All of the elements of the scene work together to create the image — the illusion — that a savage wolf has taken the prince away in order to eat him. The queen believes this, as does the king and his retinue who chase the werewolf all the way to the Strait of Messina:

116 Il saut en l'eve a tout l'enfant
Le Far trespasse, perdu l'ont
Li rois et cil qui o lui sont.
Ensi s'en va en tel maniere
[120] A tout l'enfant la beste fiere [116–20].

116 He jumps in the water with the child
And crosses the strait. They have lost him,
The king and those who are with him.
Thus in this manner the fierce beast
120 Went off with the child.

The king and queen's despair after they lose their child is real. All the rest, however, is really only an illusion, one that will soon be partially dispelled, at least for the romance's courtly audience. As for Guillaume's parents, their illusion will last for many cruel years; by the time Guillaume returns to Palermo and the truth is revealed, he will be a young man and his father King Embron will be long dead.

Faithful to the promise he made in his prologue, the poet begins to reveal some of his hidden knowledge, in this case about the werewolf. After escaping with Guillaume, the werewolf travels with the child day and night until they reach a forest outside Rome, where they rest for a week. Here the poet presents an entirely different image of the creature:

L'enfant de quanques fu mestiers
Li a porquis la beste franche:
176 Onques de rien n'ot mesestance.

Whatever the child needed
The noble beast provided for him;
176 Never did he experience any discomfort [174–76].

The werewolf is not a "beste fiere" (120), "fierce beast," after all. Not only does the werewolf not harm the child, but he also administers to his needs. The narrator's reference to the werewolf as "la beste franche" (175), "the noble beast," alludes to the wolf's noble conduct, as well as his noble origins. The poet continues to develop the image of the werewolf as a gentle caretaker in the passage that follows:

La nuit le couche joste soi
Li leus garous le fil le roi,
L'acole de ses .IIII. piés,
184 Si est de lui aprivoisiés
Li fix le roi que tot li plaist
Ce que la beste de lui fait [181–86].

At night next to himself
The werewolf puts the king's son to bed

And embraces him with his four paws.
184 In this manner he tamed the son of the king,
Who is pleased by everything
That the beast does for him.

For the first time, the narrator refers to the wolf as "li leus garous" (182), "the werewolf," thus verifying the queen's suspicions, which she voiced when she witnessed her son's kidnapping (151). In spite of this label, and contrary to what appears in *Melion,* it is not the werewolf who is referred to as "tame"; instead, the four-year-old Guillaume is "aprivoisiés" (184), "tamed," by the werewolf. Although in this passage the beast clearly occupies a dominant position of potential power, the last two verses hint at a different hierarchal relationship between them, one that prefigures Guillaume's future sovereign role. Nevertheless, the werewolf is still functioning as the boy's caretaker, but this role is about to be assumed by another. While the wolf is out searching for food for Guillaume in the nearby villages, a cowherd finds the child and takes him home with him. When the werewolf returns to his den and discovers that Guillaume is missing, he reacts in the following manner:

Onques nus hom de mere né
Ne vit a beste tel duel faire.
236 Qui li oïst uller et braire
Et les piés ensamble detordre
Et la terre engouler et mordre,
Esrachier l'erbe et esgrater
240 Et soi couchier et relever
Et comme il s'ocit et confont,
Et querre aval et querre amont
Et les larmes fondre des ex,
244 Bien peüst dire si grans dex
Ne fu par nule beste fais [234–45].

Never did any man born of a mother
See a beast demonstrate such grief.
236 Whoever might have heard him shriek and howl
And see him wring his feet together,
Bite and plunge his mouth into the ground,
Tear out and scratch the grass,
240 Lie down and get up again,
And see how he is almost dying of chagrin and how overwhelmed he is,
How he searches low and searches high,
Tears flowing from his eyes,
244 That person might well have said that such great grief
Had never been expressed by any other beast.

The werewolf reacts just as a mother would; indeed, his reaction is almost identical to that of Queen Felise when Guillaume is kidnapped, although the werewolf is unable to speak and his movements are constrained by his lupine form.[11] We see something similar in *Melion*, although on a much smaller scale; the werewolf is sad when he cannot find his wife: "Molt fu dolans, ne set que face, / qant il ne le troeve en la place" (215–16), "He was very unhappy and does not know what to do, / When he does not find her there." Likewise, in *Arthur and Gorlagon*, the werewolf is described as "overwhelmed with very great grief for the loss of his cubs and maddened by the greatness of his sorrow" (241). But each passage in the two shorter narratives is almost immediately followed by the violent acts of the werewolf, which are motivated by his grief and justified by his need for revenge. In *Guillaume de Palerne*, however, no such violence occurs. Instead, the werewolf tracks Guillaume to the cowherd's home. When he sees that the boy will be well cared for and will be happy with the cowherd and his wife, "[m]olt en est liés et fait grant joie" (265), "he is very happy about it and shows his great joy." The werewolf then disappears from Guillaume's life for several years.

From the beginning of the romance the *Guillaume* poet never hides the fact that the wolf is actually a werewolf, but instead stresses his unnatural state. Before continuing with Guillaume's story, the narrator decides to reveal the truth about the werewolf:

> Li leus warox dont je vos di
> N'iert mie beste par nature [274–75].
>
> The werewolf that I am telling you about
> Was not at all a beast by nature.

After referring to the wolf as a "leux warox" (274), "werewolf," the narrator amplifies and emphasizes the beast's abnormality with the litotes in verse 275. Obviously he wants to be sure that his audience does not miss the fact. The narrator has already referred to the wolf as a werewolf three times, "li leus garous" (182), "li garous" (197), "li garoux" (261). But before he does so, the queen, who would not be privy to this information, calls the wolf who has just kidnapped her child a "leu garoul" (151), "werewolf." Since the audience is already well aware that the wolf is a werewolf, the narrator's "revelation" in the passage above is anticlimactic. The same could probably be said of the story of Alphonse's metamorphosis that he is about to tell them:

> 280 Si com l'estoire le nos dist,
> Il estoit fix le roi d'Espaigne
> De sa feme la premeraine.
> De lui estoit morte sa mere;
> 284 Feme reprist li rois ses pere,
> Fille le roi de Portingal.
> Molt sot la dame engien et mal;
> Sorceries et ingremance

288 Avoit molt apris de s'enfance.
Bien sai que Brande fu nomee [280–89].

280 So, as the story tells us,[12]
He was the son of the king of Spain,
The firstborn of his wife.
His mother had died giving birth to him;
284 The king his father took a new wife,
The daughter of the king of Portugal.
294 Now that lady knew trickery and evil very well;
Much sorcery and magic
288 She had learned from her childhood.
Well I know that she was named Brande.

Like Gorlagon's wife, Queen Brande appears to be unequivocally evil. She is not only wicked, however; like the werewolves in the three shorter narratives, she also possesses unnatural powers. Her knowledge of sorcery and her malevolence are the worst combination possible, one which she will use against the most innocent of victims, her stepson, who is just a little boy, so that her own son Brandin may inherit the throne. Although Brande is perhaps motivated by motherly devotion, her ambition is nevertheless linked to her desire for power as she robs Alphonse of his heritage and identity by using sorcery to transform him into a werewolf:

Oiés que fist la male feme:
296 Vit que issi faitement regne;
De son fillastre a tele envie
N'enportera, s'el puet, la vie
Ou en tel point le metera
300 Jamais roiaume ne tenra.
D'un oingnement li oint le cors
Qui tant estoit poissans et fors;
Tant par estoit de grant vertu,
304 Si tost com l'enfes oins en fu,
Son estre et sa samblance mue,
Que *leus* devint et *beste mue.*
Leus fu *warox* de maintenant;
308 Ce que de lui fu aparant
A tout perdu, *son essiënt* [295–309, emphasis added].

Hear now what that wicked woman did.
296 She saw how her stepson would reign;
She has such a strong hatred for him
That she will take away his life, if she can,
Or she will put him in such a position
300 That he will never rule the kingdom.
She anoints his body with an ointment
Which was very strong and powerful;

It was so very potent that
304 As soon as the child was anointed with it
His condition and appearance changed;
304 A *wolf* he became and he was *transformed* into a *beast.*
At once he became a *werewolf*;
308 Everything that was visible of him
He has lost, *he believes.*

Brande's plot against her stepson parallels the conspiracy against Guillaume by his uncle. In addition, her evil maneuver adds a marvelous element to the romance and highlights the difference between the male and female exercise of power. Magic has become a substitute for the prowess which she, as a woman, does not possess. In the three shorter werewolf narratives, the treacherous wives are motivated either by fear or by their adulterous love for another man. Here, however, Queen Brande is motivated by her hatred and greed. Moreover, according to the narrator she is even willing to kill Alphonse, if necessary, in order to accomplish her goal. Although she manages to instantly change his "condition and appearance" by transforming him into a werewolf, she has only changed him outwardly. Even so, the poet emphasizes the importance of this metamorphosis with a triple repetition of its physical results in two consecutive verses: "leus" (306), "wolf," "beste mue" (306), "transformed beast," and "leus warox" (307), "werewolf," terms which he will henceforth use as synonyms for one another. On the other hand, the phrase "son essiënt" (309), "he believes," immediately reveals to the romance's courtly audience that the werewolf has retained his human understanding and intelligence. The last two verses (308–09) of this passage will be particularly significant as we work toward an understanding of the werewolf's role in the romance. The phrase "he believes" at the end of these verses suggests that the werewolf is wrong; all in fact has not been lost and there is still something remaining that can be seen of him, something that is not concealed by his lupine form, his behavior. It is his courtly and very human behavior that will point to the illusion of his metamorphosis. In the scene that follows, however, Alphonse appears to be acting entirely like a wolf, at least at first glance:

Volt s'enfuïr isnelement,
Car tres bien set, se or est pris,
312 N'escapera ne soit ocis.
Mais ains que gerpesist la terre,
Vers sa marastre *mut tel guerre*
Seure li cort *geule estendue*,
316 Se la gens n'i fust acourue
Qui de la mort l'ont bien tensee [310–17].

He wants to flee immediately,
For he knows very well that if he is taken now

312 He will not escape and might be killed.
But before he leaves that land
Against his stepmother he *begins a war*;
Toward her he runs, his *mouth stretched open.*
316 He would have hurt Brande had her people not run to her;
From death they truly protected her.

After Gorlagon is transformed by his treacherous wife, he is pursued by the dogs that she releases to hunt him down.[13] Alphonse, too, is about to run for his life as he is be chased by Brande's household throughout the city and more than three miles out of town. Indeed, he will be hunted down from early morning until late that night by men who are trying to kill him (316–326). But Alphonse's first and immediate response to his transformation, before he escapes, is an aggressive one as he attempts to attack his stepmother. As we saw with Melion, the narrator justifies Alphonse's violence by describing it in chivalric terms: "he begins a war against his stepmother" (314). This scene is particularly noteworthy in that it is one of only three or four in the romance depicting the werewolf engaged in what might be considered violent acts.

The narrator also motivates and justifies the first violent episode depicted in the romance, Guillaume's kidnapping. Explaining how the werewolf came to Apulia "after one season" (328), he tells his courtly audience:

En la terre fu puis .II. ans;
332 Molt devint fiers et fors et grans,
Bien sot le plait et le desroi
Que dut faire du fil le roi
Ses oncles, li *traïtres* lere,
336 De son neveu et de son frere.
Ne pot souffrir la grant dolor,
Ne le buffoi au *traïtor*:
Por ce l'enfant ensi ravi,
340 Si comme arrier avés oï [331–40, emphasis added].

He had been in that land for two years
332 Where he grew very fierce, strong, and big.
He found out about the guilty deed and the serious wrong
That was to be done to the son of the king
By his uncle, that *treacherous* thief,
336 To his nephew and his brother.
He could not tolerate this great suffering,
Nor the arrogance of the *traitor*.
Because of this he kidnapped the child,
340 Just as you have already heard.

So although they did not know it, what King Embron and Queen Felise witnessed was not really a kidnapping; it was a rescue. Like Marie de France, the *Guillaume* poet transforms the werewolf's behavior into the deeds of a knight by providing the werewolf with a noble motive for "kidnapping" Guillaume. With his feudal diction: "traïtres" (335), "treacherous" and "traïtor" (338), "traitor," the poet justifies this deed even more and emphasizes the chivalric nature of the werewolf's conduct. After he is transformed into a wolf by his stepmother, Alphonse is no longer a helpless child; he now has not only the means to defend himself, but also the ability to defend others. Thus we see him enacting chivalric justice in this scene.

The poet's early divulgence of and insistence on Alphonse's situation has been strongly criticized by literary scholars. Charles Dunn reproaches the author for having revealed the true identity of the werewolf too soon:

> [T]he poet quite unnecessarily informs the reader about the werwolf's identity at the very beginning of the romance; and the reader's interest in the discovery of Alphonse's true nature by the characters in the romance is needlessly minimized by the fact that on two dramatic occasions those who see the transformed Alphonse speak of him as a *werwolf* although they can have no idea that he is anything more than a normal wolf [115].

Alexandre Micha reacts similarly: "Enfin en informant, dès le début, le lecteur de l'identité réelle du loup, le romancier enlève de l'intérêt à son récit et manque un effet de surprise dans la scène où la bête est délivrée de l'enchantement."[14] "Finally, by informing the reader from the beginning about the real identity of the wolf, the author makes his account less interesting and fails at creating a surprise in the scene in which the beast is set free from the enchantment." If Dunn and Micha are correct, the poet has been terribly careless with the use of these terms, as well as with the exposition of his plot. Micha does attempt to explain the early revelation of Alphonse's history: "Mais comment, sans cette précaution, faire admettre le comportement de cet étrange garou?"[15] "But without this precaution, how can the behavior of this strange werewolf be accepted?" The audience's concern, however, does not have to revolve around the true identity of the werewolf, as Dunn and Micha suggest, but may instead focus on how Alphonse will manage to regain his human identity.[16] This interest mirrors the curiosity generated by Guillaume's situation: how will he recover his birth identity? As we have seen, the authors of the shorter werewolf tales also never hide the "werewolfness" of their heroes and divert the suspense of their stories in a similar manner. The *Guillaume* poet, however, has another reason for revealing Alphonse's identity, one related to his didactic intent. In *Guillaume de Palerne*, the narrator's early disclosure of the werewolf's identity and continued use of different forms of the term *loup garou*, "werewolf," call immediate attention to the presence of this motif and its significance in the romance: appearance is not always a reliable indicator of core identity.[17] As was shown earlier, according to the Church, werewolves were not real but merely illusions.[18] Dunn and Micha fail to take this theological perspective into account. The opposition between Alphonse's fierce appearance and his gentle conduct indicates that his true nature is hidden. His savage exterior cannot be trusted; it is only a disguise imposed on him by his stepmother. Nonetheless, many characters who see only his external aspect are deluded by this image and react with fear, just like Felise did.

In keeping with his didactic intent, the *Guillaume* poet portrays the beast in a chivalric role throughout the romance, while at the same time reminding the audience that this "knight" is, after all, a beast. The first instance appears when the narrator says that the werewolf, after secretly observing the cowherd and his wife and concluding that Guillaume is safe in their care, bows and then leaves on his *aventure* (adventure):

> Parfont encline et vait sa voie,
> Ne sai quel part, en *s'aventure* [266–67, emphasis added].
>
> The werewolf bows down low and goes on his way,
> I know not where, off on his *adventure.*

The last verse is almost identical to one occurring in Chrétien de Troyes' *Erec* et Énide:

> Erec s'an va, sa fame an moinne,
> ne set ou, mes en avanture [2762–63].[19]
>
> Erec goes off, his wife he leads away,
> he knows not where, but on an adventure.

According to Mario Roques, *avanture* (adventure) within the context of the passage in *Erec* et Énide specifically means "circonstance étrange et dangereuse" (a strange and dangerous circumstance.)[20] For Glyn Burgess, this use of *aventure* in *Erec* et Énide implies that the adventure is "entreprise pour et malgré ses dangers" (undertaken for and in spite of its dangers.)[21] With his echo of Chrétien's famous verse, the *Guillaume* poet alerts his audience to the implied quest and danger that subtend the phrase *en aventure.* By adding the possessive adjective, he renews Chrétien's verse and individualizes the concept of adventure; the werewolf does not leave on just any adventure, but on "*s*'aventure," "*his* adventure" (emphasis added). The werewolf's courtly gesture, "parfont encline" (he bows down low), reinforces his knightly image. The poet thus begins to point out early in the romance that external signs are not always reliable. Later, when he comments about the werewolf's disappearance after he delivers food to Guillaume and Melior, the poet again echoes Chrétien:

> 3296 Puis si se rest arriere mis
> En la forest grant aleüre,
> Ne sai quel part[,][22] *querre aventure* [3296–98, emphasis added].

3296 Then he retreated again
Into the forest at a rapid pace,
I know not where, *to seek adventure.*

This time the werewolf does not merely leave on his *aventure*, but rather, like Erec, Yvain, and Calogrenant and other knights in the romances of Chrétien de Troyes, he actively seeks it. The poet establishes a parallel between the Arthurian knight and the werewolf with these echoes and implies that the latter behaves like a knight in spite of his appearance.

The werewolf is always there when Guillaume needs help. His assistance, however, is not merely coincidental but seems to have a divine connection. Alphonse briefly reappears in the romance four years after the prince's kidnapping, just before the emperor finds the eleven-year-old Guillaume watching his adopted father's herd. The emperor of Rome, who is out hunting, has been separated from his men:

408 Atant es vos que li garous
Vient devant lui .I. cerf chaçant;
De pren en pren la va sivant
Et l'empereres cort aprés;
412 Tant l'a suï tot a eslés
Que sor l'enfant s'est embatus,
Mais il ne set qu'est devenus
Li cers ne li garox andui,
416 Si li torne a molt grant anui [408–16].

408 Here comes the werewolf
Chasing a stag in front of him;
He is following closely on the heels of the stag
And the emperor runs after them.
412 He followed as fast as he could
Until by chance he came upon the child.
He does not know what has become of
Either the stag or the werewolf,
416 So he turns to the boy with great chagrin.

In this scene the poet obviously borrows and plays with elements from Morganian tales, in which a fairy sends an animal, often a white doe or stag, to lead a knight to her. The knight normally pursues the animal until he comes upon the fairy, at which point he abandons his pursuit of the animal. Here, however, the fact that the werewolf miraculously appears just for this scene and then disappears immediately afterward suggests that he is deliberately leading the emperor to Guillaume. Of course there is no fairy waiting for the emperor, nor is there any in the entire romance, but when the emperor sees the child, he reacts with wonderment and marvel at the boy's great beauty and "cuide chose faëe soit" (423), "[h]e believes that the child might be an enchanted creature." Although there is nothing in this particular scene to connect Alphonse's activity to the divine, with other interventions of the werewolf the divine connection soon becomes apparent. After Guillaume and Melior escape from Rome disguised in bearskins, they are very hungry and ask God to watch over them (3234–37). Unbeknownst to the young lovers, the werewolf has followed them from Rome and, according to the narrator, he is well aware that they need food:

3256 Garde u chemin, voit .I. vilain
Qui portoit blanc pain et char cuite:
Ja ert, s'il puet, d'aus .II. la luite.
En .I. sachet l'ot estoïe,
3260 Se le portoit a sa maisnie.
Li vilains vint et li leus saut;
Cil voit la beste et crie en haut:
"Aidiés, biau pere glorious!
3264 Hui me deffent, que cis garous
De moi ocire n'ait poissance."
Et li garous vers lui s'avance,
As dens l'aert et saut d'encoste,
3268 Tres bien le tient par le hargote;
Tot estendu le vilain rue,
La viande li a tolue
Que il portoit a sa maisnie.
3272 Mais se sa feme en ert irie,
De ce n'ert gaires a la beste.
En la place plus ne s'arreste,
Le vilain laist, atant s'en torne [3256–75].

3256 He watches on the road, sees a peasant
Who was carrying white bread and cooked meat:
Soon there will be, if possible, a battle between the two of them.
In a small sack he had enclosed the food,
3260 In that manner he was carrying it to his household.
The peasant comes and the wolf leaps out:
The man sees the beast and shrieks loudly:
"Help, sweet glorious Father!
3264 Protect me today, that this werewolf
Might have no power to kill me."
And the werewolf advances toward him,
With his teeth he seizes him and jumps to the side,
3268 He has a good hold on him because of the pleat in his garment;
He throws the peasant flat on the ground, all stretched out.
He seized the meat
That he was carrying to his household.
3272 But if the peasant's wife will be angry about it,
This will not matter very much to the beast.

In that place he does not stay any longer,
He leaves the peasant, then goes away.

This scene is noteworthy for several reasons. First of all, the poet sets it up as a potential "luite" (3258), "fight or battle," which gives it ominous overtones, but the werewolf and the peasant end up fighting over a bag of food. Second, the peasant, who correctly identifies the wolf as a "garous" (3264), "werewolf," is so frightened that he believes he is about to be killed and, like the two lovers, prays to God for help. In spite of what we have learned about this beast's gentle nature, the next two verses cause us to wonder just how far the werewolf will go to help Guillaume: "Et li garous vers lui s'avance, /As dens l'aert et saut d'encoste" (3266–67), "And the werewolf advances toward him, / With his teeth he seizes him and jumps to the side." But the following verse dispels any doubt and leaves Alphonse's gentle image intact: "Tres bien le tient par le hargote" (3268), "He has a good hold on him because of the pleat in his garment." The scene not only degenerates into comedy as the werewolf goes off with the cooked meat, leaving the peasant unharmed, "flat on the ground," but also stands in stark contrast to the scenes depicting the violent and lethal activities of the werewolves in *Melion* and *Arthur and Gorlagon*. Since the beast appears with food immediately after their appeal to God for help, Guillaume considers the werewolf the answer to their prayer:

"Bele, sachiés, ne nous oublie
Li rois de toute creature.
3308 Bele, or oiés quele aventure!
Fu mais tex merveille veüe,
Quant Diex par *une beste mue*
No soustenance nos envoie?" [3306–11, emphasis added].

"My dear, you know, He does not forget us,
The King of all creatures.
3308 Sweetheart, now hear what an adventure!
Has such a miracle ever been seen,
When God by means of *a transformed beast*
Sends us our sustenance?"

For Guillaume, Alphonse is not a monster; he is a miracle. Like his mother Queen Felise, and like the peasant whose food was stolen, Guillaume also recognizes that Alphonse is a werewolf: *une beste mue*, "a transformed beast." But when Felise witnesses her son kidnapped by the werewolf, she is deluded by appearances. The peasant is also terrified of the werewolf because he sees only his external aspect. Guillaume and Melior are not frightened by the beast however, when they see him bringing food, "Chascuns s'asseüre et conforte" (3288), "[e]ach one feels safe and is comforted." Like a faithful servant, the werewolf also manages to provide them with something to drink:

.I. clerc encontre a .I. prouvoire
Qui li portoit a sa maison
3336 .I. barisel de vin molt bon;
Mais, je quit bien, n'en goustera
Li provoires qui le manda.
Quant li clers voit le leu venir
3340 Ne set en fin que devenir,
Tout rue jus quanqu'il portoit,
En fuies torne a tel esploit
Comme cil qui ne cuide mie
3344 Que il em puist porter la vie.
Et li garox le barril prent,
Qui du clerc n'avoit pas talent
Qu'il li face nul autre mal [3334–47].

A cleric who was going to meet a priest
Was bringing to his house
3336 A small cask of very good wine;
But, I truly believe, the priest
Who ordered it will not taste it.
When the cleric sees the wolf coming
3340 He does not know what will happen in the end,
Everything that he was carrying he throws on the ground,
He turns in flight at such a speed
Like one who does not believe at all
3344 That he will be able to save his life.
And the werewolf picks up the cask,
For regarding the cleric he had no desire
To do him further harm.

Here the werewolf is able to take advantage of his ferocious appearance in order to assist Guillaume and Melior. He never intends to harm the terrified cleric; rather, his only purpose seems to be to help the prince and princess. After the werewolf tosses the cask in front of Guillaume and Melior, Guillaume thanks him:

3352 "Hé, dist Guillaunes, *franche beste*,
Com me faites grant cortoisie
Qui secourés moi et m'amie!
Cil qui a nos t'a ci tramis
3356 En ait et graces et mercis
Et il garisse le tien cors" [3352–57].

3352 "Oh, said Guillaume, *noble beast*,
How you do me a great courtesy
When you help my beloved and me!
May He who sent you to us

3356 Receive our gratitude and our thanks
And may He protect you.

Alphonse is no ordinary werewolf; when Guillaume calls him a "franche beste" (3352), "noble beast," it is obvious that he has recognized Alphonse's inherent nobility. Moreover, in this passage Guillaume explicitly identifies the werewolf's role in the romance, at least from his point of view: like a guardian angel, the werewolf has been "sent by God" to watch over him and protect him. Later, the narrator's reaction to the plight of the two fugitives confirms the werewolf's role as heavenly agent:

Or les gart Diex de cest peril!
Mien esciënt si fera il,
Car li garox pas nes oublie,
Ains lor garist sovent la vie [3763–66].

May God protect them now from this peril!
3764 I believe He will do it,
For the werewolf has not forgotten them,
Thus he often protects their lives.

Here we see the poet at play; the narrator's wish, presented in the jongleuresque style of Béroul[23]—"Or les gart Diex de cest peril," "May God protect them now from this peril!"—is immediately followed by the omniscient assertion that God will protect the two lovers since the werewolf is always there to divert the attention of the hunters. The beast's behavior as he continues to provide for Guillaume and Melior's needs supports the interpretation of Guillaume and the narrator.

The werewolf also routinely puts his life *en aventure*, "in danger, at risk," for Guillaume and Melior as he leads them southward. After the two lovers escape from Rome, they are pursued by the Lombards, Romans, and Greeks, all vassals of Melior's father and of the Emperor of Greece, whose son Melior was supposed to marry. Every time one of the hunting parties gets close to the young couple, the werewolf comes to their assistance:

Car quant li questor aprochoient
3768 La ou li dui amant estoient
A tout lor chiens, li leus sailloit;
En aventure se metoit
Por eus garandir et deffendre.
3772 Tos les faisoit a lui entendre,
Que tos les avoit desvoiés
Des jovinceus et eslongiés [3767–74].

For when the hunters would get close
3768 With their dogs to the place where
The two lovers were, the wolf would leap out;

He would put himself at risk[24]
In order to protect and defend them.
3772 He would keep them all busy with him,
Until he had led them all away
And distanced them from the young people.

Like the mother bird who makes herself a target in order to focus attention away from her nestlings, the werewolf risks his life for the young people he is protecting. The poet develops and amplifies this motif in a later scene in which Guillaume and Melior have been discovered asleep in a grotto in Benevento by quarry workers who have heard of the reward that the emperor has offered for the two white bears that have escaped from Rome. Melior awakens from a dream in which they are about to be attacked by wild animals, but their "beste que Jhesus gart" (4014) 'beast that Jesus watches over' saves them by capturing the lion's cub. While Melior and Guillaume are trying to decide what to do about the armed men about to enter the grotto, Alphonse once again comes to their rescue. This time he finds a distraction just as effective as the lion's cub in Melior's dream:

4080 Atant es vos par mi la roche
Le garoul *la gole baee.*
Tres par mi outre l'assamblee
Va le fil au prevost aerdre,
4084 Mix velt l'ame de son cors perdre
C'as .II. amans secors ne face [4080–86].

4080 At that moment appeared in the middle of the rocks
The werewolf with his *gaping mouth.*
Right through and beyond the army
He goes and seizes the provost's son,
4084 He would rather lose the soul from his body
Than not bring aid to the two lovers.

In a scene echoing the kidnapping of Guillaume, the werewolf rushes in, with his "goule baee" (4081), "gaping mouth,"[25] and kidnaps the provost's son. Sharing his insight into Alphonse's thoughts in these verses—"Mix velt l'ame de son cors perdre" (4084), "He would rather lose the soul from his body"—the narrator reminds the romance's courtly audience of the great disparity between Alphonse's inner and outer realities; he may be a werewolf, but he still has the soul of a man. More important, this phrase indicates how committed Alphonse is to protecting Guillaume and Melior; he is willing to lose his soul, but that is what makes him a man and his werewolf condition an illusion. If Alphonse were to lose his soul, he would also lose his human intelligence and understanding, any hope of recovering his human form and ultimately his hope for salvation. While this kidnapping echoes the original, there is a subtle change: Alphonse does not take the child to protect him, but rather to protect Guillaume. Again, everything is just an illusion and he does not harm the provost's son: "nul mal ne sent / De riens que la beste li face" (4106–07), "he feels no pain / From anything that the beast does to him." Nevertheless, everyone believes that this monstrous creature will hurt the child and the werewolf is consequently able to lead everyone on a merry chase:

4108 Aprés la beste est grans la chace;
Li leus s'en va auques fuiant
Et cil le vont aprés sivant.
Quant d'eus est pres, puis les eslonge,
4112 Molt set bien faire sa besoigne,
Et puis vers ceus a pié repaire,
Mais n'i voelent lancier ne traire,
Car l'enfant doutent a blecier [4108–15].

4108 The chase after the beast is enormous;
With the beast fleeing a little
And the men following after him.
When he is near them, then he distances himself from them,
4112 He knows well how to do his task,
And then come back toward those on foot,
But they do not want to throw their lances or shoot their arrows,
For they are afraid they will wound the child.

In this scene the werewolf demonstrates his human intelligence; he is clearly manipulating and controlling the actions of his pursuers as he leads them away from the lovers. Even though he puts his life in jeopardy for them, his superior intelligence allows him to minimize the risk, setting just the right pace to keep a safe distance from those who are pursuing him. After the werewolf leads everyone away from the grotto, Guillaume marvels again that God has sent them aid in the form of "une beste mue" (4128), "a transformed beast." Guillaume thus emphasizes the link between God and the wolf. As the romance continues, the werewolf begins to take on an almost Christ-like quality as the narrator insists on the beast's suffering[26]:

Ensi la beste les enmaine
O *grant travail* et o *grant paine*
Et garde de lor anemis
Que il nes ont perçus ne pris.
Mainte *perilleuse* jornee
En a *soufferte* et *enduree* [3777–82, emphasis added].

In this manner the beast leads them
With *great fatigue* and with *great difficulty*
And protects them from their enemies
3780 So that they are neither seen nor captured.

Many a *perilous* journey
Did he *suffer* and *endure.*

The poet's choice of words in this sequence, *grant travail* (great fatigue), *grant paine* (great difficulty), *perilleuse* (perilous), *soufferte* (suffer), and *enduree* (endure), reinforce one another and underline the danger of the werewolf's *aventure* (adventure). In one more notable instance, the werewolf risks his life again and jumps into the sea in order to divert attention away from the lovers, who have stowed away on a boat to Messina and are afraid they'll be observed when it arrives in port:

Cil de la nef trestuit fors saillent,
4608 La beste ruent et assaillent,
Sovent le font en mer plungier,
Prendre le quident et noier.
Por les .II. jovenciaux garir
4612 *Est en grant doute de morir,*
En aventure a mis son cors
Por ceus geter de la mer fors;
Ensi les maroniers demaine [4607–15, emphasis added].

All those on the ship jump out,
4608 They kick and attack the beast,
Often they make him dive into the sea,
They believe they will capture and drown him.
To save the two young people
4612 *He is in great fear of dying,*
In danger has he put his life
In order to deliver them from the sea;
Thus he leads the sailors away.

The poet intensifies the atmosphere of danger in this passage with the actions verbs *ruer* (to kick), *assaillir* (to attack), *plungier* (to dive), *noier* (to drown), *morir* (to die), and the description of the violence directed at the werewolf. In addition, for the first time the poet refers to the beast's fear; he is "en grant doute de morir" (4612), "in great fear of dying." Later, after he is recognized as the long-lost Spanish prince and transformed back into his human form, Alphonse reveals Guillaume's identity. The Spanish prince then recapitulates Guillaume's kidnapping. Echoing the poet's prologue, he introduces his tale with this comment: "Te voel mostrer tot en apert / Que j'ai por toi fait et souffert" (8165–66), "I want to show you openly / What I did and suffered for you." As he describes how he was forced into the sea by Embron and his men, the Spanish prince firmly inscribes himself in Guillaume's story and makes himself the hero of this retelling:

8176 Ne poi guenchir ne champ ne voie,
Venir au bos ne d'aus sevrer

Ne *m'*enbatissent en la mer.
S'en la mer ne *me* fuisse mis,
8180 Molt tost *m'*eüst li rois ocis.
Par mi le Far de mer autaine
*M'*estut passer a molt grant paine,
Par mi la mer passai a nage.
8184 Molt par i oi grevex passage,
Molt en souffri *mes* cors d'ahan,
Car ainc n'i oi nef ne chalan,
N'ainc n'i eüs mal de ton cors.
8188 Quant *je* fui outre arrivés fors,
Onques de riens n'oi si grant joie [8176–89, emphasis added].

8176 *I* could not avoid fields or paths
Or get into the woods or distance *myself* from them
And they pushed *me* into the sea.
If *I* had not gone into the sea,
8180 Very quickly would the king have killed *me.*
Through the Strait of Messina in high seas
I had to cross with very great difficulty,
Through the sea *I* passed by swimming.
8184 There *I* had a very painful crossing,
Greatly did *my* body suffer from the effort,
For *I* never had a ship or barge,
And yet you never suffered any harm to your body.
8188 When *I* arrived on the other side and got out,
Never had *I* been so happy about anything.

Other than one brief mention of the king and one reference to Guillaume, the entire passage is devoted to Alphonse, as the proliferation of first-person markers and verb forms indicates. In order to rescue Guillaume and keep himself from being killed by Embron and his men, the werewolf had to swim across the Strait of Messina — no small task, especially with a four-year-old child in his mouth.[27] Through the use of key words, *a molt grant paine* (with great difficulty), *grevex passage* (painful crossing), *souffri* (suffer), and *ahan* (effort), Alphonse insists on his own ordeal, which he contrasts with Guillaume's relatively painless experience, "N'ainc n'i eüs mal de ton cors" (8187), "And yet you never suffered any harm to your body." The joy that he feels when he reaches the other side of the Strait magnifies the hardship he endured. His story thus becomes proof of his own nobility and selflessness. As he tells Guillaume, "Ainc beste ne fist ce por home / Que jou ai, sire, por toi fait" (8194–95), "Never has a beast done this for man / As I have, sire, for you." As he retells their adventures, Alphonse again reminds Guillaume and Melior that he put his own life in jeopardy to help them:

Si com *por lor delivreüre*
8236 Se mist de mort *en aventure* [8235–36, emphasis added].

And how *for their deliverance*
8236 He put himself *at risk* of death.

The phrase "por lor delivreüre" (for their deliverance) is significant and forms part of a pattern; the other two occurrences of *en aventure* are accompanied by similar explanations: "Por eus garandir et deffendre" (3771), "In order to protect and defend them." and "Por les .II. jovenciax garir" (4611), "To save the two young people." By adding this motivation to the idea that the beast was sent by God and by using the expression *en aventure* to describe only the activities of the werewolf, the poet reinforces his portrayal of the latter as a knight embodying the Christian concept of selfless service to others.[28]

As we have seen, the werewolf frequently takes advantage of his fierce appearance to protect Guillaume and Melior. This modification of the werewolf motif appears nowhere else. Bisclavret and Melion act only for their own benefit and Gorlagon's assault on the queen's lover, while motivated by unselfish concerns, is not presented as deliberate and intentional. Moreover, Gorlagon actually harms the man, whereas Alphonse never injures anyone. By having Alphonse alternate between his roles of wild beast and guardian angel, the *Guillaume* poet mimics the cycle of metamorphosis typically associated with the popular image of the werewolf. But the impression of Alphonse as a *loup garou* that emerges from the narrative is one of a clever man, not a beast, who manipulates for the benefit of others the disguise, the false identity, that he is forced to wear. No one is strong enough or smart enough to withstand or overcome the werewolf's combined prowess and ingenuity, as we saw with the two kidnappings, the episode at the quarry, and the debarkation at Messina. Although trapped in the body of a beast, a monster, Alphonse proves that he is a valorous knight; his triumph over perilous circumstances makes his inner worth obvious to the discerning observer. The werewolf is thus skillfully played off the stereotype in a way that accentuates his humanity and emphasizes not only the idea that noble victims transform themselves into heroes through service to other people, but also that there is no absolute correlation between appearance and core identity.

The *Guillaume* poet amplifies the incongruity between the werewolf's appearance and his behavior by consistently using marked phrases in surprising juxtaposition to depict the beast as a knight in spite of his lupine condition. He thus repeatedly reminds the audience of the creature's double nature. In the following passage, the narrator relates the werewolf's reaction after he discovers that Guillaume is missing:

Lors est saillis ens el markais,
Si met a la terre le nés;
248 Tout si com l'enfes ert alés,
Desi ou le mist li vilains
Le siut *li leus de rage plains.*
Tant l'a suï a esperon
252 Que venus est a la maison
Ou li enfes portés estoit [246–53, emphasis added].

Then he jumped into the marsh
And put his nose to the ground;
248 Just exactly as the child had gone,
From that spot to where the peasant took him,
The wolf follows him full of rage.
He charged after him at such a high speed
252 That he came to the house
Where the child had been carried.

This description of the enraged wolf with his nose to the ground following a scent accentuates his animal side. The phrase "a esperon" (252), "charging at high speed," however, evokes a knight spurring his horse and echoes the narrator's earlier description of King Embron in pursuit of the werewolf: "Li rois le siut a esperon" (103), "The king charges after the wolf." This phrase is also used later in descriptions of Guillaume in combat (6861–63, 6900–01). When used to describe the werewolf, these lexical choices create a striking juxtaposition that points to the beast's dual nature.

The poet further develops the image of the werewolf as a knight, while at the same time insisting on his bestiality, with the phrase "goule baee" (mouth gaping open), a *leitmotif* that is unique to *Guillaume de Palerne*. After Melior awakens from a dream, she tells Guillaume how "ors et lupart et sengler fier" (4006), led by a lion, were threatening them until the werewolf arrived and captured the lion's cub:

4012 Si me sambloit que je veoie
Venir et traire ceste part
Nostre beste que Jhesus gart.
Tres par mi toute l'assamblee
4016 *Venoit fendant, goule baee,*
Desci au lyoncel sans faille [4012–17, emphasis added].

4012 It seemed to me that I saw
Coming and heading this way
Our beast that Jesus watches over.
Right through the middle of the mêlée,
4016 *He came cutting through, his mouth gaping open,*
Right to the lion cub without fail.

Coming to their rescue, the werewolf emerges as the hero of Melior's dream. Since the beast is in the midst of many other wild animals, the phrase "goule baee" (4016), "mouth gaping open," might seem appropriate. But its juxtaposition with "Tres par mi toute l'assamblee" (4015), "Right through the middle of the mêlée," a phrase often used to describe a knight's progress through the mêlée of a tournament or battle, sets up an unexpected contrast. Similar to the knight who charges in with his sword raised, the werewolf arrives with his mouth open in an attack gesture. Unlikely parallels can now be drawn not only between knight and werewolf, but also between sword and mouth. The poet strengthens the parallel with the verb *fendre* (to cut, split, also to rush), which he frequently uses to describe Guillaume's actions in battle as he splits the helmets and heads of his enemies. For instance, the verb appears twice in the narrator's account of Guillaume's victory over the Spanish knight Meliadus (6883, 6885), as well as in numerous battle scenes throughout the romance. The juxtaposition of "goule baee" (mouth gaping open) with the verbal phrase "venoit fendant" (he came cutting through / rushing) in verse 4016 transforms the wolf's *goule* into a heroic weapon, while at the same time ironically reminding the audience of the animal nature of this "knight." Acting as a *leitmotif* throughout the romance, "goule baee" not only reminds the audience of Alphonse's bestial nature as a werewolf, but also functions in other ways. First, it announces that he is about to attack. Seeing his stepmother for the first time in Palermo, his instinct for revenge takes over and he lunges at her, "goule baee" (7638).[29] Another modification of the *leitmotif* appears when Felise dreams that she is surrounded by many wild animals: these creatures are described as having their "geules baees" (4728), whereas the white wolf and the two white bears that "[l]i venoient faire secors" (4732) '[c]ame to bring her aid' are not. Here the presence of the *leitmotif* in the description of the attackers emphasizes their bestiality; its absence in the description of the rescuers — the werewolf, Guillaume, and Melior — minimizes their feral nature. The *leitmotif* also points to a contradiction: although the werewolf's mouth is frequently "gaping open" in an attack posture to facilitate the catching of prey, he is never depicted eating or even biting any living creature. Thus, his gaping mouth is also an empty mouth signifying the absence of cannibalized flesh. In other passages, "goule baee" underscores Alphonse's contradictions and limitations: although his mouth is open, he cannot speak. Unable to carry a sword, he employs his animal features to defend those he loves: with his mouth open and his teeth exposed, he presents a more frightening spectacle. This interpretation of the werewolf's mouth as a chivalric weapon allows us a new reading of his abrupt arrival when he kidnaps Guillaume from the palace park at the opening of the romance. We have already noted that this scene depicts in fact a rescue and not a kidnapping. From our privileged position as leisurely readers of the text, we understand that in this first scene the poet is actually portraying the heroic deed of a knight, not the monstrous act of a beast. To Guillaume's distraught mother, he is a ferocious animal, the monster with a gaping mouth that must be feared. Yet when the narrator reveals the creature's true nature and motives to his listeners, their view, and ours, of the werewolf and his role in the romance undergoes a metamorphosis. He is the hero that must be exalted and imitated. In the light of this privileged information, his "goule baee" becomes the heroic weapon of a true knight.

Although most of the characters who see the werewolf are terrified of him, Guillaume is never frightened or fooled by Alphonse's lupine appearance. As Harf-Lancner notes, writers of medieval tales of werewolves and apologetic literature always provide a saint-like character who is able to see through the illusion that others accept as real[30]; in *Bisclavret*, *Melion*, and *Arthur and Gorlagon* this person is the king who protects the werewolf. In *Guillaume de Palerne*, it is of course the eponymous hero who pierces the illusion. In the romance the motif is complicated by the fact that Guillaume is not the protector of the werewolf but instead is protected by the werewolf. Guillaume's perceptiveness reflects his exemplary status: he can see what others cannot. Although the kings in the shorter tales note that the wolf has human understanding and intelligence, Guillaume, as we have already seen, goes one step further and identifies him as a "beste mue" (3310), "transformed beast." Like these rulers, Guillaume also detects Alphonse's "raison et sens" (reasoning and intelligence) and realizes that there is a man concealed behind his bestial appearance. This becomes especially clear to him after he and Melior abandon their bearskins at the grotto of Benevento and have to find a new way to conceal their identities. Suddenly the werewolf arrives chasing a stag, which he kills in front of them. Moments later, he arrives with a doe, which he also kills, and then he leaves.[31] Knowing that they'll be able to use the deer skins as new disguises, Guillaume addresses the werewolf thus:

Et dist Guilliaumes: "Franche beste,
As tu donques doute de moi?
4372 Ja ne puis je garir sans toi.
Se Diex ne fust et li tiens cors,
Pieça que fuisse oci et mors.
Ne sai se as de moi doutance,
4376 En toi est toute ma fiance.
Bien pens et croi que *entendés*
Et que *raison* et *sens* avés.
Je ne sai que ce est de vous,
4380 Quë en *nule riens ne fus lous* [4370–80, emphasis added].

And Guillaume said: "Noble beast,
Have you therefore fear of me?
4372 I will never be safe without you.
If it were not for God and for you,
For a longtime I would have been killed and dead.
I know not if you are afraid of me,
4376 In you I place all my trust.
Well do I think and believe that *you understand*
And that you possess *reasoning* and *intelligence.*
I know not what you are,
4380 Except that *in no way are you a wolf.*

Like the king in *Bisclavret* and Gargol in *Arthur and Gorlagon*,[32] Guillaume recognizes and acknowledges that the werewolf has the mental powers and understanding of a human being, although this acknowledgment does not occur during or after a submission scene, as it does in the shorter tales. This passage is also noteworthy in that it portrays the werewolf behaving in an apprehensive manner in the presence of Guillaume; indeed, he is timid enough to cause Guillaume to ask the werewolf if he is afraid of him. This is another side of the werewolf; one that never appears in the other tales.

In *Bisclavret, Melion*, and *Arthur and Gorlagon*, the werewolf enacts the feudal ceremony of homage in order to secure the king's protection when his life is in danger; in *Guillaume de Palerne*, however, the werewolf has no need of protection when he enacts this ceremony and he does not do it at Guillaume's feet. In the romance the submission motif opens with a sequence of odd behaviors by the beast on three consecutive days after Guillaume and his knights return from battle. The poet first establishes a norm for the werewolf's conduct through two scenes in which he briefly appears in the palace park beneath Felise's window. On both occasions, Guillaume is relaxing by the window with the queen, her daughter Florence, and Melior:

Ensi comme ilueques parloient,
Gardent aval, el vergier voient
Ou li garox i ert venus;
5840 Mais tel merveille ne vit nus:
Les piés ot joins et sor la teste
Les avoit mis la fiere beste;
Si se drece sor ceus derriere.
5844 A simple vis, a simpe chiere
Encline la chambre et la tor
Et les dames et le signor,
Puis se refiert en la gaudine [5837–47].[33]

Thus as they were talking there,
They look down, in the orchard they see
That the werewolf had come there.

5840 But such a marvel has no one ever seen:
He had his front paws joined together and on his head
The fierce beast had placed them,
So he is standing up on his rear paws.
5844 With an affable visage, with a gentle face
He bows in greeting toward the chamber and the tower
And the ladies and the lord,
Then he hurries away back into the wood.

Like the knights in Marie de France's *lai* who are amazed at Bisclavret's courtly demeanor, the observers all marvel at the unusual display of such chivalrous behavior by a wolf, especially Queen Felise who then finds herself compelled to recount the story of her son's kidnapping by a similar beast. The following day, the werewolf reappears:

Ensi comme il iluec parloient,
Gardent aval, el vergier voient
Ou revenus ert li garox;
6376 A terre ot mis les .II. genous
Devant Guilliaume et la roïne
Et les puceles, ses encline
Molt simplement .II. fois la beste,
6380 Puis tient sa voie, ne s'arreste [6373–80].

Thus as they were speaking there,
They look down, in the orchard they see
That the werewolf had come back there.
6376 On the ground he had put his two knees
Before Guillaume and the queen
And the maidens, the beast bows down to them
Two times very simply,
6380 Then goes on his way, he does not linger.

Verses 6373–74 repeat 5837–38, while verse 6375 inverts the terms of 5839 and emphasizes the werewolf's return with *revenus* (come back). Using repetition to make the two scenes parallel, the poet underscores their significance. Moreover, the wolf has changed his gesture. The numeral two, ".II.," which appears twice in this second passage, announces the second step of a *gradatio* and reinforces the pattern. The queen's reaction indicates her awareness of this progression; she does not question the wolf's courtliness, but asks instead why he bowed to them twice this time and only once the day before (6389–91). The poet thus sets up the audience's anticipation for a third sequence that will outdo the first two. On the third day the werewolf enters the great hall instead of the palace park and greets the king of Spain, who is, unbeknownst to everyone except the werewolf himself, his father:

Atant es vos que li garox
7208 Par mi la sale, voiant tous,
Tres devant le roi s'agenoille,
De lermes tot les piés li moille.
A ses .II. poes prent son pié,
7212 Estroitement l'a embracié;
Ensement par samblant l'opose
C'on l'aprovast d'aucune chose.
Atant s'en part et puis l'encline
7216 Et puis Guilliaume et la roïne
Et les puceles ensement [7207–17].

At that moment came the werewolf
7208 Right through the hall, in the presence of everyone,
Near the king he kneels before him,
He wets his feet with his tears.
With his two paws he picks up his foot,
7212 And he tightly embraces it.
Moreover, he seems to be asking
That he grant him something.
Then he gets up to leave and bows down to him
7216 And then to Guillaume and the queen
And to the maidens as well.

This third step of the *gradatio*, this enactment of the feudal ceremony of homage, completes the motif of the werewolf's odd behavior. The new set of gestures alerts Guillaume, who then demands an explanation of the werewolf's behavior. The beast's presence in the great hall has several effects. The immediate reaction is one of general bedlam as the knights run for their weapons:

De totes pars saillent la gent;
As lances corent et as dars,
7220 Prendent guisarmes et faussars;
Aprés le leu est grans li cris.
Ja fust de totes pars ocis,
Quant li bers Guilliaumes saut sus
7224 Et jure Dieu et ses vertus,
Se nul i a qui mal li face,
Ja n'iert tex hom, tres bien le sache,
N'en prenge de son cors venjance [7218–27].

From all directions the men leap out.
They run to their lances and to their javelins,
7220 They pick up their halberds and their falchions.[34]
The shouts following the wolf are great.
He would already have been killed from all directions,
When Guillaume the baron jumps up
7224 And swears to God and His miracles,

If there is anyone who harms him,
Never will there be a such a man, know this very well,
That he will not take vengeance on him

The turbulence of the passage, which the poet emphasizes with the verbs *saillir* (to leap out), *core* (to run), and *ocire* (to kill) and the substantives *dars* (javelins), *lances* (lances), *guisarmes* (halbards), *faussars* (falchions), and *cris* (shouts), contrasts markedly with the tranquility of the previous scene and its more sedate lexicon: *agenoiller* (to kneel), *moiller* (to wet, moisten), *embracier* (to embrace), *encliner* (to bow down), *lermes* (tears). This opposition highlights the incongruity between the wolf's courtliness and his fierce appearance. The scene represents a turning point in the narrative as Guillaume is finally able to help the creature that saved him from harm so many times; he and the werewolf, who is able to function as knight-protector only outside the confines of civilization and is now himself in need of assistance, have reversed roles. In the preceding two passages we see how significantly the *Guillaume* poet has modified the submission scene and motif of the king-protector. The werewolf's enactment of the homage ceremony appears almost at the end of the romance, at a time when his life is not in jeopardy. Moreover, it occurs between Alphonse and his father, the king of Spain, who is himself a prisoner and in no position to help anyone. Until he throws himself at his father's feet, Alphonse is in no danger whatsoever; it is then Guillaume, not the king of Spain, who prevents anyone from harming the beast (7218–27). Since the service of protection is traditionally provided by the king, the poet uses his variation of the motif to foreshadow Guillaume's future rank. This split in the role of the king-protector also reflects the narrative complexity of the romance. In spite of these differences, Alphonse's actions almost duplicate those that we find in *Bisclavret*.[35] The *Guillaume* poet's unique treatment of this motif resides not in content or form, then, but in narrative placement and purpose. In the three tales the submission scene preserves the werewolf from mortal injury by immediately establishing rapport between him and the king. In *Guillaume de Palerne*, however, the scene serves a different purpose: it provokes curiosity and supplies a clue to the werewolf's identity. As the werewolf, Alphonse initiates his relationship with Guillaume, his eventual protector, by providing sustenance, protection, and guidance. The poet thus emphasizes the reciprocity of the feudal contract and the primacy of deeds and service over ceremony, which, like appearances, may be illusory. The submission scene is a scene of recognition, albeit one-sided, and accentuates the notion of identity. Moreover, it reveals Alphonse's emotional reaction to seeing his father for the first time since his metamorphosis and, in so doing, underscores his humanity. The werewolf's unusual behavior also causes the onlookers to question his identity and true nature. Suddenly remembering the story his men had told him about how his wife Brande had transformed his son into a *loup garou* (7247–58), the king decides that this wolf must be the lost Prince Alphonse but keeps this information to himself. For his part, Guillaume is convinced that the king of Spain holds the key to the creature's true identity and insists that the king tell him "[q]ue cele beste senefie" (7270), "[w]hat this beast signifies." Guillaume voices the questions that the romance's courtly audience must be asking itself by now: what is the significance of the werewolf in this narrative? What is the truth that is hidden behind his appearance? When the king tells Guillaume that he thinks the wolf is his missing son (7275–7340), Guillaume immediately accepts this explanation for the werewolf's behavior.

In *Guillaume de Palerne,* the poet also modifies the motif of the sudden violent behavior of the werewolf, for in the romance it is his docile behavior, not his violent behavior, that triggers the investigation into his identity. Alphonse's only truly hostile acts in the romance are his two attempts to attack his stepmother Brande.[36] The first attempted attack occurred just after Brande transformed him (vv. 313–317). When the queen is forced to come to Palermo, the werewolf immediately recognizes her:

De mautalent li cuers li tramble,
Quant del tot l'a reconneüe.
7636 Les iex roeille et la veüe;
N'i fait plus longe demoree,
Tot a eslais, *goule baee,*
Laisse corre por li aerdre [7634–39, emphasis added].

His heart trembles from rage
When he thoroughly recognized her.
7636 He saw her and his eyes roll;
He does not delay any longer,
At top speed, his *mouth gaping open,*
He runs as fast as he can to seize her.

Although Alphonse undergoes a total metamorphosis here, from his normal docile and courtly behavior to a ferocious beast, we have already seen how his *goule baee* (mouth gaping open) may be interpreted as a chivalric weapon. If we read this scene as a sequel to Alphonse's first attempted attack on his stepmother, in which he is described as beginning a war against her, "Vers sa marastre mut tel guerre" (314) "Against his stepmother he begins a war," then we can conclude that he is merely attempting to finish what he had begun so many years before. The attack reveals Alphonse's anger, which is a human rather than a bestial response; his reaction is that of a knight seeking vengeance. For those who witness Alphonse's actions, they need no explanation, since the king of Spain has already revealed that the wolf is probably his long-lost son who had been transformed into a *leus garox* 'werewolf' by Queen Brande. The werewolf's violent behavior does not trigger a search for his identity, as it does in Bisclavret, *Melion*, and *Arthur and Gorlagon*; instead, it confirms his identity. Indeed, at this point Brande admits that she recognizes the wolf and addresses him by name:

> "Biax sire Anphons," dit la roïne,
> "Avec moi ai ci la mecine
> Dont vos serés trestos garis.
> 7684 Damoisiax, sire, chiers amis,
> Bien sai sans faille ce es tu,
> Bien t'ai del tot reconneü" [7681–86].

> "Good sir Alphonse," says the queen,
> "With me I have the remedy
> By which you will be completely cured.
> 7684 My lord, sire, dear friend,
> I know indeed without a doubt that it is you,
> Well did I recognize you completely."

Note Brande's initial use of the formal *vos* (you), as she attempts to placate the beast that tried to kill her, followed by her use of the informal *tu* (you), as she admits to their familial relationship and tries to ingratiate herself with him. Her choice of words, *sire* (sir), *damoisiax* (my lord), *sire* (sire), and *amis* (friend), reflects this progression. The poet's adaptation of the motif of the werewolf's violent behavior also stresses recognition and its correlative, identity. Finally, by echoing Alphonse's first attempt to attack Brande immediately after his metamorphosis (308–17), the scene announces that the story of the werewolf is about to come to a resolution.

Unlike what we find in *Bisclavret*, *Melion*, and *Arthur and Gorlagon*, in which the recovery of the werewolf's human form is essentially a reversal of the initial metamorphosis once the instrument of transformation has been retrieved, in *Guillaume de Palerne*, the process is more complicated. In the romance, the sorceress Queen Brande and her use of magic are the only elements common to both Alphonse's original metamorphosis and his second and final metamorphosis. When he was a small boy, she "anoint[ed] his body with an ointment" (301). The fact that she does not use the same ointment to retransform him is perhaps due to the scruples of the poet when faced with the sensual image of the queen rubbing it on the werewolf's body as it changes into the naked body of her stepson, now a young man. Nevertheless, the poet does not hesitate to deal with Alphonse's nudity after his transformation, as we shall see. Brande begins by announcing that she has come to heal him and that when she has finished everyone will be able to see "[q]uel beste ceste piax acuevre" (7692), "what beast this skin is hiding." The queen makes a full confession of what she did to him, saying "Te fis fuïr *com* leus boscage" (7696, emphasis added), "I made you flee *like* a wild wolf." This verse is particularly significant because she does not say that she turned him into a wild wolf, just that she made him flee *like* one. Throughout the romance, Alphonse appears to be acting *like* a wolf from time to time, but it is obvious that he never becomes one. It is just an illusion, as Brande has just confirmed. Throwing herself at the werewolf's feet, she then asks him for mercy and pledges her future loyalty to him (vv. 7693–7717). Brande's gestures of remorse recall the modified ceremony of homage enacted earlier by the werewolf; here, however, the poet offers a bizarre, world-upside-down image with the queen's submissive posture before this "monstrous" creature. Brande's repentance in particular represents an important divergence from the werewolf tales in which the wicked woman is always punished or condemned. After everyone pleads with the werewolf to pardon Brande, "a tos boinement l'otroie" (7723), "he gladly granted it to everyone." Brande then leads the werewolf into "une chambre painte a flor" (7728), "a chamber painted with flowers." When she hangs a golden ring with a magic stone on a red silk thread around his neck, the narrator tells us "[m]olt en maine li leus grant joie" (7746), "the wolf displays great joy." Although no other details are given, it is fairly easy to imagine how a man trapped in a lupine form might express happiness, perhaps by jumping up excitedly, or by wagging his tail as a dog might. This is the last image we have of the werewolf, for he is about to become a man again:

7748 Dont a la dame .I. livre trait,
Tant a porlit et conjuré
Le vassal a deffaituré
Et tot remis en sa samblance.
7752 Cil qui senti sa delivrance,
Quant il s'escoust, s'est devenus
Li plus biax hom, mais tos fu nus,
Qui adont fust, mien essiënt,
7756 Fors Guilliaume tant seulement;
N'en sai fors lui plus metre fors.
Cil voit son samblant et son cors
Qui tous sans dras et nus estoit
7760 Et devant lui la dame voit;
Tel honte en a tos en tressue [7748–61].

7748 Then the lady pulled out a book;
She read it entirely and conjured until
She changed the form of the vassal
And totally restored his appearance.
7752 He who sensed his deliverance,
When he shook himself, became,
Although he was completely naked, the most handsome man

Who ever was, to my knowledge,
7756 With the exception of only Guillaume;
I do not know anyone else I can exclude.
He sees his appearance and his body
That was totally without clothing and naked
7760 And he sees the lady before him.
He is so ashamed that he becomes violently agitated.

Thus Alphonse recovers his human form by means of a combination of Brande's magic ring and her incantations. And of course he is exceptionally handsome. But he also feels terribly ashamed. Alphonse's shame regarding his nakedness is an echo of a motif that appears in both *Bisclavret* and *Melion*. In these *lais*, the werewolf is transformed in a private space so that he will not experience public embarrassment.[37] Although Alphonse is not transformed in public, he is nevertheless humiliated by Queen Brande's presence. Her presence, however, was absolutely essential for his metamorphosis. As we see below, rather than ignoring or shrinking from the awkward situation in which he has placed Alphonse, the poet instead profits from it by inserting some tongue-in-cheek humor into the passage. In doing so, he ultimately magnifies its sensuality by calling more attention to it, while at the same time downplaying it with the queen's remarks:

La dame en est toute esperdue,
A li l'apele, se li dist:
7764 "Sire, por Dieu qui tos nos fist,
Ne te vergoigne pas de moi
Se je tot nu, sans dras, te voi:
N'a ci se nos seulement non.
7768 Ne voi en toi riens se bien non
Ne chose qui estre n'i doie" [7762–69].

The lady is quite distraught because of this,
She calls to him and tells him:
7764 "My lord, in the name of God who made us all,
Do not be ashamed because of me,
If I see you naked, without clothing:
There is no one here but the two of us.
7768 I see in you nothing that is not good
Nor anything that is not as it should be."

Changing the subject, perhaps to ease his distress about his nudity, Brande tells Alphonse that he will be knighted that very day. After the queen puts her own mantle on him and leads him to a bath, Alphonse gives her instructions regarding his dubbing ceremony and requests clothing. Unlike Bisclavret, who must put on his own clothing in order to transform himself,[38] and unlike Pliny's Arcadian werewolves who become men again after swimming across a march,[39] Alphonse bathes and receives clothing after his transformation, not in order to bring it about. These events have nothing to do with the recovery of his human form, as Carolyn Walker Bynum seems to suggest when she says, "Small wonder that Alphonse's restoration is bathing and receiving new clothes; it's as if the human body were there under the wolf skin all along" (109). Alphonse needs clothes because he is naked. As for the bath, cleaning oneself is not an unusual thing to do before putting on clothes for the first time in over twelve years.[40] In this scene Alphonse has indeed come full circle. The naked prince in the presence of his stepmother evokes that long-ago scene when she first transformed him into a werewolf, but now Brande herself has also undergone a metamorphosis; she is no longer the "wicked stepmother."

Marie de France and the authors of *Melion* and *Arthur and Gorlagon* downplay the violent side of their werewolf heroes but never totally conceal it. Unlike the werewolves in the three tales, Alphonse the werewolf is never portrayed as a ferocious creature, with the exception of the incident involving his stepmother. Furthermore, Alphonse is never successful in his attempts against his stepmother and never harms her or anyone else. More significant, the *Guillaume* poet goes one step further in his presentation of the werewolf and makes the gentleness of the beast the key that unlocks the door to his human identity; his werewolf identity is only a disguise. As Ménard describes Alphonse, "Une fois métamorphosé, il reste doux comme un mouton, raisonnable, bienveillant" (214), "Once he has been transformed, he remains as gentle as a lamb, reasonable, benevolent." Francis Dubost comes to a similar conclusion:

> A plusieurs reprises, il [le loup] joue du pouvoir qui lui confère son apparence mais ne s'abandonne jamais à la férocité d'instincts qui ne sont pas les siens. La métamorphose n'est ici qu'une forme d'exclusion: la nature humaine, la noblesse, la générosité se sont maintenues merveilleusement intactes sous la peau de l'animal [562–3].
>
> Several times he [the wolf] makes use of the power that his appearance confers on him but he never gives in to the ferociousness of instincts that are not his. Metamorphosis is only a form of exclusion here: human nature, nobility, generosity are marvelously maintained intact beneath the skin of the animal.

Alphonse had already established himself as a "franche beste" (noble beast), but his manner in the presence of his father the king of Spain exceeds mere courtliness; it demonstrates familiarity and intimacy. The werewolf's new display of submissiveness and affection, not his attempted assault on his stepmother, leads to the recovery of Alphonse's human form and thereby restores the lost harmony between his behavior and his appearance. The hatred of the werewolves in the three tales ultimately reveals their identity, whereas it is Alphonse's love for his father that provides the clue to his. With his reworking of the traditional motifs of the werewolf tale, the *Guillaume* poet thus accords supremacy to that most human of emotions: love.

As we have seen, the *Guillaume* poet uses the werewolf to underscore the ambiguity of appearances by eliminating any suspense about the werewolf's true nature and by constantly portraying the beast as a knight, while at the same time reminding the audience that this "*chevalier*" is, after all, a wolf. The poet also calls into question the reliability of external signs by setting up an opposition between the werewolf and the true villains of the romance, as well as a parallel between Alphonse and Guillaume. The figure of the werewolf in *Guillaume de Palerne* suggests at first glance the outlaw who is forced to take refuge in the forest because he has broken society's rules. Smith writes that an ancient Teutonic custom associated criminals with the predatory wolf; the lawbreaker was accordingly called a "wolf" or a "wolf's head" and the body of a wolf was frequently hung on the gallows beside that of the executed criminal.[41] Wolves, because of their attacks on people and livestock, were also hunted down like thieves and murderers throughout the Middle Ages.[42] The werewolf's savage appearance, then, both causes and reflects his exclusion from society. According to Charlotte Otten, the presence of the werewolf motif in folklore indicates a societal concern about internal sources of violence: "[t]he shape-changing may indicate that evil was not always regarded as external; that humans in the shape of wolves were responsible for the terrorizings in their communities" (138). In her study of *Bisclavret,* Benkov offers a similar explanation:

> Part-man, part-beast, the dual nature of the werewolf epitomizes the dilemma of humankind which must battle the forces of good and evil within. Often the creature is depicted in an ambiguous way: an unwilling victim of some evil or sorcery who through no fault of his own turns into a beast. And, although the human side is repressed when the beast takes over, remorse and regret may follow the periods of rampage. Yet even when pity is felt for the werewolf, it is at best ephemeral. These man-beasts wreak havoc when let loose in society; they are destructive forces which subvert the social system [27].

Although this description might be appropriate for Gorlagon and at times possibly Melion, any "havoc" that Bisclavret wreaks is carefully concealed, if it exists at all; Benkov's description of the werewolf certainly does not apply to Alphonse. I would argue instead that the *Guillaume* poet uses the figure of the werewolf to set up a false parallel between Alphonse and the evil forces in the romance. Although Alphonse's motives are pure when he kidnaps Guillaume, his act is construed as a crime. He has actually done no wrong, but it seems that he has and his ferocious appearance reinforces this impression. Alphonse does not conform to the stereotype of the werewolf; the "beast" in him never takes over. He is not both man and wolf; he is merely a man caught in a disguise that he cannot remove. Unlike the other werewolves that we have examined, Alphonse never runs wild. In fact, like Guillaume, he always remains true to the chivalric code. Alphonse's noble behavior not only resembles Guillaume's, but also contrasts sharply with and becomes an inverted reflection of the behavior of the noblemen who, in a weak moment, forget chivalry and its code of conduct. While Alphonse is innocent of any evil deeds, the duke of Saxony who breaks his oath of fidelity to the emperor of Rome and the king of Spain who attacks Felise's kingdom are not. Even though they do not assume the shape of wolves, they do become predators. Like the man-beast Benkov describes, they sometimes "repress" their more civilized nature and, metaphorically turning into wild animals, "wreak havoc when let loose in society." Later, however, they express "remorse and regret." With the exception of Guillaume's unnamed uncle, all the individuals responsible for wrongdoing in the romance, the duke of Saxony, the king of Spain, Alphonse's stepbrother Brandin and stepmother Brande, and even Guillaume's nursemaids, regret and confess their crimes. This succession of repentances, all of which may be considered moral transformations of the villains and a return to their true nature, as opposed to an evolution in their character, is an important trait of the romance, as evidenced by the fact that it survives in the sixteenth-century prose reworkings of *Guillaume de Palerne*. The remorse expressed by these noble villains and the forgiveness they receive reinforce the poet's upbeat portrait of the aristocracy and provide additional examples of appropriate behavior for noblemen and noblewomen. In addition, these repentances contribute to the romance's underlying Christian themes of divine providence and the possibility of salvation. Although the duke of Saxony dies from his battle wounds and the two nursemaids do penance in a hermitage until their deaths, the king of Spain, Brande, and Brandin all return to Spain and resume their lives. Relinquishing at last their claims to what is not rightfully theirs, they are pardoned and harmony is restored between their core identity and their conduct. These moral transformations remind the noble audience of the possibility for change and redemption available to those who recognize their faults and return to the obligations imposed on them by their high birth.

Participating in the clerical and literary tradition of the twelfth- and thirteenth-century moral guides known as the *miroir des princes* (mirror for princes), *Guillaume de Palerne* emphasizes the virtues required of the nobility, primarily through the example set by its eponymous hero. Moralizing passages also appear throughout the romance, just before combat scenes, in which an authority figure presents his or her view of the responsibilities of a knight. Without regard for their personal safety, the noblemen are expected to serve their lord in the profession for which they have been trained. Other didactic passages appear frequently at moments of separation in which parents or parent-figures give advice to their children, telling them that they must be noble and gracious. But there is another layer of instruction in this romance. Constantly risking his life and putting Guillaume's needs before his own, Alphonse embodies the Christian concept of selfless service to others. Through his example and through his own retelling of his sacrifice, the werewolf functions as a metaphorical *miroir des princes*. As Alphonse reminds Guillaume, "Ainc beste ne fist ce por home / Que jou ai, sire, por toi fait" (8194–95), "Never has a beast done this for man / As I have, sire, for you." The figure of the werewolf in *Guillaume de Palerne* thus challenges the romance's aristocratic audience to conform to the high standards for noble sacrifice that he has set. This chivalrous werewolf is indeed an exemplar for all to follow.

Chapter Eight

A New Renaissance for the Wicked Werewolf

During the sixteenth century in France, an era so celebrated for its rebirth of culture that it is more commonly called the Renaissance, a new werewolf arrives on the scene — or rather the traditional werewolf from antiquity is reborn. This werewolf has replaced the chivalrous knight, the hero portrayed in the *lai* and the romance; he has once again undergone a metamorphosis. This werewolf is now a rough, dirty peasant who savagely attacks, kills, and then eats his victims, who are usually children. He is indeed the terrifying monster of our nightmares. Worse yet, we do not find the story of this Renaissance werewolf recounted in the pages of courtly literature; instead, we find it reported in court trials. He is real. Or is he? To trace the history of the werewolf in the sixteenth century, we must delve into that of witches, for their histories, and the theoretical treatises that discuss them, are forever bound together and intertwined.

In the waning years of the fifteenth century, more precisely on December 9, 1484, Pope Innocent VIII issued his famous decree against the heresy of sorcery, *Summis desiderantes affectibus*, which specifically authorized the Dominican inquisitors Heinrich Kramer and Jakob Sprenger to imprison and punish anyone they found guilty of the practice of witchcraft.[1] Just two years later in 1486, Kramer wrote the *Malleus maleficarum* (*The Hammer of Witches*),[2] which served as a manual for other inquisitors and provided the theological groundwork for heresy trials. As Sydney Anglo notes:

> The *Malleus* was written to demonstrate precisely what witches were doing, and how they could be stopped. It first establishes the truth of the existence of witchcraft and its heretical nature; then elucidates the principal evils practised by witches and demons; and finally lays down formal rules for initiating legal action against witches, securing their conviction, and passing sentence upon them ["Evident Authority," 15].

Although Kramer quotes repeatedly throughout the *Malleus* from St. Augustine and St. Thomas Aquinas and refers frequently to the *Canon Episcopi*, he deviates remarkably from them — especially from the *Canon Episcopi*— on one major point; instead of stating that it is blasphemous to believe in the existence of witches and their ability to fly and transform themselves, he declares that witches really exist and that it is heretical to believe the opposite: "Whether the belief that there are such beings as witches is so essential a part of the Catholic faith that obstinately to maintain the opposite opinion manifestly savours of heresy."[3] The scope of the *Malleus* was limited to Germany and its content was extremely misogynistic; indeed, Anglo even labels it "scholastic pornography" ("Evident Authority," 17). In addition, Kramer's logic is circular and he often contradicts himself.[4] Nonetheless, the *Malleus* had a profound and widespread influence on beliefs and behavior throughout Europe during the sixteenth century. According to Gaël Milin, the *Malleus* was a "texte fondamental dans le développement en Europe de la croyance au satanisme et dans la répression," "fundamental text in the development in Europe of the belief in Satanism and [a fundamental text] in repression" (119).[5] As evidence of its importance, twenty-eight editions of the *Malleus* appeared during the fifteenth and sixteenth centuries. In addition to affecting attitudes regarding witchcraft, the text shaped opinion about werewolves, for belief in witches and their ability to transform themselves into animals also made the belief in werewolves permissible.

Although the *Malleus maleficarum* deals almost exclusively with witches, Kramer addresses the issue of metamorphosis in Part I, Question 1, at the very beginning of his work, immediately after stating that "no operation of witchcraft has a permanent effect among us"[6] because if it did that would mean that the devil had powers that would be contrary to the teachings of the Church. He continues his argument thus:

> Moreover, every alteration that takes place in a human body — for example, a state of health or a state of sickness — can be brought down to a question of natural causes, as Aristotle has shown in his 7th book of *Physics*. And the greatest of these is the influence of the stars. But the devils cannot interfere with the movement of the stars. This is the opinion of Dionysius in his epistle to S. Polycarp. For this alone God can do. There it is evident the demons cannot actually effect any permanent transformation in human bodies; that is to say, no real metamorphosis. And so we must refer the appearance of any such change to some dark and occult cause.[7]

Here Kramer reiterates Augustine's theory of metamorphosis: it is not real, but merely appearance or illusion. Yet he opened the *Malleus* by stating that witches were real. Set within the context of this text and its detailed discussion of the practices of these witches, Kramer's statement about metamorphosis paradoxically lends some credence to the very belief that he is attacking.

Further on in the *Malleus*, Kramer devotes an entire section to metamorphosis, even though it would seem that he had already settled the issue, and asks "Whether Witches can by some Glamour Change Men into Beasts."[8] He begins by quoting the passage from the *Canon Episcopi* that states witches cannot transform men into animals and that anyone who believes such a thing is an infidel. After reviewing Thomas Aquinas' arguments about whether or not demons can delude men's senses, Kramer concludes "that the devils can in no way deceive the imagination and senses of a man" (152). He continues, however, by quoting St. Augustine's statement "that the transmutations of men into brute animals, said to be done by the art of devils, are not actual but only apparent" (153). It follows, then, as Kramer notes, that the devils must be deceiving men's senses and he arrives at a new conclusion: "let us say in agreement with the opinions of the three Doctors, that the devil can deceive the human fancy so that a man really seems to be an animal" (153). Further on, in the "Solutions" section of this question, Kramer reinforces this conclusion with his discussion of the different meanings of the word "made":

> And as to where it says that no creature can be made by the power of the devil, this is manifestly true if Made is understood to mean Created. But if the word Made is taken to refer to natural production, it is certain that devils can make some imperfect creatures. And S. Thomas shows how this may be done. For he says that all transmutations of bodily matters which can be effected by the forces of nature, in which the essential thing is the semen which is found in the elements of this world, on land or in the waters (as serpents and frogs and such things deposit their semen), can be effected by the work of devils who have acquired such semen. So also it is when anything is changed into serpents or frogs, which can be generated by putrefaction.
>
> But those transmutations of bodily matters which cannot be effected by the forces of nature can in no way be truly effected by the work of the devils. For when the body of a man is changed into the body of a beast, or a dead body is brought to life, such things only seem to happen, and are a glamour or illusion; or else the devil appears before men in an assumed body [156–57].

According to Kramer, then, devils and witches can make some imperfect creatures, if the semen and "germs" (157) necessary for their production are available, but they cannot transform a man into an animal; they can only make it seem that this has happened. He adds one more caveat: they must also have God's permission to perform these acts. Indeed, as Kramer noted earlier in his discussion of the devil's power to deceive, "the devil can do none of these things without the permission of God" (155). Before moving on to an entirely new subject, Kramer asks another question related to metamorphosis that is of particular interest to our study: "What is to be Thought of Wolves which sometimes Seize and Eat Men and Children out of their Cradles: whether this also is a Glamour caused by Witches" (158). He initiates his discussion in this manner: "There is incidentally a question concerning wolves, which sometimes snatch men and children out of their houses and eat them, and run about with such astuteness that by no skill or strength can they be hurt or captured" (158).[9] According to Kramer, natural explanations such as famine or the wolf's great strength or fierceness are not the real cause of such behavior. Instead, he declares that "such things are caused by an illusion of devils, when God punishes some nation for sin" and that the wolves are not devils who have taken on the appearance of wolves but are "true wolves ... [that] are possessed by devils" (159). Nevertheless, Kramer cites one case that did not involve real wolves "possessed by devils" and refers to a story recounted by William of Paris in which a man thought he had been transformed into a wolf that attacked and ate children.[10] In this case, Kramer states that this was "an illusion caused by witches" (159). He concludes his discussion by reiterating his declaration that "such things only happen by the permission of God alone and through the operation of devils, and not through any natural defect; since by no art or strength can such wolves be injured or captured" (160). It is exactly this issue of the permission bestowed on devils and witches by God that Anglo criticizes so aptly since it employs circular logic and creates the illogical situation in which inquisitors, men of God, hunt down, try, and punish witches who are supposedly doing only what God has allowed them to do:

> [T]he whole argument for persecution rests upon a monstrous paradox, since witches are merely serving God's mysterious purposes and might, on that account, be deemed more worthy of praise than of blame. God, we are told, frequently allows devils to act as His ministers and servants (p. 8). Were the devil completely unrestricted he would destroy the works of God. But he cannot destroy the works of God (p. 11). Therefore whatever he does can only be with divine permission ["Evident Authority," 20].

Following Kramer's "logic" to its conclusion, since the wolf or the werewolf cannot be injured or captured, God also must be using the illusion of werewolves — as well as the werewolves themselves — for his own purposes. Certainly we saw in our study of *Guillaume de Palerne* that Alphonse the werewolf is an agent of God.[11] In spite of his circular logic, Kramer may not be so very far from the truth, at least in regards to some werewolves.

Over the next hundred years, Europe was caught up in a frantic witch hunt as thousands were put on trial for sorcery and burned at the stake. At the same time, a handful of men and women, primarily in the Franche-Comté region of France, confessed to being werewolves. Their court cases are referred to and recounted in the writings of jurists, theologians, and doctors who wrote about sorcery and lycanthropy. In 1563, Johann Weyer, a Lutheran physician, wrote *De Praestigiis Daemonum*.[12] He is most famous for condemning the burning of witches and advocating instead the persecution of magicians. For Weyer, however, Catholic priests are no different from demon-worshipping magicians and should be condemned. As Christopher Baxter notes, Weyer's fifth book is "an ideological attack on Catholic idolatry and superstition" (54). Citing Weyer's comments regarding how the devil uses "idoles" 'idols' in the Catholic Church to get Christians to serve and honor him, Baxter declares:

> The devil has, then, turned the Roman Church into a front organisation [sic]. For instance, the baptism and exorcism of bells, ceremonies overtly designed to prevent the devil getting hold of them, are in fact devilish deceits to fill the organisation's [sic] coffers. We should however note that Weyer does think that exorcism of people *is* legitimate if carried out by those who 'ont puissance et don particulier de chasser les diables hors de leur siege,'[13] that there is, in other words, a good (Protestant) Christian magic as well as a bad (Catholic) pseudo-Christian magic [55]

Weyer's attitude reflects, of course, the schism between the Catholics and Protestants and the wars of religions that had just started to rip France apart. Although Weyer focuses *De Praestigiis Daemonum* almost exclusively on the devil, magicians, and witches, he devotes one chapter of the text to werewolves, Chapter 23 of Book Four: "Concerning the disease of lycanthropy, in which men believe themselves to be turned into wolves." According to Weyer, lycanthropes suffer from an imbalance in their melancholic humor, are deluded by the devil, and exhibit the following physical symptoms:

> They therefore go out of their houses, especially by night, imitating wolves or dogs in their every action. They are pale, and their eyes are sunken and dry. They see but dimly and have a dry tongue and a great thirst, while their mouth lacks saliva. Their legs are so covered in sores that they cannot be healed — because of frequent injuries and dog bites [343].

Weyer was not the first to suggest a medical cause for lycanthropy; in the second century the Alexandrian physician Paulus Aegineta described werewolves in almost the same way and also attributed their disease to melancholy, or an "excess of black bile" (Douglas, 9).[14] Nor will Weyer be the last; in the twentieth century, other medical explanations will be proposed, such as porphyria. For those suffering from the delusion of lycanthropy, Weyer offers the following treatment:

> These individuals are cured by the letting of blood (even to the point of losing consciousness), and also by good juicy foods, fresh water baths, buttermilk, the "sacred antidote" of Rufus or Archigenes or Justus (made from

> colocynth), and all the other remedies useful against melancholia. Before the accession of the illness their heads are rinsed with sleep-inducing agents and their nostrils are rubbed with opium. Sometimes, too, a soporific must be taken by mouth. It is probable that this flaw of nature, this aberration of the human mind, provided the occasion for Ovid's story about Lycaon, the king of Arcadia, whom he represented as being changed into a wolf by Jupiter because of his crimes ... Avicenna has remarked that many persons who are corrupted by black bile imagine themselves to be lions or demons or birds. And according to Herodotus, the Neuri, a people of Scythia, were convinced that they changed into wolves [343].

Although Weyer states that lycanthropy is caused by a combination of melancholia and delusion, he offers a different diagnosis later on when discussing the incident in 1521 at Poligny in which two men, Pierre Bourgot and Michel Verdung, confessed during their trial that they were werewolves. Chapter 13 of Book Six, "The confession of certain men who believed that they had been transformed into wolves," details this confession. According to Weyer, Bourgot and Verdung were charged with the heretical crime of *maleficium* or sorcery and were consequently put in prison. They confessed during the month of December 1521 after being tortured on several occasions. On December 31, 1521, they "repeated [their confession] in its essential details ... in the presence of many eyewitnesses" (511).[15] According to Bourgot, while looking for stray cattle "about nineteen years earlier, on the day of the Poligny Fair" (512), he had encountered three black men dressed in black and riding horses. One of them offered to help him find the cattle, protect them from wolves, and give him money, if in turn Bourgot would promise to serve his master. Bourgot agreed and returned four days later as agreed, only to learn that the master that he would serve was the Devil. Nevertheless, Bourgot paid him homage, asking only that the demon keep his promises. Bourgot renounced all his Christian beliefs and served the Devil for two years. Afterward, he returned to the Church for some eight or nine years, until Verdung persuaded him to resume serving the Devil. Bourgot accepted, asking only that he receive the money that had been promised to him before. Verdung anointed Bourgot with an ointment that caused him to change into a wolf. While the two of them were werewolves, Bourgot and Verdung killed a woman gathering peas, killed and ate a little girl who was only four, killed another girl and drank her blood and ate her neck, and killed a fourth girl who was eight or nine. Bourgot said that he "had broken her neck with his teeth because she had once refused his request for alms; and as soon as he had done the awful deed, he begged then and there for alms in honor of God" (513–514). They also mated with wolves, "with as much pleasure as if they had been having relations with their wives" (514). In the following chapter, "The confession explained and refuted point by point, Chapter 14," Weyer never mentions melancholia, but merely says that Bourgot and Verdung were deceived by the devil:

> In this case, everything hinges upon the question of whether the entire confession is true. And I hope to show plainly, with the help of God, that in its essentials it is opposed to the clear truth, and that accordingly it is not only erroneous but totally false, and that appearances of things which are perceived only through dreams or are presented to the eyes by trickery are substituted for the things themselves [514].

Weyer reinforces his argument by noting how quickly Bourgot returns to his Christian faith when he is no longer a herdsman and no longer so isolated and vulnerable to the illusions created by the devil:

> I still want to mention briefly at this point that the bonds of the pact were so weak and insignificant that when Peter [Bourgot] completed his job of grazing cattle he lived piously in his old religion for eight or nine successive years — leading me to say all the more quickly that his confession represented only the foolish beliefs of a man who was deluded by appearances. While he played the role of herdsman and dwelled apart in the solitude of the fields where the Devil had a better opportunity to deceive him with his illusions, he was harassed by idols of this sort more by reason of the solitude than because of his renunciation of faith. In this way also the demon sometimes called up wolf-images which did no harm — nor could they do harm, being mere appearances of things. Or, if we should grant that they were real wolves, it is likely that Satan drove them there and back again, designing the whole drama for the purpose of binding Peter more closely to himself by means of his mad and misleading suggestions. This he could not do so easily when Peter had ceased from his duties as a herdsman and no longer frequented those lonely places [515].

Weyer buttresses his argument even further by recounting an incident involving a pack of real wolves that seemed to invade, or at the very least, attack Constantinople about twenty years after Bourgot's and Verdung's confession:

> So, too, in the year 1542, a huge pack of wolves appeared in Constantinople, wolves so hostile and so harmful to the inhabitants that they were unwilling to go out of their houses. Therefore, the Turks first fortified the walls of the city with a guard detail and on the following day went about the city with a great troop of horsemen and foot soldiers, finally encountering about a hundred and fifty wolves at one corner of the wall. Being attacked without delay, the wolves seemed to leap instantly through the wall, and not one was later seen in the city or in the vicinity [515].

Real wolves? Supposedly so, but the wolves are in such an astounding quantity and, in addition, figure in an account that is juxtaposed with Weyer's suggestion that Satan "drives" real wolves here and there for dramatic effect.

Certainly, the fact that these wolves in Constantinople "seemed to leap instantly through the wall" lends credence to the idea that there was something supernatural going on and that this is just another demonic illusion. Returning to his refutation of Bourgot's and Verdung's confession, Weyer declares:

> If, then, I have succeeded in proving that this metamorphosis did not really take place — as every sane person must admit — and that the confession is therefore imaginary and in this respect false, what credence should be given, I ask you, to the other things that they have confessed — the outrages and the murders? They have already admitted that these were only perpetrated during the course of the transformation, and in their wolfish form, and that they could not have done otherwise. But this is assuredly nothing but raving; more than nonsense, it is madness [516].

As we saw earlier, Weyer states that lycanthropy is caused by a combination of melancholia and delusion. Faced with Bourgot's and Vendung's confession as werewolves, however, Weyer attributes their lycanthropy only to delusion. His inconsistency is somewhat troubling, yet the medical explanation that he proposes for the men's confession is much more significant: according to Weyer, the ointment that the men had used to transform themselves into werewolves was a drug that induced sleep and hallucinations:

> The liniment with which they anointed themselves when about to take on the form of wolves was no doubt a sleep-producing agent, such as I have also described in book three, chapter 17, because it achieved its effects when it was spread upon the exposed parts of the body and then activated by the body's innate heat. When they were overwhelmed by deep sleep, the arch-contriver thrust upon them images of their being changed into roving wolves that attacked others, killed and ate maidens, and copulated with female wolves — and all sorts of similar images. ... [T]he other liniment with which they anointed themselves when they wanted to return to human form was either imaginary (and they were asleep when they thought they were using it), or else it might have been effective against the harmful effects of the sleep-producing ointment; or it might even have done nothing at all, save that by means of it the demon deceived his clients — as though it had some special powers with regard to the metamorphosis [516–17].

In spite of the fact that Bourgot and Verdung were convinced that they were werewolves and had committed atrocious crimes, Weyer believes that none of these things had ever happened. They were merely experiencing nightmarish delusions while they were asleep. Weyer was certainly not the first to say that werewolves were merely people deceived by the devil, but he was most likely the first to write of the link between the ointments that they used to "transform" themselves into wolves and their delusions.[16]

Less than twenty years later, in 1580, the French jurist Jean Bodin wrote

De la démonomanie des sorciers (Demonomania of Witches). The sixth chapter of the second book is entitled "De la Lycanthropie et si le Diable peut changer les hommes en bestes," "About Lycanthropy and if the Devil can change men into beasts." Unlike others who wrote about werewolves at this time, Bodin took the radical position of believing that the devil could really transform man's physical form into that of a wolf; Bodin also believed, however, that the werewolf retained his human understanding:

> Et par ce moyen la Lycanthropie ne seroit pas contraire au canon Episcopi xxvi. q.v. ny à l'opinion des Theologiens qui tiennent pour la plurpart que Dieu non seulement a crée toutes choses, ains aussi que les malins esprits n'ont pas la puissance de changer la forme, attendu que la forme essentielle de l'homme ne change point, qui est la raison, ains seulement la figure.[17]

> And by this means Lycanthropy would not be contrary to the Canon Episcopi xxvi. q.v. nor to the opinion of most Theologians who believe that God not only created all things, but also that evil spirits do not have the power to change form, considering that the essential form of man does not change at all, which is his understanding, but that only his body changes [in the condition of Lycanthropy].

The unknown author of the *Canon Episcopi* rationalizes sorcery, while at the same time condemning belief in it, by explaining that witchcraft, like metamorphosis, is not real but only illusion and the result of demonic trickery.[18] Bodin's belief that the physical transformation actually occurs runs contrary to the *Canon Episcopi,* yet he manages to remain within its theological boundaries by insisting that the mind of the victim of the metamorphosis is untouched. Moreover, God always has a hand in the transformation:

> Mais en quelque sorte que ce soit, il a pert que les hommes sont quelques fois transmuez en bestes demeurant la forme et raison humaine. Soit que cela se face par la puissance de Dieu immediatement, soit qu'il donne ceste puissance à Satan executeur de sa volonté.[19]

> But however it may be, it appears that men are sometimes transformed into beasts but they retain their human understanding and intelligence. Either it is done by the power of God immediately or he gives this power to Satan as the executor of his will.

Thus, like the werewolf heroes of the medieval tales, Bodin's theoretical "werewolf" retains his human understanding and reasoning and, like Alphonse, serves God's purpose.

In addition to offering his own very different opinion on the reality of werewolves, Bodin's chapter on lycanthropy in *De la démonomanie des sorciers* also provides us with accounts of "real" werewolves of that era. The first werewolf whose story he relates is that of the famous self-professed werewolf Gilles Garnier:

> Et sans aller gueres loing de ce Royaume, nous avons un procez fait au Parlement de Dole, et l'arrest donné le XVIII Janvier 1574 contre Gille Garnier Lyonnois, qu'il n'est besoin de mettre icy au long, puisqu'il est imprimé à Orléans par Eloy Gibier, et à Paris chez Pierre des Hayes, et à Sens; mais je mettray les poincts principaux dont il a esté accusé et convaincu. C'est à sçavoir que ledict Garnier le jour sainct Michel, estant en forme de Loup garoup print une jeune fille de l'aage de dix ou douze ans pres le bois de la Serre, en une vigne, au vignoble de Chastenoy pres Dole un quart de lieue, et illec l'avoir tué et occisé, tant avec ses mains semblans pattes, que avec ses dents, et mangé la chair des cuisses, et bras d'icelle, et en avoit porté à sa femme. Et pour avoir en mesme forme un mois apres pris une autre fille, et icelle tué pour la manger, s'il n'eust esté empesché par trois personnes, comme il a confessé. Et quinze jours apres avoir estranglé un jeune enfant de dix ans au vignoble de Gredisans, et mangé la chair des cuisses, jambes, et ventre d'iceluy. Et pour avoir depuis en forme d'homme, et non de Loup, tué un autre garçon de l'aage de douze à treize ans, au bois du village de Perouse, en intention de le manger, si on ne l'eust empesché, comme il confessa sans force ny contraincte, il fut condamné d'estre bruslé tout vif, et l'arrest fut executé.[20]

> And without going far from this kingdom, we have a trial conducted in the Parlement of Dole, and the judgment given on January 18, 1574 against Gille Garnier of Lyons, that there is no need to give here in length, since it is printed in Orléans by Eloy Gibier and in Paris by Pierre des Hayes and in Sens; but I will put down the principal points for which he was accused and convicted. That is that the said Garnier on the day of Saint Michael, being in the form of a Were Wolf took a young girl ten or twelve years old near the woods of Serre, in a vineyard, in the vineyard of Chastenoy a quarter of a league from Dole, and there he killed and butchered her, as much with his hands in the semblance of paws as with his teeth, and ate the flesh of her thighs and arms, and had carried some to his wife. And for having taken another girl, and killed her in order to eat her, if he hadn't been prevented by three people, as he has confessed. And fifteen days later, for having strangled a young child ten years old in the vineyard of Gredisans, and eaten the flesh of his thighs, legs, and belly. And since then for having killed, while in the form of a man, and not that of a Wolf, another boy twelve to thirteen years old, in the woods of the village of Perouse, with the intention of eating him, if he hadn't been prevented from doing so, as he confessed without being forced or coerced. He was condemned to be burned alive, and the sentence was carried out.

According to this account, Gilles Garnier confessed to killing four children, ate of the flesh of two of them, and would have eaten the other two if he hadn't been prevented from doing so. Interestingly, his behavior remained the same whether he was in his human form or in his werewolf form. In other words, he did retain his own particular human understanding. His last crime was his undoing, for it was then that he did not transform himself, was seen by others — he was "prevented" from eating the child — and identified by them. Indeed, his true nature was finally recognized; he was a child murderer, he was a werewolf, he was a monster, he was a cannibal, and so Garnier was brought to trial.[21]

After relating the account of Gilles Garnier, Bodin then turns to a werewolf trial that occurred more than fifty years earlier, one that we have already encountered, that of Pierre Bourgot and Michel Verdung:

> Il se trouve encores un autre proces faict à Bezançon, par l'Inquisiteur Jean Boin l'an 1521, au mois de Décembre, et envoyé en France, Italie et Allemaigne, et que Vierus defenseur des Sorciers a mis bien au loing au livre VI, Chap. XIII des Prestiges : c'est pourquoy je le trancheray court. Les accusez estoient Pierre Burgot, et Michel Verdun, qui confesserent avoir renoncé à Dieu, et juré de servir au Diable. Et Michel Verdun mena Burgot au bord du Chastel Charlon, ou chacun avoit une chandelle de cire verte, qui faisoit la flamme bleue, et obscure, et faisoient les danses, et sacrifices au Diable. Puis apres s'estans oinctz furent tournez en Loups courant d'une legereté incroyable; puis qu'ils estoient changez en hommes, et souvent rechangez en Loups et couplez aux Louves avec tel plaisir qu'ils avoient accoustumé avec les femmes. Ils confesserent aussi, à sçavoir Burgot, avoir tué un jeune garçon de sept ans avec ses pattes, et dents de Loup, et qu'il vouloit manger, n'eust esté que les païsans luy donnerent la chasse. Et Michel Verdun confessa avoir tué une jeune fille cueillant des poids en un jardin, qui fut chassé par le Seigneur de la Cuvée. Et que tous deux avoient encores mangé quatre filles, et remarqua le temps, le lieu, l'aage particulièrement des enfans. Et qu'en touchant d'une poudre, ils faisoient mourir les personnes.[22]
>
> There is yet another trial that took place in Bezançon, by the Inquisitor Jean Boin in the year 1521, in the month of December, and sent to France, Italy and Germany, and that Vierus defender of the Witches set down at length in Book VI, Chapter XIII of the Prestiges: that is why I will cut it short. The accused were Pierre Bourgot and Michel Verdung, who confessed that they had renounced God and had sworn to serve the Devil. And Michel Verdung led Bourgot to the side of the Charlon Castle, where each one had a candle of green wax, which made the flame blue and dark, and they danced and made sacrifices to the Devil. Then after having put ointment on themselves, they were transformed into wolves and ran with an unbelievable lightness; afterward they changed into men, and often changed back into Wolves and coupled with female Wolves with the same pleasure that they customarily had with women. They also confessed, that is Bourgot did, to have killed a young boy seven years old with his paws, and his Wolf teeth, and that he wanted to eat the boy and would have, if it hadn't been for the peasants who had chased him. And Michel Verdung confessed that he had killed a young girl gathering peas in a garden, and was chased away by Seigneur de la Cuvée. And that both of them had eaten four other girls and noted the time, the place, and the particular age of the children. And that by touching them with a powder, they caused the people to die.

Not only do both Verdung and Bourgot confess that they worship Satan and that they transform themselves into wolves, but they also confess to killing children and eating them. They are werewolves and they are cannibals. The fact that Verdung and Bourgot are aware of the pleasure they experience when, as wolves, they "couple" with female wolves, indicates that they, like the medieval werewolves, retain their human understanding while in their lupine forms. Unlike the medieval werewolves, however, they are not heroes but are truly wicked monsters.

Finally, Bodin also writes very briefly about two other werewolves. The lack of details in these two accounts is frustrating, yet the similarity in them is noteworthy and justifies their inclusion in our study:

> Il me souvient que M. Le Procureur général du Roy Bourdin m'en a recité un autre, qu'on luy avoit envoié du bas pays, avec tout le procez signé du Juge et des Greffiers, de un loup qui fut frappé d'un traict qui luy fut arraché, estant rechangé en forme d'homme, et le traict cognu par celuy qui l'avoit tiré, le temps et le lieu justifié par la confession du personnage. Et Job Fincel au livre XI des Merveilles escrit, qu'il y avoit aussi à Padoue un Lycanthrope qui couroit d'une vitesse incroyable, toutefois enfin, à force de chevaux, il fut attrapé, et ses pattes de loup luy furent coupées, et au mesme instant il se trouva les bras et pieds coupez.[23]
>
> I remember that Monsieur Bourdin, the King's General Prosecutor, told me about another one, that they had sent him from the lowlands, with the entire judgment signed by the judge and by the court clerks, about a wolf that was hit by an arrow that was pulled out of him, changing him back into the form of a man, and the arrow recognized by the man who had shot it, the time and the place confirmed by the person's confession. And Job Fincel in Book XI of the Marvels writes that there also was in Padua a Lycanthrope who ran at an incredible speed, however it was finally caught using horses and its wolf paws were cut off and at the same moment he found that his arms and feet were cut off.

Similar motifs can be found in the eleventh- and thirteenth-century Latin poems and in the Middle Irish tales of Irish werewolves.[24] All these accounts tell of men who have the ability to change themselves at will into wolves; if they are injured while in their lupine form, their human bodies show the same marks or wounds of injury. In the early thirteenth century Gervase of Tilbury also relates in *Otia Imperialia* the story of a werewolf, Raimbaud de Pouget, who recovers his human form after a woodcutter chops off one of his paws.[25] But the motif is much older; Petronius is perhaps the first to use it in his *Satyricon* when he relates the tale of Trimalchio's dinner party in which Niceros finds the soldier in bed with a neck wound the morning after the werewolf is stabbed in the neck. This injury, which is an important motif in folklore, shows continuity between the bestial and human life and makes the identification of the werewolf possible.[26]

In 1584, just four years after Jean Bodin insisted that the physical transformation of man into werewolf was not only possible but a reality, the English scholar and horticulturalist Reginald Scot wrote *The Discoverie of Witchcraft*, in which he attacks the ideas of Bodin, as well as those found in Kramer's *Malleus Maleficarum*. Although Scot's text does not include any "new" accounts of werewolves, it is worth examining because it contributes to our understanding of the multi-faceted attitude toward witches and werewolves in the sixteenth century. According to Anglo, Scot's book grew out of his "horror at the prejudice of the judges in witch trials; the fatuity of the charges brought against helpless and often senile women; the way in which ... the evidence adduced in trials was totally inadequate and unsubstantiated ... and the fact that his own religious convictions ... seemed to invalidate even the possibility of magical activity" ("Reginald Scot's *Discoverie*," 108). Scot devotes one book of his *Discoverie of Witchcraft* to the question of metamorphosis.[27] After summarizing the werewolf accounts related by Bodin in *De la démonomanie des sorciers*, Scott launches his assault. Following Bodin's logic, Scott wonders if every "asse, woolfe, or cat that we see" is really a human being, since according to Bodin, the metamorphosis of man into animal is possible, but then responds in the following manner:

> But to what end should one dispute against these creations and recreations; when Bodin washeth away all our arguments with one word, confessing that none can create any thing but God; acknowledging also the force of the canons, and imbracing the opinions of such divines, as write against him in this behalfe? Yea he dooth now (contrairie to himselfe elsewhere) affirme, that the divell cannot alter his forme. And lo, this is his distinction ... [t]he essentiall forme (to wit, reason) is not changed, but the shape or figure. And thereby he prooveth it easie enough to create men or beasts with life, so as they remaine without reason. Howbeit, I thinke it is an easier matter, to turne Bodins reason into the reason of an asse, than his bodie in to the shape of a sheepe: which he saith is an easie matter; bicause Lots wife was turned into a stone by the divel. Whereby he sheweth his grosse ignorance. As though God that commanded Lot upon paine of death not to looke backe, who also destroied the citie of Sodome at that instant, had not also turned hir into a salt stone. And as though all this while God had beene the divels drudge, to go about this businesse all the night before, and when a miracle should be wrought, the divell must be faine to doo it himselfe [Otten, 118–119].

Scott not only criticizes Bodin for contradicting himself, but does it with humor and in a way that turns Bodin's ideas as a weapon against him, implying that it would be easier to transform Bodin's reason or human understanding into that of an ass, which of course Bodin insists does not and cannot occur during diabolical metamorphosis, than to transform his human body into that of an animal. In other words, Scott is implying that Bodin has the reasoning of an ass. In this passage, he also points out Bodin's ignorance regarding the story of Lot's wife, since it was certainly God and not the Devil that turned her into a pillar of salt (Gen. 19.26). Finally, Scott insinuates that Bodin is at the very least showing disrespect toward God in attributing this miracle to the Devil; he has put God in a subservient position by making him the "divils drudge."

After relating at length the story of a young Englishman who was turned into an ass by a witch who lived in the city of Salamin in the kingdom of Cyprus, Scott declares that Bodin believed that the story was true. Indeed, according to Bodin, the old woman restored the young man's human form when the Inquisitors commanded her to do so. Scott, however, objects vehemently to Bodin's account:

> I answer, that as the whole storie is an impious fable; so this assertion is false, and disagreeable to their owne doctrine, which mainteineth, that the witch dooth nothing but by the permission and leave of God. For if she could doo or undoo such a thing at hir owne pleasure, or at the commandement of the inquisitors, or for feare of the tormentors, or for love of the partie, or for remorse of conscience: then is it not either by the extraordinarie leave, nor yet by the like direction of God; except you will make him a confederate with old witches [Otten, 123].

Scott once again attacks the irreverent and demeaning attitude toward God displayed by Bodin in his writing, noting that he has in effect made God the partner or accomplice of "old witches." Continuing his criticism of Bodin, Scott turns to the spiritual nature of the human body:

> What a beastlie assertion is it, that a man, whom GOD hath made according to his owne similitude and likenes, should be by a witch turned into a beast? What an impietie is it to affirme, that an asses bodie is the temple of the Holy-ghost? Or an asse to be the child of God, and God to be his father; as it is said of man? Which Paule to the Corinthians so divinelie confuteth, who saith, that Our bodies are the members of Christ. In the which we are to glorifie God: for the bodie is for the Lord, and the Lord is for the bodie. Surelie he meaneth not for an asses bodie, as by this time I hope appeareth: in such wise as Bodin, may go hide him for shame; especiallie when he shall understand, that even into these our bodies, which God hath framed after his owne likenesse, he hath also brethed that spirit, which Bodin saith is now remaining within an asses bodie, which God hath so subjected in such servilitie under the foote of man [Otten, 125].

As Scott points out, Christians believe that the human body is a temple in which the Holy Spirit, the Spirit of God, dwells. Bodin, however, believes that the human body can be transformed into the body of an ass or a wolf, for example, but that the reason — the spirit — remains intact within the animal body. For a Christian, the idea of God's Holy Spirit dwelling within the body of an animal is unthinkable, even blasphemous. Scott also notes that if diabolical transformation were possible "Gods work should not onelie be defaced and disgraced, but his ordinance should be woonderfullie altered, and thereby confounded" (Otten, 125). According to Scott, only God has the power to bring about such miraculous transformations, such as those of Lot's wife and of King Nebuchadnezzar.[28] Scott concludes his discussion of metamorphosis by stating that the transformations of human beings into animals through sorcery can be attributed to "a disease proceeding partlie from melancholie, wherebie manie suppose themselves to be woolves, or such ravening beasts. For Lycanthropia is of the ancient physicians called *Lupina melancholia,* or *Lupina insania*" (Otten, 126). In giving this medical diagnosis, Scott thus joins ranks with Weyer.

In 1595, Claude Prieur, a Franciscan monk living at the order's house in Louvain, wrote the *Dialogue de la Lycanthropie, ou transformation d'hommes en loups, vulgairement dit loups-garous, et si telle se peut faire (Dialogue of Lycanthropy, or Transformation of men into wolves, commonly called werewolves, and if such a thing can be done)*, which was published the following year under the authority of the king and with the approval of Bishop Cuyek and Gilles Cheheré, professor of theology. As the title suggests, the text is written in the form of a dialogue, more specifically between three men: Eleion, Scipion, and Proteron. The first two argue that the transformation of a human being into a wolf is possible, whereas the latter presents Prieur's point of view that metamorphosis is not possible. They begin their conversation with Scipion lamenting the miseries of the times:

> "Sans doubte noz miseres sont si communes, qu'il n'y a personne, soit grand, soit petit, qui ne s'en resente; ou qui par succession de temps n'estime tomber en vn mesme desastre, ou plus grief. Et semble le comble de noz miseres venir tout a coup; selon les fleaux, & punitions, que iamais nostre Dieu a envoyé aux hommes. Car qui est celuy qui n'auroit occasion de se plaindre, voiant vne intemperie du temps engendrant vne infinité de maladies, voire telles, que de semblables on n'a iamais ouy parler? Ou bien qui est celuy d'entre nous qui n'apperçoit les saisons renuersées ne nous presagier autre chose sinon une sterilué future? Ioint le degast que font encore les hommes, se menant guerre les vns aux autres, estant acharnez contre le sang de leurs propres voysins" [13b–14].

> "Without a doubt our miseries are so common that there is no one, whether he be noble or peasant, who doesn't feel the effects of it; or who by the passage of time doesn't consider that he will fall into the same disaster or more trouble. And the depth of our misery seems to come suddenly; according to the scourges and punishments that God has forever sent to men. For who is he who would not have had the occasion to complain, seeing bad weather

> causing an infinite number of maladies, indeed such maladies of which no one has ever heard the like before. Or then who among us doesn't see the reversed seasons foretelling anything other than a sterile future? Add [to all this] the damage that men are still causing, waging war against each other, so fiercely against the blood of their own neighbors."

The war to which Scipion refers is of course one of the wars of religion, which were still tearing France apart. Begun in 1560, they did not end until the proclamation of the Edict of Nantes by Henri IV in 1598.[29] But the miseries of the times extended well beyond Catholics and Protestants killing one another, as famine and plague were also widespread in France and beyond. Proteron then discusses various stories from the Bible and reviews all the ways God punishes man "ou par peste; ou par famine; ou par guerre" "either by plague, or by famine, or by war" (14b). Afterward he begins to speak of animals, noting that the Holy Scripture is full of examples of how "les bestes avoir autrefois aussi bien guerroyé l'homme" "in the past animals have also waged war against man." (15) The three men speak of various animals and then Proteron brings up the subject of wolves:

> "Et pour reprendre le fil de nostre discours, tout ainsi que nous voions les loups reuestrez d'vn manteau de simplicitié au commencement doux & appriuoysez; mais peu apres ayant quitté ceste peau de faintise & simulation, il n'est possible de raconter quel degast, quel rauage, quelle cruauté ilz exercent enuers les pauures brebis: Ainsi ces faux prophetes vsent de flaterie aux simples, pour soudain les prenant à la gorge les empescher, ou de loüer Dieu, faire confession, ou prendre la pasture accoustumée dans la prée verdoyante de l'eglise: a cause de quoy nostre Sauueur particulierement taschoit nous detourner de ceux cy, preuoiant l'horrible desastre qu'au dernier temps ilz deuoient executer contre son troupeau" [19b].

> "And to pick up again the thread of our discussion, just as we see wolves at the beginning garbed in a cloak of gentle and tame simplicity; but a little later having discarded this skin of pretense and simulation, it is not possible to recount what damage, what devastation, what cruelty they wreak against the poor sheep. In the same way these false prophets use flattery on simple people, suddenly taking them by the throat in order to prevent them either from praising God, making their confession, or taking their accustomed pasture in the green meadows of the church: because of this our Savior tried particularly to turn us away from them, foreseeing the horrible disaster that they recently carried out against his flock."

Proteron thus uses the metaphor of the wolf in sheep's clothing to compare false prophets to wolves. The false prophets to whom he is referring are most likely Protestant ministers; the horrible disaster would then of course be the wars of religion. Proteron continues his discourse by stating that these false prophets are worse than wolves, for a wolf "bien souuent se contentera d'emporter vn mouton ou aigneau sans faire tort au reste; mais vn faux predicant ne fera point a son aise qu'il n'aye perdu tout le troupeau Catholique" (19b–20), "will very often content himself with carrying off a sheep or a lamb without harming the rest; but a false preacher will not be at ease until he has caused the entire Catholic flock to perish." But as Proteron notes, this urge to physically harm others is nothing new; even the first-century Roman philosopher Seneca wrote about it: "Ceste rage, dit il, peut bien estre appellée brutale, se resiouir & prendre plaisir au sang, & au playes, & ayant reietté l'homme changer en beste sauuage" (20). "This rage, he said, can certainly be called brutal, to delight & take pleasure in blood & in wounds, & having rejected the man change into a savage beast." Proteron's commentary then triggers the following dialogue regarding metamorphosis itself:

SCIPION. Les homes donc peuuent ilz laisser leur forme de nature humaine, pour en reuestir vne autre?

PROTERON. Il n'y a personne qui le peut soustenir.

ELEION. Ne croyez vous point de transformation, à sçauoir que l'homme peut prendre vne autre forme corporelle , ou se transmuer en autre figure qu'il n'est?

PROTERON. Il ne se sçauroit faire sinon par la puissance diuine, & ne le croy autrement.

SCIPION. Toutesfois vous auez desia proposé vne autorité de Seneque, par laquelle il semble que de son temps se trouuassent hommes qui se delectants au sang humain, changeoient la forme humaine en guise d'animaux farouches.

PROTERON. En cela n'ay ie pas entendu qu'il laissast la forme humaine, mais bien qu'il se pouuait trouuer des hommes si cruelz, qu'ilz meritoient plustost d'estre appelez bestes brutes, que creatures raisonnables, pour se delecter à toute impieté. Au surplus s'il nous faut passer plus outre, nous dirons que Seneque pouuoit avoir experiementé telle cruauté & barbarie en cest abominable & detestable tyran Neron, qui non content de persecuter, & affliger les Chrestiens de mille morts & supplices, oloit bien encore (chose horrible a ouyr) se vestir de la peau recentement escorchée d'vne beste sauuage, pour aller soubz ceste couuerture manger les cuisses des crucifiez encore viuants. (20–20b)

SCIPION. Then can men leave their natural human form to take on another?

PROTERON. There is no one who can defend it [the idea].

ELEION. Don't you believe at all in transformation? That is, that man can take on another corporal form or transmute into a form other than the one he has?

PROTERON. He would not be able to do it except by divine power, and I do not believe it [can happen] any other way.

SCIPION. However you have already mentioned an authentic story of Seneca, according to which it seems that in his time men could be found who, taking delight in human blood, changed their human form into that of savage animals.

PROTERON. About that I have not heard that he [they] left his [their] human form[s], but rather that men could be found that were so cruel that they merited being called brutal beasts rather than reasonable creatures, in order to delight in all ungodliness. Moreover, if we must go on even further, we will say that Seneca could have experienced such cruelty and barbarity in this abominable and detestable tyrant Nero, who not content with persecuting and afflicting the Christians with a thousand deaths and forms of torture, used to also (a horrible thing to hear) garb himself in the pelt of a savage beast that had recently been skinned, in order to go beneath this covering and eat the flesh of the crucified who were still alive.

Proteron thus insists that metamorphosis is possible only at the hand of God; anything else is merely metaphor. Men can be said to behave like beasts but they do not become beasts. Nero remained a man, even while perpetrating horrendous cannibalistic crimes. Interestingly enough, he disguised himself to do so; he put on an animal skin. The importance of this will become clear later in the dialogue. Proteron then continues his argument by discussing the "sortes de monstres approchants a l'espece humaine, d'ou auriez occasion de tomber en erreur" (20b), "kinds of monsters similar to the human species, by which you would have cause to fall into error." According to Proteron, however, the kinds of monsters that might make someone believe in metamorphosis are more common in other climates and are very rare "en ce païs icy" (21b), "in this country here." Scipion then raises the question of men who transform themselves into wolves:

SCIPION. Nous en auons tant d'exemples, qu'il me semble impossible de dire le contraire, a sçauoir d'hommes qui se tournans & conuertissans en forme strangere, deuorent les personnes qu'ilz rencontrent, les autres bestes mesme, & sur tout les ieunes enfants. Et quant est de moy, ie ne dis que ce soient monstres, ains des hommes vrayement, & naturellement de mesme espece que vous & moy.

PROTERON. En quelle forme?

SCIPION. Tantost en l'vne, tantost en l'autre, mais la plus commune, & experimentée en ce païs est en forme de loups; car ilz sont loups en vn temps, quand ilz veulent, & retournent hommes quand ilz veulent.

PROTERON. Croyez vous cela?

ELEION. Il est trop certain, & ont deuoré, & deuorent encore ordinairement, non seulement le bestial ains plustost s'adressent aux hommes, & particulierement aux petits enfants.

PROTERON. Ha! Bon Dieu combien vous errez grandement de vous persuader telle phantasie estre veritable. Ie croy certes plustost que c'est vn songe que verité. Iamais les philosophes, ou naturalistes n'y ont pensé, principalement ceux qui ont eu parfaicte cognoissance de la nature, moins encore les vrays historiens ne consenziront a telle transformation; au contraire nous apprennent que tout ce qui est au monde (excepté les cieux & les choses spirituelles) appete (appere?) & desire vne autre forme, & non indifferenment telle qu'elle, mais vne plus parfaicte. Et pour vne resolution absoluë, & en peu de parolles, souuienne vous de ceste sentence du philosophe; *Species non mutatur,* que l'espece jamais ne se change [21b–22].

SCIPION. We have so many examples of them that it seems impossible to me to say the contrary, that is, of men who, turning and changing themselves into a foreign form, devour the people that they meet, even other beasts, and especially young children. And as for me, I do not say that they are monsters, but truly men, and by nature of the same species as you and me.

PROTERON. In what form?

SCIPION. Sometimes in one, sometimes in another, but the most common and the one that is experienced the most often in this country is in the form of wolves; for they are wolves for a time, when they want, and return [to their form] as men when they want.

PROTERON. Do you believe that?

ELEION. It is too certain, and they have devoured and are still normally devouring, not just beasts but instead seek out men, and particularly small children.

PROTERON. Ha! Good God, how greatly you err in persuading yourself that such a fantasy is true. Indeed, I believe that it is a dream rather than truth. Never have philosophers or naturalists thought it, principally those who have perfect knowledge of nature, less still will true historians consent to such a transformation; on the contrary they teach us that that everything which is in the world (except for the heavens and spiritual things) is ready for and desires another form, and not indifferently one just as it is, but one more perfect. And for an absolute resolution, and in few words, remember this sentence of the philosopher; *Species non mutatur,* that the species never changes.

Using Proteron to voice his opinion, Prieur insists that the transformation of man into wolf is only fantasy and that those who believe in its possibility and reality are in error and are dreaming. Human beings would never lower themselves by taking on animal form, although they may seek to perfect their form. Continuing this train of thought, Proteron scolds the two men for their absurd beliefs and for having such a low opinion of man, "[c]ar celuy qui mesprise l'ouurage d'vn maistre, par consequent il contemne, & mesprise le maistre & l'ouurier" (24b) "for he who scorns the work of a master, consequently condemns and scorns the master and the worker." In other words, Eleion and Scipion are scorning God as the Creator of man. Eleion, however, immediately denies Proteron's accusation:

ELEION. Ia à Dieu ne plaise, que nous entendions faire aucune iniure a l'homme, ou luy deroger en les droits, moins encore a son Createur. Car nous ne disons point Dieu estre la cause de telle mechanceté, non plus que dire l'homme de bien s'en vouloir mesler, mais plustost la malice de quelques vns, ou le peché.

PROTERON. Si vous tenez que pour le peché, ou malice de l'homme, il puisse ou doive prendre autre forme, ou autre corps que le sien, vous tomberez en vne opinion fort erronée, & qui n'est de peu d'importance, veu qu'elle meine le droict chemin au pagamime, comme nous vous monstrerons [24b–25].

ELEION. May it never please God that we might intend to offend man, or go against his rights, less still offend his Creator. For we are not at all saying that God is the cause of such wickedness, no more than we are saying that good men want to get involved in it, but rather the malice of some men, or sin.

PROTERON. If you insist that because of the sin, or the malice of man, he might be able or might have to take on another form, or another body than his own, you are falling into a very erroneous opinion, & which is not of little importance, seeing that it leads directly to paganism, as we will show you.

Proteron then proceeds to review various writings from antiquity, including the writings of Pythagoras regarding metempsychosis, or the transmigration of souls, Ovid's *Metamorphoses*, and the writings of St. Augustine, inevitably ending up with the same message that "la loy diuine ne permettre tel changement de l'esprit humain au corps des bestes" (28b–29), "divine law does not permit such a change of the human spirit into the body of beasts." Proteron also mentions the axiom of many philosophers, according to which "chasque forme substantielle requiert certaines dispositions pour informer la matiere qu'elle pretend, & d'autant plus grandes que la perfection de ladicte forme est plus souueraine" (29b), "each substantial form requires certain arrangements to inform the matter that it maintains, & so much greater when the perfection of the said form is more sovereign." According to Proteron, the soul is too noble and too perfect to "inform" a body that is as different from a human body as that of a wolf. Elieon denies that he and Scipion believe in anything against the Christian faith, such as the transformation or transmigration of souls into another body, but still believe in the possibility of metamorphosis and "transformation corporelle" (30), "bodily transformation." Proteron, however, states that if they believe that men can transform themselves into wolves and then change back immediately into their human form, then therefore they must also believe that stories such as Ovid's *Metamorphoses* are true. In response to Scipion's question "Quelle est donc vostre opinion que puissent estre ce genre de bestes, exerçant telle cruauté sur le genre humain" (31b), "What is your opinion then about what this kind of beast might be, wreaking such cruelty on mankind?" Proteron replies that God uses these wolves to punish his enemies and those who break his commandments. Of special interest to our study is the section that follows, in which Proteron describes his personal experiences with wolves:

> A celle fin donc que vous pensiez que ce puissent estre loups naturels, comme ie les pense estre, je vous reciteray ce que moymesme ay experimenté depuis quelques années. Me souuient que l'an 1587 estant en Perigort, & seiournant quelques mois en vn petit conuent & ville de Rions, asçavoir cinq lieues de Bordeaux, fus envoyé le jour S. Iean par le pere Gardien dudict lieu en quelque village distant enuiron trois lieues, d'ou m'en retournant, & transuersant certain aultre petit village, aduisé vne pauure femme fort contristée, laquelle me dissuadoit de tenir le mesme chemin, dautant disoit elle, qu'il n'y auoit pas encores demie heure quand sur le sueil de sa porte luy auoit esté rauie du loup vne petitte fillette, qui pour quelques tourments ou crys que ladicte femme & plusieurs de ses voysins peussent mener, iamais ne peut estre recouurée. C'est le premier duquel entendis parler, mais non le dernier. Me transportant de la à Toloze, pour mon cours d'estudes, le susdict pere Gardien escriuit a celuy de nostre conuent, feu de bonne memoire le Reuerend pere de Roca, lettres de recommandation aux prieres des Religieux, touchant telle pauureté & miseres, asçauoir comme plusieurs hommes, femmes, & petits enfants, s'estans perdus, & desquels on n'auoit sçeu nouuelle, auroient esté deuorez par les loups, ou autres bestes sauuages, en signe dequoy venant a sier les bleds, on trouuoit caches des tez & os des bras & iambes: Ce n'est encore tout. Car peu a peu en ce mesme païs, & encore plus entre leurs voysins les Gascons & aultres païs d'alentour, ces loups prindrent telle hardiesse que personne n'oloit doresenauant aller par les champs sans compagnie. Car peu a peu en ce mesme païs, & encore plus entre leurs voysins les Gascons & aultres païs d'alentour, ces loups prindrent telle hardiesse que personne n'oloit doresenauant aller par les champs sans compagnie. Dont trois ou quatre ans apres ayant parachevé mon dit cours, & me commençant a retirer vers noz cartiers, fuz employé de mon office a Rhodez ville capitale de Rouergue & limitrophe d'Auuergne, ou semblablement courroient ces loups a grandes touppes, de sorte qu'enuiron dix heures du soir estudiant en nostre chambrette, entendis vn bruit & hurlement de tel accord, que iamais n'auois ouy le semblable. Dequoy cupide sçavoir que pouroit estre, apres auoir paracheue mon discours, m'en vois promptement enquerir de ceste nouuelle & inaudite harmoniё a la sentinelle du conuent, laquelle trouuay encore toute effroyée de peur, me disant qu'il n'auoit veu oncques telle compagnie, ny de loups si enragez, le nombre estoit dix-huict ou vingt, comme il auoit peu remarquer au cler de la lune. Au Reste si hardis, qu'ils sembloient despiter tout ce qu'il y auoit d'habitans en la ville, approchans iusques aux fossez. Et quant est de la hardiesse, je peux dire ce que m'est arriué. En ce mesme pays pres Villefranche, y en rencontray vn

tout proche de moy en vn chemin estroit, qui a peine pour clameur que ie peusse faire, se vouloit destourner, en fin toutefois s'en alla lentement comme Dieu voulut. Et a present en tous ces pays là, on ne parle dautre chose, sinon d'aller a la chasse au loup, ce qu'on faict tous les iours de dimanches, & festes apres auoir assisté au seruice divin, les paroissiens s'assemblants autour d'vn bois assigné auec vne fourchefiere a trois pointes en triangle, car c'est le baston qu'on a cogneu le plus propre pour resister a la rage de telles bestes, & en ceste façon en ont desia despeché vn grand nombre. Le vulgaire est d'opinion que la faim pressant tels animaux pour la paucité du bestail qui est presque tout pery par la guerre, ont esté poulsez en ceste rage de s'adresser aux hommes, & ceulx que i'entendis hurler, qui estoit enuiron la Saint Martin, on les disoit estre descenduz des montaignes d'Auuergne, comme ilz faisoient tous les ans, pour trouuer a manger, Ce qui estoit vray-semblable, car quelques mois auparauant la Toussaincts les bergers ne pouuants plus demeurer en ces montaignes pour les froidures excessiues, s'en retournoient aux maisons auec leurs troupeaux: & voila comment les loups estans pressez de la faim, peuuent s'attacquer aux hommes naturellement.... [P]our plusieurs occasions arriuvent ces incursions des loups, quelquefois par la faim, aultrefois par leur grande force, aucunefois lors qu'ilz ont des petits, aultresfois aussy par la viellesse, car daultant qu'ilz ne peuuent plus chasser ou courir apres les bestes, lors sont ilz plus dangereux contre les hommes: Aussy s'adressent ils plus volontairement pour l'experience qu'ilz ont de la chaire humaine, laquelle comme ainsi soit qu'elle est mieulx complexionnée que des aultres creatures, c'est pourquoy elle est plus doulce & sauoureuse, le mesme sont ils aussi lors qu'ils sont enragez [31b–33b].

So that you might therefore think that they might be natural wolves, I will recite for you what I myself experienced in the last few years. I remember that in the year 1587 being in Perigord, and staying for a few months in a small monastery in the town of Rions, that is five leagues from Bordeaux, I was sent on the day of Saint John by the Gardien father from said place to a village about three leagues away. While I was returning from there, and crossing through another small village, I noticed a poor woman who was very sad. She dissuaded me from following the same path, all the more, said she, since it had not been a half hour since a wolf had carried off her little girl from the threshold of her door.[30] She can never be recovered, in spite of the torment and shrieking this woman and several of her neighbors had been able to stir up. That is the first one I heard about, but not the last. Traveling from there to Toulouse, for my course of study, the above-mentioned Gardien father wrote to the one at our monastery, the late Reverend Father de Roca who had a good memory, letters of recommendation for the prayers of the Religious, touching on such poverty and misery, to tell how several men, women, and small children, being lost, and of which no one had any news, were probably devoured by the wolves, or other savage beasts, as a sign of which while coming to cut the wheat, they found hidden skulls and leg and arm bones: This is still not all. For little by little in this same region, & even more among their neighbors the Gascons & other border-

> ing regions, these wolves took on such boldness that henceforth no one went to the fields alone who used to do so. Then three or four years after having put the finishing touches on my course that I mentioned, & beginning to go back toward our area, I was engaged in ecclesiastical duties in Rhodez, the capital city of Rouergue & adjoining Auvergne, where similarly were running these wolves in great bands, so that at about ten o'clock in the evening while studying in our small bed chamber, I heard a noise and howling in such a chord that never had I heard anything like it. Greedy to know what it could be, after having finished my discourse, I promptly went to inquire of the monastery's watchman about this new and unheard of harmony, whom I found still entirely agitated with fear, telling me that he had never seen such a band, nor wolves so enraged, the number was eighteen or twenty, as he had been able to observe by the light of the moon.[31] [They were] so bold in Reste, that they seemed to defy all the inhabitants that there were in the town, going right up to the moat. And as for boldness, I can tell what happened to me. In this same region near Villefranche, I encountered one of them very close to me on a narrow path, who scarcely wanted to get off the path regardless of the clamour that I made. Finally however it slowly went away as God wanted. And at present in all those regions, no one speaks of anything else except of going hunting for wolves, which they do every Sunday and feast day after having attended mass, the parishioners assembling around a designated woods with a pitchfork that has three points in the form of a triangle, for that is the weapon that is known to be the most suitable for resisting the rage of such beasts, & in this way they have already dispatched a great number. Common people are of the opinion that such animals, hunger tormenting them because of the paucity of livestock that have almost all perished because of the war, have been pushed into this rage of going after men, & those that I heard howling, which was around the feast of Saint Martin, are said to have come down from the mountains of Auvergne, as they did every year, to find something to eat. Which was plausible, because a few months before All Saints Day the shepherds no longer being able to stay in these mountains because of the exessive cold, returned home with their flocks: & here is how the wolves being tormented by hunger, can naturally attack men.... For several reasons these incursions of wolves happen, sometimes because of hunger, other times because of their great strength, sometimes when they have little ones, other times because of old age, because as much as they can no longer hunt or run after animals, then they are most dangerous against men: Also they attack them more voluntarily because they have experienced human flesh, which is in this way so much better constituted than that of other creatures, that is why it is sweeter and more delicious, they are also the same when they are enraged.

In spite of Proteron's stories of his experiences with very real wolves, Scipion remains unconvinced that werewolves do not exist and continues to engage him in a dialogue about them, first turning to those about cannibals, which he associates with metamorphosis:

Toutesfois les exemples que nous en trouuons & apperceuons, ne nous permettent de croire que ce soient seulement loups, agitations diaboliques, ou corps prins par les demons, mais ce sont certainement Lycanthropes & transformez, comme nous le sçauons par leur descharge, lorsqu'ils sont menez au dernier supplice. Car il ne fault faire instance, pour ce que les hommes ne mangent, ou n'ayent iamais mangé chair humaine, veu qu'il s'en trouue vne infinité d'exemples. Et pour en faire preuue, ie sçay que n'estes ignorant de ce que Bodin raconte d'vne sorciere, laquelle fut mise sur la rouë pour auoir estranglé & puis deuoré vn petit enfant. Et derechef, au chap. 5 du 4. auquel lieu il recite d'vn certain patissier, qui faisoit[32] manger la chair humaine en paste, & la mesme qu'Apulée gaigna pour vne nuict six escus a garder vn corps mort, parce que en ce païs la, il n'y auoit corps mort qui ne fust mangé, iusques aux os par les sorciers, qui se mettant en forme de petites bestes commettoient tel horreur & cruaulté. Et derechef il dict que Philostrate Lemnien a laissé par escrit comment Appollonius Tymeus chassa de Corinthe vne lamie qui viuoit de telle viande.... Le mesme autheur recite que certaine sorciere couppala gorge a deux filles, desquelles l'vne estoit sienne (il faict mal auoir de telles meres) l'autre de sa voysine. Le Baron de Raiz fut conuaincu, d'auoir tué & sacrifié au diable huict enfants, & que Sathan luy auoit encore commandé de sacrifier son propre enfant, & le tirer du ventre de la mere. Ce qu'il n'auoit peu mettre a chef, par ce que sa femme se doutant d'vn oeuure si pernicieux & detestable, s'enfuit.... Cela est horrible a entendre, ce nonobstant, c'est pour nous monstrer n'estre d'à present que telle barbarie commence a se practiquer, mais pour n'estre recognuz (comme ilz pourroient estre, ou allant aux maisons de nuict, ou en aultre lieu commettre quelque meschancheté) ils se transforment & se rendent en tel semblant, quittans la forme humaine par art diabolique [34–35].

However the examples that we find and observe do not permit us to believe that these are only wolves, diabolical agitations, or bodies taken by demons, but they are certainly Lycanthropes and transformed people, as we know by the charges against them when they are taken to the final torture. For one must not be insistent, because men do not eat, or have never eaten human flesh, seeing that an infinity of examples can be found. And to give proof of this, I know that you are not ignorant of what Bodin recounts of a witch, who was put on the wheel for having strangled and then devoured a small child. And once more, in chap. 5 of 4, in which place he tells of a certain pastry maker, who was making[33] [people] eat human flesh in pie crusts, & similarly that Apuleius earned six crowns[34] for watching a dead body one night, because in that country there was no dead body that was not eaten up to its bones by the witches who, putting themselves into the form of small beasts, committed such horror and cruelty. And once more he says that Philostrate Lemnien left in writing how Appollonius Tymeus chased from Corinth a lamia[35] who was living on such meat. The same author recites that a certain witch cut the throat of two girls, one of whom was her daughter (it hurts to have such mothers); the other was his neighbor's. The Baron de Raiz was convicted of having killed and sacrificed eight children to the devil, & that Satan had even ordered him so sacrifice his own child and pull it out of its mother's belly. Which he had not been able to achieve, because his wife fled, suspecting a deed so pernicious and detestable. That is horrible to hear, nevertheless, it is to show us that it is not only at present that such barbarity is beginning to be practiced, but in order to not be recognized (as they could be, or in going to their home at night, or to another place to commit some wickedness) they transform themselves and make themselves into such a semblance, leaving their human form by means of diabolical arts.

According to Scipion, then, metamorphosis is not the primary goal of lycanthropes and other shape-shifters — in other words, they do not transform themselves because they want to be a wolf or another animal — but metamorphosis is instead a disguise they use to protect their identities so that they may perpetrate crimes such as cannibalism without being detected. Proteron concedes that unnatural people do exist who carry out such atrocities but denies that they are werewolves. He then proceeds to give Eleion and Scipion examples of recent acts of cannibalism against children:

Ie vous concederay qu'il se puisse trouuer des personnes si desnaturées, qu'elles s'addressent aux corps humains morts ou vifs, pour les deuorer & manger, particulierement les petits enfants, & estre en apparence de loups, dequoy vous peux confirmer d'exemples tous recents, comme l'auons entendu depuis n'agueres par lettres expresses de Paris datées du 20e d'Aoust, auquel iour auoient esté mangez deux petits enfans par ceux desquelz vous entendez parler, & desquels comme on dit il en y a 17 au mesme lieu, & aultant aux aultres villes circonuoisines: Mais ie n'accorderay iamais (comme aussi ne font les peres de l'Eglise) que telles gens prennent autre forme, pour par ce moyen cacher la forme humaine, car nous auons ia prouué le contraire par iceulx docteurs [35–35b].

I will concede to you that there might be found people acting so much against nature that they attack human bodies, dead or alive, in order to devour and eat them, especially small children, and that they might have the appearance of wolves, of which I can confirm for you some very recent examples, as we have heard recently by reliable letters from Paris dated the 20th of August, on which day two little children had been eaten by the ones about which you have heard spoken, & about which as one says there are 17 of them in the same place, and as many in the other neighboring towns: But I will never agree (as the Church fathers also will not do) that such people take on another form, in order to hide by this means their human form, for we have already proved the contrary through those doctors.

Proteron persists in his belief that there is no real metamorphosis. He thus draws a distinction between the reality of Nero putting on a physical animal skin as a disguise and the possibility of man-to-animal transformation. Reviewing the writings of the Church fathers and other texts, Scipion and

Eleion attempt to convince him that he is wrong. Proteron, however, repeatedly tells them that they have misread or misunderstood the writings of the Church fathers and that the other texts were written by pagans and were not to be trusted. He thus reaffirms the doctrines of Saint Augustine and all those who followed him. At the end of the dialogue, Proteron summarizes all of his resolutions, "pour mieux l'imprimer en la memoire" (72) "in order to imprint them better in your memory":

> La premiere resolution sera donc, que pour le peché & punition d'iceluy, les animaux irraisonables vengeans leur Createur, par sa permission, & quelquesfois expres commandement, assaillent les hommes pour en faire punition.
>
> La seconde, que ce peuuent estre des loups naturels, lesquels on void ainsi deuorer les hommes; le faisant ou par rage; en laquelle ils sont; pour la faim de laquelle ils sont pressez; pour l'agitation des diables; ou autres raisons dictes cy dessus.
>
> La 3. que ce peuuent estre des hommes naturels, lesquels ou sans charmes, ou auec charmes, viuent de chaïr humaine, comme l'auons prouué par exemples.
>
> La 4. que ny Lycanthropie, ou reale transformation est admise aucunement en l'eglise Catholique; & que si l'homme se transforme (s'il est toutesfois loisible d'vser du mot) c'est plustost en bien qu'en mal, & non se transformer, ou changer en vne beste , veu que ny onguens, ny ... ny parolles, ny ceintures, ny le diable ... aucun pouuoir de le faire; trop bien ... exterieurement autres qu'ils ne font....[36] persuader euz mesmes, voire cacher par enchantement la forme & figure humaine, à fin qu'on ne cognoisse quelles gens sont. Mais on ne scauroit admettre telle transformation; sinon que par consequent on admettre ou la metempsichose Pythagorique, ou les metamorphoses d'Ouide, & autres telles absurditez fabuleuses.
>
> La 5. resolution est, que selon la foy qu'on y adiouste, les hommes par magie, ou les diables en un corps prins, se peuuent faire veoir, ou aussi les autres, en forme estrangere, enchantant ou esblouissant & la veuë, & les autres sentimens, tant interieurs, qu'exterieurs.
>
> La 6. & derniere est, que detestant & reiettant tous charmes, & toute superstition, & vsant des benedictions de l'eglise, (& specialement de la croix) soit grans ou petits, qui en seront signez, non seulement peuuent euiter telle sorcelerie, & enchantements, mais aussi le danger qui leur pourroit ensuiuir; veu que le diable n'a point tant de pouuoir sur les vrais fideles, lesquels Iesus Christ conserue triomphant (par la croix) de ses ennemys, & des nostres [71–71b].

> The first resolution will therefore be that, for the sin and punishment of this one, irrational animals avenging their Creator, with his permission and sometimes his express command, attack men to punish them.
>
> The second, that these can be natural wolves that one sees devouring men in this way; doing it either because they are enraged,[37] because of the hunger that torments them, because of diabolical agitation, or other reasons mentioned above.

> The third, that these can be natural men, who either without or with charms, live off of human flesh, as we have proved through examples.
>
> The fourth, that neither Lycanthropy nor real transformation is at all accepted in the Catholic church; and that if man transforms himself (if however it is permitted to use the word) it is in a good way rather than in a evil way, & does not transform himself or change into a beast, seeing that neither unguents nor *haunted streams* nor belts nor the devil *himself has* any power to do it.... But no one would be able to accept such a transformation; other than that with the consequence of accepting either the metempsychosis of Pythagoras or the metamorphoses of Ovid, & other such fabulous absurdities.[38]
>
> The fifth resolution is that according to the faith that one adds to it, men through magic, or the devils in a possessed body, can make themselves seen, or also others seen, in a foreign form, enchanting or dazzling the vision and other sensations, interior as much as exterior.
>
> The sixth and last is, that detesting and rejecting all charms, & all superstitions, & using blessings of the church, (& especially of the cross) whether big or small, which will be signs of it, not only can they avoid such sorcery and enchantments, but also the danger which could pursue them; since the devil does not have at all as much power over true believers, whom Jesus Christ keeps triumphant (by the cross) over his enemies and over ours.

Anchored firmly within the social, historical, and theological contexts at the end of the sixteenth century, Prieur's *Dialogue de la Lycanthropie* remains a unique and important document, devoting 120 pages to the subject of metamorphosis that is frequently only a footnote or at best a chapter in other works of the time. It not only provides an exhaustive theoretical review, but also offers new anecdotal evidence that sheds light on the basis for the fear of wolves, which resulted in the irrational fear of werewolves. Moreover, Scipion's belief that werewolves deliberately transform themselves in order to hide their identities while committing crimes adds another facet to the interpretation of metamorphosis as a disguise; the disguise is now intentional. This new interpretation has a twofold effect: it gives the transformation a motive and links it with cannibalism.

In 1597, just one year after the publication of Prieur's *Dialogue de la Lycanthropie*, another treatise on sorcery appeared, *Daemonologie,* which was written by James VI of Scotland and I of England. As Stuart Clark notes in his study of the *Daemonologie*, the treatise offers nothing new or insightful to the study of demonology. In consequence, if the work were anonymous its only significance would consist in the fact that it was one of the first in England to defend "Continental beliefs about witchcraft" (156). But the work is not anonymous; it was written by the king of England—"someone with enormous potential influence over the incidence and severity of prosecution" (Clark, 156)—and this fact alone gives it unique status. Like Heinrich Kramer's

Malleus maleficarum, James' *Daemonologie* insists that witchcraft is real and that because of this witches must be sought out and punished. In his preface, King James introduces the purpose of his treatise and attacks the beliefs of both Reginald Scot and Johann Weyer:

> The fearefull aboundinge at this time in this countrie, of these detestable slaues of the Deuill, the Witches or enchaunters, hath moved me (beloued reader) to dispatch in post, this following treatise of mine, not in any wise (as I protest) to serue for a shew of my learning & ingine, but onely (mooued of conscience) to preasse / thereby, so farre as I can, to resolue the doubting harts of many; both that such assaultes of Sathan are most certainly practized, & that the instrumentes thereof, merits most severly to be punished: against the damnable opinions of two principally in our age, wherof the one called SCOT an Englishman, is not ashamed in publike print to deny, that ther can be such a thing as Witch-craft: and so mainteines the old error of the Sadducees, in denying of spirits. The other called VVIERVS, a German Phisition, sets out a publick apologie for al these craftesfolkes, whereby, procuring for their impunitie, he plainely bewrayes himselfe to have bene one of that profession [xi–xii].

After describing the general outline and contents of his treatise, James specifies the exact purpose of the work:

> My intention in this labour, is only to proue two things, as I haue alreadie said: the one, that such diuelish artes haue bene and are. The other, what exact trial and seuere punishment they merite: & therefore reason I, what kinde of things are possible to be performed in these arts, & by what naturall causes they may be, not that I touch every particular thing of the Deuils power, for that were infinite [xii].

Like Kramer in his *Malleus maleficarum*, James declares that Satan receives his powers from God and is always subordinate to God:

> But one thing I will pray thee to obserue in all these places, where I reason upon the deuil's power, which is the different ends & scopes, that God as the first cause, and the Devill as his instrument and second cause shootes at in all these actiones of the Deuil, (as Gods hang-man:) For where the deuilles intention in them is euer to perish, either the soule or the body, or both of them, that he is so permitted to deale with: God by the contrarie, drawes euer out of that euill glorie to himselfe, either by the wracke of the wicked in his justice, or / by the tryall of the patient, and amendment of the faithfull, being wakened up with that rod of correction [xiii–xiv].

According to King James I, then, the devil functions as an instrument or servant of God, who uses him to punish sinners and warn the faithful when they are tempted. Thus, God uses the malevolence of Satan for His own glorification. Before concluding his preface, James declares that a discussion of the rites and practices of witchcraft is not within the scope of his work and refers those who are curious about such things to Bodin's *De la démonomanie des sorciers,* as well as to Weyer's *De Praestigiis Daemonum.* Like Prieur, James wrote his treatise in the form of a dialogue, this time a dialogue between two men: Philomathes, who voices the beliefs of Weyer and Scot, and the demonologist Epistemon, who counters with the more orthodox beliefs of James. Toward the end of the work, in the course of their conversation regarding the spirits of the dead, Philomathes eventually turns the discussion to werewolves:

> EPISTOMEN. What more is the reste troubled of a dead bodie, when the Deuill carryes it out of the Graue to serue his turne for a space, nor when the Witches takes it vp and joyntes it, or when as Swine wortes vppe the graues? The rest of them that the Scripture speakes of, is not meaned by a locall remaining continuallie in one place, but by their resting from their trauelles and miseries of this worlde, while their latter donjunction againe with the soule at that time to receaue full glorie in both. And that the Deuill may vse aswell the ministrie of the bodies of the faithfull in these cases, as of the vn-faithfull, there is no inconvenient; for his haunting with their bodies after they are deade, can no-waies defyle them: In respect of the soules absence. And for anie dishonour it can be vnto them, by what reason can it be greater, then the hanging, heading, or many such shameful deaths, that good men will suffer? for there is nothing in the bodies of the faithfull, more worthie of honour, or freer from corruption by nature, nor in these of the vnfaithful, while time they be purged and glorified in the latter daie, as is dailie seene by the vilde diseases and corruptions, that the bodies of the faythfull are subject vnto, as yee will see clearelie proued, when I speake of the possessed and Daemoniacques.
>
> PHILOMATHES. Yet there are sundrie that affirmes to haue haunted such places, where these spirites are alleaged to be: And coulde neuer heare nor see anie thing.
>
> EPISTOMEN. I thinke well: For that is onelie reserued to the secreete knowledge of God, whome he wil permit to see such thinges, and whom not.
>
> PHILOMATHES. But where these spirites hauntes and troubles anie houses, what is the best waie to banishe them?
>
> EPISTOMEN. By two meanes may onelie the remeid of such things be procured: The one is ardent prayer to God, both of these persones that are troubled with them, and of that Church whereof they are. The other is the purging of themselues by amendement of life from such sinnes, as haue procured that extraordinarie plague.
>
> PHILOMATHES. And what meanes then these kindes of spirites, when they appeare in the shaddow of a person newlie dead, or to die, to his friendes?
>
> EPISTOMEN. When they appeare vpon that occasion, they are called Wraithes in our language. Amongst the *Gentiles* the Deuill vsed that much, to make them beleeue that it was some good spirite that appeared to them then, ether to forewarne them of the death of their friend; or else to discouer vnto them, the will of the defunct, or what was the way of his slauchter,

as is written in the booke of the histories Prodigious. And this way hee easelie deceiued the *Gentiles*, because they knew not God: And to that same effect is it, that he now appeares in that manner to some ignorant Christians. For he dare not so illude anie that knoweth that, neither can the spirite of the defunct returne to his friend, or yet an Angell vse such formes.

PHILOMATHES. And are not our war-woolfes one sorte of these spirits also, that hauntes and troubles some houses or dwelling places?

EPISTOMEN. There hath indeede bene an old opinion of such like things; For by the Greeks they were called λυκανθρωποι which signifieth menwoolfes. But to tell you simplie my opinion in this, if anie such thing hath bene, I take it to haue proceeded but of a naturall super-abundance of Melancholie, which as wee reade, that it hath made some thinke themselues Pitchers, and some horses, and some one kinde of beast or other: So suppose I that it hath so viciat the imagination and memorie of some, as *per lucida interualla*, it hath so highlie occupyed them, that they haue thought themselues verrie Woolfes indeede at these times: and so haue counterfeited their actiones in goeing on their handes and feete, preassing to deuoure women and barnes, fighting and snatching with all the towne dogges, and in vsing such like other bruitish actiones, and so to become beastes by a strong apprehension, as *Nebucad-netzar* was seuen yeares: but as to their hauing and hyding of their hard & schellie sloughes, I take that to be but eiked, by vncertaine report, the author of all lyes [59–62].[39]

Like Kramer, James insists on the reality of witches, although he firmly denies the existence of werewolves. In addition, James does not blame wolf-like behavior on diabolical trickery; instead, like Weyer and Scott, he posits an excess of melancholy as the culprit that causes some men to believe that they are wolves and to "counterfeit" the actions of these animals. James' treatment of the subjects of werewolves and metamorphosis is perhaps most notable for its brevity; indeed, Philomathes' response to Epistomen's question is so perfunctory that it almost causes one to wonder one why James even bothered to included the item in the dialogue. Nevertheless, his text adds further weight to the growing argument against werewolves.

In 1599, two years after James' *Daemonologie*, Beauvoys de Chauvincourt's *Discours de la lycantropie* [sic] *ou de la transmutation des hommes en loups* (*Treatise on Lycanthropy or on the Transformation of Men into Wolves*) was published in Paris. According to Summers, the text adds little to the body of knowledge, since Chauvincourt, like others before him, merely attributes lycanthropy to a "glamour" brought on by the Devil that deceives both the man who believes he has been transformed and those who witness his behavior (98). Chauvincourt does, however, include some new anecdotes regarding werewolves. The first relates an incident involving a hungry nobleman:

Un seigneur du païs escorté d'un grand nombre de ses serviteurs domestiques, traversant une ample et spatieuse forest, surpris par la nuict, et esloigné des maisons, fut contrainct de se loger à la haye, ou ayant soubs un arbre faict dresser ses tentes et pavillons, delibera y passer le reste de la nuit. Lors l'un de ses serviteurs, voyant que les vivres leur manquoient, encouragea ses compagnons sur l'espoir qu'il leur donna qu'en brief il leur apporteroit de quoy mettre soubs la dent: et de faict ayant espié non loing de là un troupeau de moutons se retira quelque peu avant, en la forest le plus secrettement qu'il peut et là se transforma en loup, puis d'un viste pas et d'une hardiesse furieuse se lanceant sur la bergerie en ravit un mouton, lequel incontinent il apporta en mesme forme de loup a sa compagnie, puis retournant en la forest reprist sa première forme.[40]

A lord from the region escorted by a large number of his household servants, crossing a vast and spacious forest, surprised by nightfall, and far from any houses, was forced to lodge outdoors and having had his tents and pavilions put up under a tree, decided to spend the rest of the night there. Then one of his servants, seeing that they were lacking provisions, encouraged his companions with the hope that he gave them that soon he would bring them something to put between their teeth: and in fact having observed not far from there a flock of sheep he went off a little ahead, into the forest as secretly as he could and there he transformed himself into a wolf, then, with a quick step and a ferocious boldness, rushing in to the sheepfold he carried off one of the sheep, which he brought forthwith to his companions while still in the form of a wolf, then returning to the forest recovered his original form.

Although Milin suggests that this account is a variant of the medieval tale *Melion* (103), the similarities between the two are slim and indeed difficult to find. This werewolf evidently has the ability to transform himself at will without the assistance of anyone else, whereas Melion needs someone to touch his head with his magic ring in order to become a werewolf and then later recover his human form. In addition, *Melion* relates only one metamorphosis and there is no indication that the eponymous hero has ever undergone a previous transformation. Chauvincourt's tale, which Milin indicates was first reported by Olaus Magnus, Bishop of Uppsala, most likely in his 1555 treatise, the *Historia de gentibus septentrionalibus,* shares one motif with *Melion,* that of hunger as the cause for transformation; it lacks, however, the motif of the demanding wife.[41] The werewolf in this tale also calls to mind the werewolf Alphonse in *Guillaume de Palerne,* who constantly provides for the sustenance of the eponymous hero and his beloved Melior, but Alphonse is trapped in his lupine form and is not able to transform himself at will.[42] The account related by Chauvincourt is most remarkable for the benevolent nature of the werewolf, for this is a man with charitable motives who transforms himself with the sole motive of feeding his companions. Among the sixteenth-century werewolves we have examined thus far, this unnamed werewolf stands alone.

In a second anecdote, one that Chauvincourt once again attributes to Olaus Magnus, we find still another kind of werewolf story. Although atypical of the sixteenth century, it too is one that we have seen before:

> Il en raconte un autre d'une Damoyselle du païs de Livonie, laquelle disputant avec l'un de ses serviteurs, sçavoir s'il était possible que l'homme se peust transformer en forme de loup et d'autant qu'elle le revocquoit en doubte, ce serviteur pour luy en faire plus ample preuve, luy demanda permission de se faire loup; ce que luy estant par elle octroyé il se retira en une chambre secrète de la maison, de laquelle peu après il sortit en forme de loup et après lequel une meute de chiens s'eslancea et le poursuyvant jusques au boys prochain, luy arracherent un oeil et le lendemain ayant repris sa figure humaine s'en retourna privé d'un oeil en la maison.[43]

> He told another story about a young noble woman from the region of Livonia,[44] who was arguing with one of her servants as to whether it was possible for a man to transform himself into a wolf and since she called it into question so much, this servant, to give her more extensive proof, asked her permission to make himself a wolf; that being granted to him by her, he retired into a secret chamber in the house, from which a little later he left in the form of a wolf, and after which a pack of dogs rushed in and pursuing him into the next woods, tore out one of his eyes and the next day having recovered his human form he returned to the house deprived of one eye.

Although Milin states that this tale is "plus proche encore de *Melion*" (103), significant similarities between the two are almost non-existent.[45] Both involve a strong-willed noblewoman and a man who transforms himself into a wolf, but the resemblance seems to end there. *Melion* is of course hunted down by the Irish king, along with the rest of his pack of wolves, but he is never caught or injured. The story retold by Chauvincourt is much more reminiscent of other tales of werewolves, such as the story of the werewolf of Padua in Bodin's *De la démonomanie des sorciers*, the Middle Irish tales of Irish werewolves, Gervase of Tilbury's story of Raimbaud de Pouget, and finally Niceros' tale of the soldier-werewolf in Petronius's *Satyricon*. All these accounts tell of men who not only have the ability to change themselves at will into wolves, but are also injured while in their lupine form. In each case when they recover their human form, their bodies retain these same marks or injuries. Like the werewolf in the other tale recounted by Chauvincourt, this werewolf appears to have a benevolent nature; at the very least, if he has a malevolent nature, it is not revealed in this anecdote.

In a third werewolf anecdote, one that was apparently told to Chauvincourt by a peasant, an altogether different type of werewolf appears. According to Milin, it attests to the existence in sixteenth-century folklore of the motif of the "meneur de loups" (wolf-leader) or leader of the pack:

> Comme je tramois le fil de ce discours, un certain personnage, non menteur, et duquel la vie et les moeurs sont assez approuvées, m'a racompté une chose très espouvantable, et neantmoins asseurée pour véritable. C'est que depuis peu de temps un certain homme de qualité marchanda à un passager de l'un des prochains ports d'une ville de Touraine, à le passer en son basteau luy quarantiesme, d'une rive à l'autre la nuict ensuyvant, et pour cest effect luy delivra et avançea quarante souls pour la recompense de son passage. La nuict estant venüe, cest homme appelle le bastelier qui l'attendoit, lequel descendu jusques à son basteau, apperceut trente-neuf loups en une troupe; il eut frayeur, le marchant l'asseure, et à son possible luy oste la peur, luy promettant le guarantir de tout outrage; les loups entrent tous dans le basteau, le marchant après, estant au port tout fort, et le marchant le dernier, qui comme les autres se transmua en loup. Le pauvre bastelier ayant le cœur serré tombe tout pasmé et cheut en syncope, y demeura jusqu'au jour, où estant trouvé par ces voisins et secouru, il revint quelque peu à soy, conta toute l'histoire et nomma le marchant, parce qu'il le cognoissoit, et deux ou trois jours après il mourut.[46]

> As I was weaving the thread of this treatise, a certain person, who was not a liar, and whose life and morals are approved enough of, recounted to me something very frightening, and nevertheless assuredly true. It seems that a short time ago a certain man of quality bargained for passage from one of the ports near a town in the Touraine region, to ferry him in his boat as the fortieth passenger, from one bank to the other on the following night, and for this purpose he delivered and advanced to him forty sous as compensation for his passage. That night having come, this man calls the ferryman who was waiting for him, who went right down to his boat and noticed thirty-nine wolves in a group; he became frightened, the man who made the bargain with him assures him, and as much as he can takes away his fear, promising him that he will protect him from any harm; the wolves all get in the boat, then the man who made the bargain, being very strong at the port, and the man who made the bargain was last, who like the others transformed himself into a wolf. The poor ferryman, his heart sinking, fell into a swoon and blacked out, remaining there until the next day, where found by his neighbors and given aid, he came back to himself little by little, related the entire story and named the man who made the bargain with him, because he knew him, and two or three days later he died.

This folktale is unique in that the werewolves, other than frightening the "poor ferryman"—evidently to death—do not intentionally harm him. Their relationship with the man seems to be nothing more than a simple business transaction, one, unfortunately, that is so disturbing for him that it leads to his death.

Another werewolf account related by Chauvincourt, that of Jacques

Roulet, has received more attention; in this one we see only the dark side of the beast. At first sight, Roulet would appear to be just another madman with cannibalistic tendencies claiming to be a werewolf. What sets him apart from the others is the verdict that was rendered in his case. Since Chauvincourt's account is primarily concerned with this verdict, for the details regarding Roulet's crime, we must turn to a treatise that was published two decades later in 1622, Pierre de Lancre's *L'Incrédulité et mécréance des sortilèges* (*The Incredulity and Skepticism of Magic Spells*).[47] According to his report, in 1598 a group of men discovered a boy about fifteen years old in an isolated spot near Angers. His mutilated and bloody body was still warm. Nearby they found Jacques Roulet, half-naked, "his hands dyed in fresh blood, his long nails clotted with garbage of red human flesh."[48] Roulet confessed his crimes in court before Judge Pierre Hérault:

> JUDGE HÉRAULT. What is your name and what your estate?
>
> ROULET. My name is Jacques Roulet, my age thirty-five; I am poor and a beggar.
>
> JUDGE HÉRAULT. What are you accused of having done?
>
> ROULET. Of being a thief; of having offended God. My parents gave me an ointment: I do not know its composition.
>
> JUDGE. When rubbed with this ointment, do you become a wolf?
>
> ROULET. No. But for all that, I killed and ate the child Cornier. I was a wolf.
>
> JUDGE. Were you dressed as a wolf?
>
> ROULET. I was dressed as I am now. I had my hands and face bloody, because I had been eating the flesh of the said child.
>
> JUDGE. Do your hands and feet become paws of a wolf?
>
> ROULET. Yes, they do.
>
> JUDGE. Does your head become like that of a wolf—your mouth become larger?
>
> ROULET. I do not know how my head was at the time; I used my teeth. My head was as it is today. I have wounded and eaten many other little children. I have also been to the sabbat.[49]

Roulet's confession is perhaps most remarkable for its inconsistency — or rather his lack of clear understanding — regarding the nature of his bodily form while committing his crimes. Did he or did he not become a wolf? Although he says that he did not "become" a wolf, he almost immediately says that he "was" a wolf. Roulet also acknowledges that his hands and feet "become paws of a wolf," but when asked if his "head become[s] like that of a wolf" Roulet is unsure and then declares that his "head was as it is today," indicating that his head did not change. In spite of his confusion, on one point Roulet is unequivocal; he never deviates from his statement that he killed and ate the Cornier child. In the course of his confession, he also declares that he did the same to other children. Finally, this self-professed child-killer and cannibal declares that he has "also been to the sabbat," "witches sabbath," thus implicating himself with sorcery. Reporting the confession of Roulet, Chauvincourt notes:

> [J]'ay entendu avoir éte trouvé Jacques Raollet de la Paroisse de Maumusson, Diocèse Nantois, prisonnier auparavant ce jour à Angers, lequel a confessé avoir dévoré plusieurs, tant hommes, femmes que petits enfans, et auquel estant confronté un gentilhomme, ce Raollet luy demanda s'il ne luy souvenoit point qu'un jour il avoit voulu tirer de son arquebuse sur trois loups, ce qu'estant recogneu par le gentilhomme, il advoua qu'il estoit l'un des loups, et que, sans l'empeschement qu'il leur fist, ils eussent dévoré une femme que estoit là auprès.[50]
>
> I heard that had been found Jacques Raollet of the Parish of Maumusson, of the Diocese of Nantes, previously a prisoner in Angers, who confessed that he had devoured several, as many men, women as small children, and who being confronted with a gentleman, this Raollet asked him if he did not at all remember that one day he had wanted to shoot his harquebuse[51] at three wolves, that being recognized by the gentleman, he admitted that he was one of the wolves, and that, if he had not prevented them, they would have devoured a woman that was nearby.

With Chauvincourt's brief account, a more coherent picture of Roulet emerges; here he actually admits to being one of three wolves that were prevented from devouring a woman by a gentleman who came upon them. It is not clear, though, how the gentleman could have recognized Roulet the man as one of the wolves. But there is no trace of the confusion or inconsistency regarding the nature of his bodily form that marks his confession as reported by Pierre de Lancre. In addition, we learn that Roulet not only killed children, but also killed men and women, and evidently quite a few. According to Chauvincourt, "Les juges d'Angers sur ces confessions l'ont condamné à la mort, sans avoir esgard à l'industrie diabolique de laquelle son maistre Sathan l'avoit instruict, sçavoir, de contrefaire le fol."[52] "The judges of Angers for these confessions sentenced him to death, without taking into consideration the diabolical cunning in which Satan his master had instructed him, that is, to counterfeit madness." Embedded in Chauvincourt's reporting of the facts regarding Roulet's judgment are his own suspicions that Roulet is merely claiming to have become a wolf in order to appear mad; implicit too is Chauvincourt's own attitude toward the reality of werewolves and the possibility of metamorphosis. Was Roulet's madness real or feigned? According to Chauvincourt, it was the latter:

> [V]oyant qu'il [Roulet] ne pouvait nier ce qui estoit par luy confessé, embrassant une folie simulée pour voye de son salut, advoua avoir mangé des char-

> rettes ferrées, des moulins à vents, des Advocats, Procureurs et Sergents, viande que toutefois pour leur grande dureté, et pour n'estre bien assaisonnée, il n'avoit peu digérer.[53]
>
> Seeing that he [Roulet] could not deny that which he had confessed, embracing a simulated madness as the means of his salvation, admitted having eaten iron carts, windmills, lawyers, prosecutors and sergeants, meats that because of their great hardness, and because they were not well seasoned, he had not been able to digest very well.

Thus Roulet goes much further than "merely" confessing to killing and eating men, women, and children; he also says he ate inanimate objects — carts and windmills — as well as judicial officials, which he likens to tough, unseasoned meat. This addendum to his confession presents an image of Roulet that is entirely different from the one that we see reported in Lancre's text. The confession that we find in Lancre reveals a confused man who is unable to determine the status of his bodily form, whereas in Chauvincourt's report, we see a man who is able to manipulate language in order to defend himself while simultaneously mocking the representatives of the judicial system who must decide his fate. Nevertheless, whether real or simulated, Roulet's madness earns him a new trial. After appealing his death sentence from the court of Angers to the Parlement of Paris, Roulet is moved to the Conciergerie.[54] Chauvincourt offers the following description of the prisoner:

> Il avoit les cheveux pendant jusques sur les espaules, les ongles merveilleusement grands...; si puant et infect que homme du monde ne pouvoit approcher de luy, couvert de graisse de deux doigts d'espais par tout le corps, la veuë fort esgarée, les sourcils refrongnez, et les yeux enfoncez en la teste....[55]
>
> His hair hung down on his shoulders, his nails were amazingly long...; so foul-smelling and vile that no man in the world could get near him, covered with grease one inch thick everywhere on his body, with his gaze very wild, his eyebrows scowling, and his eyes sunk in his head....

Roulet appears more bestial in appearance than human, but it is difficult to determine how much his imprisonment and resulting lack of care has affected his physical condition. Pierre de l'Estoile also describes Roulet in his journal:

> Ce loup-garou (qu'on appelait) fut mis aux cachots noirs de la conciergerie, après avoir été rasé, lequel je fus voir. Il portait les cheveux pendants jusques aux talons, la barbe de même, et les ongles aussi grands et longs que les mains.[56]
>
> This were-wolf (that they called [a werewolf]) was put in the dark dungeons of the Conciergerie, after having been shaved, which I saw. He wore his hair hanging down to his heels, his beard as well, and his nails [were] as big and as long as his hands.

With his parenthetical "qu'on appelait" (that one called), L'Estoile is careful to point out that others called Roulet a werewolf first. In this new portrait, Roulet's hair is longer and no mention is made of his odor. Although L'Estoile's depiction of Roulet does not deviate greatly from Chauvincourt's portrayal, a description of another prisoner — of one who was not a self-professed werewolf— might have been more helpful and more illuminating, at least for the modern reader. But we are left with Chauvincourt's and L'Estoile's reports. Based on these alone, it is easy to understand how anyone could have been impressed by Roulet's appearance, more specifically by his bestial resemblance. Chauvincourt, however, was not swayed by his appearance nor was he persuaded by his behavior. After noting that the Parlement of Paris nullified Roulet's original death verdict and sentenced him instead to two years in the insane asylum at the Hospital of Saint Germain, Chauvincourt offered the following commentary on their clemency:

> Je croy que mesdicts Sieurs de la Court interpretants toutes choses en bonne part, comme ils ont de costume, considérans la rusticité de l'homme, ses variations, sa manière de vivre, sa contenance, ses actions, et brief tous ses comportemens, l'ont seulement relégué pour deux ans audict lieu, afin que, pendant ce temps, l'on peust plus aisément esplucher par le menu sa condition et ses moeurs. Car si, suyvant l'observation journelle que l'on fera de ses actions l'on s'apperçoit tant soit peu de sa meschanceté, il n'est eschappé et traine seulement son collier et l'aura on bientost reserré.[57]

> I believe that said Lords of the Court interpreting all things in a good way, as they have custom to do, considering the rustic nature of the man, his fluctuations, his manner of living, his attitude, his actions, and in short his entire behavior, have only sentenced him for two years to said place, in order that, during this time, they might more easily be able to go over with a fine-tooth comb and in minute detail his condition and his morals. For if, following the daily observation that they will make of his actions, they notice so much as a little bit of his wickedness, he has not escaped and is only pulling on his choke collar and soon they will have tightened it.

Chauvincourt's uneasiness with the verdict handed down by the Parlement of Paris is evident here as he too attempts to "interpret things in a good way" and gives these judges the benefit of the doubt. But Chauvincourt's words "sa meschanceté" (his wickedness) betray him and reveal that he does not have the same charitable attitude toward Roulet. Although Roulet is evil, he is not a werewolf nor is he insane. The only opportunity that Chauvincourt will allow Roulet is the chance to incriminate himself with his own misdeeds. Thus Chauvincourt refuses to be deceived by the Devil's "glamour."

In 1602, Henri Boguet, chief judge of St. Claude in Burgundy, published his second edition of *Discours des sorciers*.[58] Although the first edition of his treatise appeared in 1590, it was not until the second edition that Boguet would add a chapter on werewolves and lycanthropy. Over the next nine years, seven more editions appeared. According to Douglas, Boguet's "fund of case histories involving witchcraft ... became a standard text for witch-hunters" (158). In his prefatory letter to François de Rye, the Vicar-General of Besançon, Boguet writes of the growing problem of witches:

> For if it be true that Trois-eschelles, one of the best informed of their sect, declared in the time of Charles IX that there were in France alone three hundred thousand or, as some read, thirty thousand witches, at what figure can we estimate the number of those which could be found in all the different countries of the world? And must we not believe that since that time they have increased by more than half? For my part I have no doubt of it: for if we but look around among our own neighbors, we shall find them all infested with this miserable and damnable vermin. Germany is almost entirely occupied with building fires for them. Switzerland has been compelled to wipe out many of her villages on their account. Travellers in Lorraine may see thousands and thousands of the stakes to which witches are bound. We in Burgundy are no more exempt than other lands; for in many parts of our country we see that the execution of witches is a common occurrence. Returning again to our neighbours, Savoy has not escaped this pest; for every day she sends us a countless number of persons possessed of demons which, on being exorcised, say that they have been sent by witches into the bodies of these poor wretches: moreover, most of the witches whom we have burned here came originally from Savoy. And what shall we say of France? It is difficult to believe that she is purged of witches, considering the great number which she had in the time of Trois-eschelles. I say nothing of other more remote lands. No, no; there are witches by the thousand everywhere, multiplying upon the earth even as worms in a garden [xxxiii–xxxiv].

Vermin, pest, infested, worms — with his choice of words, Boguet reveals his attitude toward witches and the fate they deserve — fires, stakes, execution. In his preface Boguet announces the purpose of his treatise. He also expresses his position in a more personal manner. Toward the end of the preface, after declaring that the stories people tell about witches are true, Boguet states:

> But to make this still clearer, I have founded the following Examen upon certain trials which I have myself conducted, during the last two years, of several members of this sect, whom I have seen and heard and probed as carefully as I could in order to draw the truth from them.... At the end of this Examen, I have added a short instruction for Judges who find themselves in the same case, since they must not conduct themselves in such trials as they do in those of other crimes. In this I have had the assistance of the works of the Inquisitors, of Bodin, Remy, Binsfeld, and others; but my chief help has been my own experience and my own observations of this damnable sect of people, who are the more difficult to convict in that they have always as their advocate that cunning Satan, who has the hardihood

> even to help and advise them when the Judge is speaking to them and questioning them.
>
> And if anyone takes exception to my having disclosed the names of the witches who were accused, I answer that, since their trials have been accomplished, this does not seem to matter much; for their names can always be found by going to the registers. Further, it is better that their names should be known, so that men may be on their guard not only against them, but also against their children, who usually follow their manner of life, and to protect themselves either change their names or their place of abode.... I would yet have it plainly known that I am a sworn enemy to witches, and that I shall never spare them, for their execrable abominations [xlv–xlvii].

According to Douglas, Boguet maintained that he was personally responsible for the execution of 600 witches in the eighteen-year period between 1598 and 1616.[59] Boguet's zeal for prosecuting witches extended to werewolves, for he saw no difference between them; werewolves were witches. Boguet devoted Chapter 47, "Of the Metamorphosis of Men into Beasts, and Especially of Lycanthropes or Loups-garoux," to the cases of the werewolves-witches that he tried. The first case that he describes is that of Jacques Bocquet, who was called Groz-Jacques, Clauda Jamprost, Clauda Jamguillaume, Thievenne Paget, and Clauda Gaillard. The first four confessed that they changed into wolves and then killed several children, naming them and giving details about the circumstances. They also admitted that they had eaten part of the children, although for some unexplained reason did not eat from the right side of the children. Boguet tells us that "[t]hese murders were verified both by the evidence of the parents, and by that of several others in the villages of Longchamois and Orcieres, who deposed that all these children had been caught and eaten by wolves at such a time and such a place" (137). As for Clauda Gaillard, she was accused of having changed into a wolf and of having attacked another woman by the name of Jeanne Perrin. Referring to all five as "these witches," Boguet then declares that he will discuss the issue of "lycanthropy and the metamorphosis of men into beasts" rather than deal with the fact that the witches also confessed going to the Sabbat, where they performed other foul deeds (138).

In the course of the next thirteen pages, Boguet reveals his own beliefs regarding metamorphosis. The judge has at the very least an odd—if not unique—way of going about this, for with each new declaration, he systematically unravels the argument of his previous statement, leaving the reader to wonder where this logical roller coaster ride will end. Boguet begins by noting "There is much disputing as to whether it is possible for men to be changed into beasts, some affirming the possibility, whilst others deny it; and there are ample grounds for both views. For we have many examples of the fact" (138). Thus he doesn't immediately take any position at all, but remains firmly on the fence. Boguet then proceeds to offer various "examples." Among them, he cites Ovid's tale of Lycaon, stories of wolves of unnatural size or without tails that must certainly have been witches, the account of the werewolves of Poligny in 1521, as well as that of Gilles Garnier, and then another that we have not previously encountered:

> Here it will be relevant to recount what happened in the year 1588 in a village about two leagues from Apchon in the highlands of Auvergne. One evening a gentleman, standing at the window of his château, saw a huntsman whom he knew passing by, and asked him to bring him some of his bag on his return. As the huntsman went his way along a valley, he was attacked by a large wolf and discharged his arquebus at it without hurting it. He was therefore compelled to grapple with the wolf, and caught it by the ears; but at length, growing weary, he let go of the wolf, drew back and took his big hunting knife, and with it cut off one of the wolf's paws, which he had put in his pouch after the wolf had run away. He then returned to the gentleman's château, in sight of which he had fought the wolf. The gentleman asked him to give him part of his bag; and the huntsman, wishing to do so and intending to take the paw from his pouch, drew from it a hand wearing a gold ring on one of the fingers, which the gentleman recognised as belonging to his wife. This caused him to entertain an evil suspicion of her; and going into the kitchen, he found his wife nursing her arm in her apron, which he took away, and found that her hand had been cut off. Thereupon the gentleman seized hold of her; but immediately, and as soon as she had been confronted with her hand, she confessed that it was no other than she who, in the form of a wolf, had attacked the hunter; and she was afterwards burned at Ryon. This was told me by one who may be believed, who went that way fifteen days after this thing had happened. So much for men being changed into the shape of wolves [140–141].

As Douglas notes, the account is filled with motifs from folklore, such as the werewolf's sympathetic wound that reveals the creature's true identity, the "exchange of hunting trophies between host and guest," the untrustworthy wife, Boguet's comment regarding the reliability of his source, and the lack of specific and verifiable details (178). More interesting, however, is the fact that the self-professed werewolf in this tale, whether its source is folklore or historical fact, is not a peasant woman, but rather a "gentle" woman, a woman of high birth. Thus we find in her, perhaps, the descendant of Bisclavret's wife, an untrustworthy wife who has become a werewolf.[60]

After relating the tale of the female werewolf, Boguet offers a few examples of men transforming themselves into other kinds of animals, such as cats, horses, and hares, before finally engaging in his own self-styled debate regarding metamorphosis. First he announces: "But even if we had no other proof than the history of Nabuchodonosor, that would suffice for us to believe that the metamorphosis of a man into a beast is possible" (143). Boguet cites the transformation of Lot's wife into a pillar of salt as further evidence, but then states the following:

> Nevertheless it has always been my opinion that Lycanthropy is an illusion, and that the metamorphosis of a man into a beast is impossible. For it would necessitate one of two things:—either the man who is changed into a beast must keep his soul and power of reason, or he must lose this at the moment of metamorphosis [143].

In the space of one page, Boguet has moved from the position of belief in the possibility of metamorphosis to rejecting it as illusion, using man's "power of reason" as the basis for his change. He thus joins ranks with the theologians who have been horrified over the centuries by the very idea that the human soul—the image of God—could ever be confined within the body of an animal. Boguet continues his argument by stating that "Homer was in error when, speaking of the companions of Ulysses who were changed into swine by Circe, he says that they had the hair, head and body of swine, but that their reason remained intact" (144). Here Boguet's logic twists and turns; he almost seems to accept the metamorphosis of the men in this tale while at the same time arguing that they did not retain their human intellect, unlike Augustine, who argues that it is impossible for man's soul to be transformed and that any physical transformation of the body must be an illusion.[61] But Boguet has not completed his scrutiny of the relationship between the soul and metamorphosis, for then he questions "if ... a man loses his reasoning soul when he is metamorphosed, how is it possible for him to recover it, and for it to return into him when he resumes the shape of a man?" (144). He also asks "Where does Satan put the soul when it is separated from its body?" (144). Although he concludes that God alone can cause such metamorphoses, Boguet goes one step further and declares that Nabuchodonosor was never transformed into an ox, but only thought he was an ox and behaved accordingly. Referring to the theory believed by some that a "werewolf" is actually asleep while someone, or something else, is perpetrating the crimes that he believes he is committing,[62] Boguet now declares, "[m]y own opinion is that Satan sometimes leaves the witch asleep behind a bush, and himself goes and performs that which the witch has in mind to do, giving himself the appearance of a wolf; but that he so confuses the witch's imagination that he believes he has really been a wolf and has run about and killed men and beasts" (146). Boguet adds that "this comes from the Devil confusing the four Humours of which he is composed, so that he represents whatever he will to his fantasy and imagination. This will be easier to believe when it is considered that there are natural maladies of such a nature that they cause the sick to believe that they are cocks, or pigs, or oxen" (146–147). As we saw earlier, Johann Weyer also suggested that lycanthropy was a medical condition caused by a combination of melancholia — an imbalance in melancholic humor — and delusion, although he did not attribute the imbalance to Satan. Before ending his chapter on werewolves, Boguet returns to the case with which he began, that of Jacques Bocquet, Clauda Jamprost, Clauda Jamguillaume, Thievenne Paget, and Clauda Gaillard. Noting that their faces, hands and legs were covered with scratches, that the self-professed werewolves spoke of how they would become tired after running in their wolf forms, and that the clothing of the dead children were found untorn, not as if the clothing had been ripped off them, but as if they had been undressed, Boguet finally declares the following:

> Who now can doubt but that these witches themselves ran about and committed the acts and murders of which we have spoken? For what was the cause of the fatigue which they experienced? If they had been sleeping behind some bush, how did they become fatigued? What caused the scratches on their persons, if it was not the thorns and bushes through which they ran in their pursuit of man and animals? Again, is it not the work of human hands to unclothe a child in the manner we have described? I say nothing of their confessions, which are all in agreement with one another [151].

Boguet holds the witches fully culpable for their deeds, thus reminding us that his book is after all a "text for witch-hunters." It matters little to him whether or not they have been deluded by the devil or by an imbalance in their humors into believing that they transform themselves into wolves; all that counts is that they are witches who have killed and eaten human beings. Boguet hastens to tell his readers that the fact that these witches are cannibals is not at all unbelievable.[63] But he does not accord their metamorphoses this same status, for after noting that the werewolf Pierre Bourgot supposedly rubbed himself with herbs "to lose his wolf's shape" (154), he declares "But since, as we have shown, the metamorphosis of a man into a beast is for countless reasons a very controversial subject, we must not pay much attention to these remedies" (154). Boguet closes his chapter with one last warning to his readers:

> So much have I thought good to set down concerning Lycanthropes or werewolves. Yet I should be sorry to leave this subject without reprimanding those who would excuse them and cast the blame for all that they do upon Satan, as if they were entirely innocent. For it is apparent from what I have said that it is the witches themselves who run about and kill people; so that we may here apply the Proverb which says: "Man is a wolf to man." And even if they were guilty in nothing but their damnable intention, they should still be thought worthy of death, seeing that the law takes cognisance of the intention even in matters which are not very serious, although nothing has actually resulted from such intention. I may add that such people never have this intention, except those who have first renounced God and Heaven [154–155].

Boguet has finally made a statement regarding werewolves that he does not turn around and undermine with the next. His intentions are now clear and unequivocal: werewolves are witches who must be hunted down and punished, even if "nothing has actually resulted from" their intent to cause harm. For them, only one punishment is possible: death.

In 1612, just ten years after Boguet's treatise appeared, Pierre de Lancre, jurist and King Henri IV's appointed counselor, published *Tableau de l'inconstance des mauvais anges et demons,* his report on the activities of witches in the Labourd region of southwestern France.[64] Just like so many of his predecessors, Lancre believed that witches were real and that they were dangerous. Indeed, as Milin notes, Lancre's treatise is hardly original (130). Nevertheless, it is of special interest to our study, for Discourses II, III, and IV of Book 4, "On the inconstancy of demons," deal at length with lycanthropy and more specifically with the case of Jean Grenier, a thirteen- or fourteen-year-old self-professed werewolf who was first tried in Coutras in 1603. Three months later his case was sent to the Parlement of Bordeaux for review.[65] This case is noteworthy for two reasons: first, the werewolf is himself no more than a child; and second, just three years after the close of the century that brought the world a new "renaissance" of the werewolf, Jean Grenier's was the last major werewolf case, to my knowledge, that was tried in Western Europe. During Grenier's first hearing on May 29, 1603, the first person who testified against him was Marguerite Poirier, a thirteen-year-old girl:

> She reported that one day, while she guarded her flock, a wild beast jumped on her and grabbed her dress between its big teeth, pulling on it near her right hip, and tearing it. She beat the animal on the back with a stick; it was bigger and shorter than a wolf, had red fur and a short tail. After she struck the animal, it moved away from her about ten or twelve feet and sat on its hind legs like a dog, looking at her ferociously, which caused her to run away. She said that the animal's head was smaller than that of a wolf [270].

Since Grenier had already admitted having attacked Marguerite and had said that he "would have eaten her had she not defended herself with a stick" (269), her testimony merely confirms Grenier's confession. Marguerite also testified that she had heard that Jean could turn into a wolf whenever he wanted and that he had killed some dogs and drunk their blood, but "it was not as good as the blood of young boys and girls" and that he had also eaten parts of a boy and had killed and eaten a girl (270). The second witness was Jeanne Gaboriaut, an eighteen-year-old girl, who testified that Jean Grenier had told her his father was a priest. He also told her that his skin was dark from the red wolf skin that he wore to transform himself into a wolf (270).

With this new detail — the red wolf skin that he wore — her testimony corroborated Marguerite's testimony and linked Jean to the girl's bestial attacker. According to Lancre, "Once this information was contained in a writ issued for his arrest, he was taken into custody; he was tried; and in the course of his hearing he confessed to more than the witnesses had testified about him" (271).

During the course of Jean Grenier's second hearing on June 2, 1603, he testified that his last name was not Grenier, but was instead Grainier. In addition, he now claimed that his father was not a priest, but a worker from the parish of St. Antoine de Pison by the name of Pierre Grainier, who was "commonly" called "le croquant," "rebel" (270). According to Jean, since leaving his father's home three months ago, he had traveled to several villages and had been in the service of different masters. One day, while in the forest with another boy named Pierre du Tilhaire, Jean met a man "dressed in black and mounted on a black horse" who "kissed them with an extremely cold mouth" (271). Like the men encountered by Pierre Bourgot and Michel Verdung, this man, whom Jean later referred to as the Lord of the Forest, promised him money if he would serve him. After giving them wine and marking them with a pin on their buttocks, the man left. Once again, Jean Grenier confessed to all the acts that he had been accused of, including those that Marguerite Poirier had testified to, but he claimed he had never drunk the blood of the dog that he had killed. Jean also confessed to new crimes. First he admitted that he stole a baby from its cradle and ate it. Although he remembered that there were only three dwellings in the village, he could not name the village. Grenier also admitted to killing a little girl "wearing a black dress" who was guarding a flock of sheep and then eating "as much of her as he wanted" (272). Regarding this particular crime, the judges comment:

> [I]t is remarkable that he said that it was he who lowered her dress, because he did not rip it. This is something that we observed, to show that while real wolves tear with their claws, werewolves tear with their teeth, and just like men they know how to remove the dresses of the girls they want to eat without ripping them [272].

The judges thus naively seem to accept Jean's statement as proof that the boy is a werewolf, rather than a "real" wolf. It could equally serve, however, as proof that no transformation ever took place. Jean continued his testimony by stating that:

> When he wants to run, he wears a wolf's skin, the one the Lord of the Forest brings him when he wants him to run. Then he rubs himself with some kind of grease from a pot the Lord of the Forest also gave him, after first taking off the clothes he normally wears in the fields and bushes [272].

Jean Grenier is not the only werewolf who used an ointment to facilitate his transformation; Pierre Bourgot and Michel Verdung, the werewolves of Poligny, as well as Jacques Roulet, also indicated that they used one. But Grenier also notes that he removes his clothing and he wears a wolfskin. Thus with the case of Jean Grenier we find what amounts to an embarrassment of riches in motifs or agents of transformation; even in the literary accounts of werewolves from antiquity and the Middle Ages, we don't find such excess. We encounter men who remove their clothing prior to their metamorphosis, such as the soldier in Petronius' *Satyricon,* the Arcadian werewolves in ancient Greece, as well as Bisclavret and Melion.[66] In *Guillaume de Palerne,* Alphonse's stepmother rubs an ointment on him in order to transform him into a wolf.[67] As for the wolfskin, for that motif we must turn to the Norse Volsung Saga and Gerald of Wales' tale of the Ossory werewolves, although with the latter, the skin was not actually used as an agent of transformation.[68] An echo of the wolfskin motif can also be found in the bearskin disguises worn by Guillaume and Melior in *Guillaume de Palerne.*[69] It is only in the account of Jean Grenier that we find any of the agents of transformation — or motifs — combined.

Jean Grenier also implicated his father in his "werewolfery,"[70] stating that his father knew that he would run "under the moon at one or two o'clock in the morning, and sometimes at night" and that "on three occasions he had put the grease on him and had helped him put on the wolf skin, the one the Lord of the Forest had given him" (272). According to Jean, the Lord of the Forest kept the ointment and the skin safe at his own home and would send it to Jean whenever he wanted to run as a werewolf. In other words, Jean was unable to produce either the ointment or the wolfskin as proof. Nevertheless, as Lancre notes,

> After his hearing and based solely on his deposition (it is truly remarkable that, in order to show that this crime of witchcraft and other crimes relating to demons are so privileged, the deposition and testimony of a thirteen-year-old son can be accepted as testimony against the father) the court ordered the father, Pierre Croquant, and Pierre du Thilhaire be taken prisoner. Only the father was found [273].

But of course Jean Grenier is no ordinary thirteen-year-old boy; he has already admitted that he is a werewolf who has made a pact with the "Lord of the Forest," who could be no other than the Devil.

After the arrest of Grenier's father, another investigation was conducted on June 3, 1603. During this inquiry, the fathers of the children that had been eaten by a werewolf testified at length. Just as it happened with Grenier's first hearing, the boy seemed anxious to incriminate himself:

> These witnesses and the accused completely agreed with regard to the crime, the place, and the other circumstances concerning the time, the appearance

> of the werewolf, the wounds, the help that the parents of other people gave to their boys and girls who had been hurt, the words they said to each other while screaming at the wolf, the weapons or sticks they used — everything right down to the smallest details, even including which one of the three children the wolf had chosen because he was the most delicate and the most plump [273].

In spite of the fact that the witnesses and the accused were in total agreement, the judges noted that they "were not satisfied with the information, or his confession, and [their] inquiries were inconclusive" (274). And so the investigation continued. They led Grenier through the villages where he had committed his crimes and had other witnesses, including Marguerite Poirier, identify him. Not only did Marguerite identify Grenier, but they also had him "[choose] her from among four or five other girls" (274) in an early seventeenth-century version of a police line-up, although in this case it was the criminal who was identifying his victim. Of course, the situation was absurd, since Grenier had just identified Marguerite Poirier in court less than five days before. It is inconceivable that he would have forgotten even a stranger in such a short time, much less someone with whom he used to tend livestock. During the investigation, Grenier testified that he had left home after his father beat him and that his stepmother had left his father after she saw him "[vomit] up from his throat the feet of dogs and the hands of little children" (274). He also stated that his father used to run with him sometimes as a werewolf and that "once they found a girl wearing a white dress who was tending the geese near the village of Grillault. They took her, and after they carried her into the field they ate her." (274). In spite of what Jean said about his friend Pierre du Tilhaire and his father Pierre Grenier, they were "respected by their neighbors" (282) and believed to be "good people" (282). In addition, the wolfskin was nowhere to be found. All of this was taken as possible evidence of diabolical illusion: "[I]t was in order to take advantage of this young boy that the Devil did this, that is, had him see his companion and also his father running with him, and indeed showed him his father in his house vomiting up the dogs' feet and the hands of little children" (282). In June 1603, Jean Grenier was sentenced to be hung on the gallows and then burned on the public square of La Roche Galve.

Before Jean's death sentence was carried out, however, his case was referred to the Parlement of Bordeaux. In his review of the case, Lord Daffis, first president of the court of the Parlement of Bordeaux, noted that "[s]ome will say that this is only a dream: however, this trial, which was one of the most rigorous known to man, and which took place within sight of all the villages of this area, testifies to the contrary" (276). But of course it wasn't a dream. While assessing Jean's case and attempting to determine his guilt or innocence, as well as what his punishment should be, the Parlement of Bordeaux also reviewed theories concerning the reality of metamorphosis, ranging from those of antiquity to St. Augustine and the *Canon Episcopi*. Even medical causes, such as those proposed by Weyer and Scot were considered:

> Nothing has been neglected in this affair in order to clarify the truth of this crime, for this young werewolf was visited by two doctors, who agree that this young boy is of a black [arrabilious] and melancholic humor. Still, he is not afflicted with the illness that is called lycanthropy, so that we do not have a case of an imaginary metamorphosis. Also, a person's imagination cannot change him. One cannot appear as a wolf or another beast that one imagines oneself to be.... But imagination can do much to men's lives and their ordinary actions, which are linked to their imagination. Indeed, it can produce effects on the fetus in its mother's womb, like changing its color and appearance.
>
> Still, it cannot act before the eyes of some people in order to charm them. Using his imagination, man is able to fantasize that he is a wolf; nevertheless if he just used his imagination he would never appear as a wolf to others.... And since the werewolf in question was seen to be a wolf, we are not confronting a case of an imaginary act, nor an example of the illness called lycanthropy [298].

In other words, the judges believe that Jean Grenier is a real werewolf, that he actually transformed himself into a wolf—"he was seen to be a wolf"—and while in this form committed horrendous crimes against children. But there is no testimony that anyone actually saw Jean Grenier transform himself into a wolf.[71] There also seems to be no evidence that a real wolf did not kill and eat these children, other than the fact that the little girl's black dress was not torn. Moreover, if "just like men they [werewolves] know how to remove the dresses of the girls they want to eat without ripping them" (272), then why was Marguerite Poirier's dress torn? Nevertheless, all the witnesses and his judges are convinced of the reality of his metamorphosis:

> Those who have the faces of wolves, like this young boy, have frightening and shining eyes like wolves, and commit the destruction and cruelty of wolves. They strangle dogs, cut children's throats with their teeth, and love the taste of human flesh just like wolves.... They have the dedication and determination to execute such acts in the presence of men; their teeth and their nails are as strong and sharp as those of wolves; they run on all fours; and when they run together, they usually hunt together like packs of wolves.... This young boy who was transformed into a wolf said at his trial that he shared his prey with another wolf that followed him. That they go as fast as wolves is completely verified by his trial and by the one that occurred in Besançon in 1521, as described in detail by Weyer. This should not appear incredible or impossible, for these are the effects of the evil Devil, who helps them, encourages them, and leads them to do these things. He gives them

> the means; he makes them like wolves; he attracts them and gives them a taste for this [307].

At this point, the focus of the Parlement's deliberations begins to shift away from Jean Grenier's culpability and toward placing responsibility for his deeds on the Devil. First, the judges ask "[w]hy the Devil is so taken with children" (309), then "[w]hether this young boy is capable of this evil spell since he is only thirteen' and "[w]hether or not this boy deserves to be punished as a witch, namely to be put to death" (310). To the latter question, the court replies:

> The fact that this boy was so obviously dazed was recorded not only by the doctors but also in the trial where he himself spoke. He is a country child, poorly instructed, or, more accurately, ignorant of the knowledge and fear of God. He knew even less about how to defend himself against Satan's wiles. Even the most intelligent are limited in the capacity of their minds to exercise judgment, which St. Augustine himself believes to be very difficult.... How, someone will ask, can one accuse a young boy of this age of having been unable to detect an Evil Spirit, of having failed to destroy it, of having been seduced, charmed, and overcome by him? The ways to prevent himself from falling prey to such enchantment and to stay away from the demons were unknown to him [311].

Referring to Jean Grenier as a "poor idiot" (312) because he did not even know enough to protect himself from the Devil by making the sign of the cross or by praying the Our Father, the judges indicate that his confessions are "suspect." Moreover, "judicial formalities lay so many traps for people of this age" (313) and he had no one to advise him. As a result, he cannot be put to death. All the same, his crimes cannot be overlooked; his association with the Devil especially must not be ignored:

> [T]his young boy is not so stupid or demented as not to be thoroughly taught and trained in the school of the Evil Spirit, or not to retain all that the Evil Spirit's disciples and slaves say about him: "It comes about at that age that he perceives matters, but does not yet misrepresent them." Although he varied what he said about those whom he accused, he offered consistent testimony during eight or ten interrogations, both before the judges of la Roche and Coutras and before the high court.
>
> In his case, it is not a matter of inventing and feigning the appearance of a big, black man with an extremely cold mouth. This is the language of the witches. Nor did he invent this title Lord of the Forest, which he used to designate the Evil Spirit [313–14].

The court then proceeds to enumerate everything that proves that Jean Grenier is a witch and served the Devil. First, he admitted that he ran on Mondays, Fridays, and Saturdays, including on the "eve of Pentecost, Good Friday, and during Holy Week. It is during these days of devotion that the witches have sex with the demons and that they claim to do the most evil." (315). Second, not only does he run on Good Friday, which is something that werewolves do, but he does it in the moonlight, which is "a Devil's trick to make him more susceptible to illusions" (315). He also bears the mark of the Devil: "He shows his mark, with which the Evil Spirit branded him, which is like a little circle that has no feeling inside, like that of the other witches.... One of the most certain proofs of a crime and of being the Devil's succubus is the mark, as all those who have written on this subject have observed" (315). Furthermore, the nail of Jean Grenier's left thumb is "very thick and very long" because the "Devil had forbidden him to cut [it]. This is pure folly, but it is a sign of belief in and obedience to the evil Devil, who binds hearts tightly to him by means of such superstitions" (315). Finally, the court comments on Grenier's cruelty:

> But what shows this miserable boy to be completely trained by the Devil, and won over and conquered according to the desire and intention of the Evil Spirit, is the cruelty he confessed to having committed while wearing the wolf's skin, namely, eating children. He confessed that he had taken them by the throat, just like a wolf does. The Devil had instructed him, for he had undressed them without tearing their clothing, a particular habit characteristic of the werewolf. He confessed that he has a taste for it; the Devil awakened this desire in him [317].

With these remarks, the court's attention is now turning away from the Devil and back to Jean, for he is their immediate problem. What are they to do with him? They can hardly overlook what he has done, for "[t]o excuse such a crime on account of the influence of the Evil Spirit would create a precedent for leaving all the witches unpunished" (317). But his crime is particularly unspeakable, for "[t]o eat a member of one's own species horrifies not only humans, but also animals. However ferocious they may be, animals spare their own, including wolves" (318). Jean Grenier the "werewolf" is a cannibal and as such he is much worse than a ferocious wolf, for he has done what a wolf would not do. Questioning "whether the young age of a werewolf completely or partly exempts it from punishment" (319), the court first cites examples of cases involving other young children and notes that the "degree of malice in these examples was a more important factor than age" (320). Unable to settle on an age at which a child is capable of committing a sin, the court declares that "clemency seems too dangerous in such cases. If you feed a wolf and tame it, it will always be a wolf: *Lupi pilum mutant, non mentem* [Wolves change their coat, not their nature]. Moreover, wild animals are killed for such a crime" (321). Finally, the court makes its decision:

> All these reasons have been examined and considered from many angles. But the court, in the end, took note of the age and the imbecility of this young boy, who is so stupid and so mentally impaired, that children of seven or eight normally show more reasoning than he. Badly fed in all ways, and so small that he is undersized, one would not think him ten years old.
>
> The opinion of those seems superior who submit to the deliberation of the judge if the pupil is capable of fraud, regardless of his age. Here is a young boy abandoned and driven out by his father, who had a stepmother for a mother, who roamed the fields, without a guide and without anyone in the world to look after him, begging for his supper, who had no instruction whatsoever in the fear of God, whose nature was corrupted by evil seduction, daily necessities, and despair, all conditions that the Evil Spirit exploited.
>
> The court did not want to contribute further to the despair of this young boy; whom the Devil had armed against other children. It preferred, after due consideration of all matters, including the inconsistencies of his testimony and other aspects of the trial, to save this soul for God rather than judge it to be lost.
>
> Moreover, according to the report of the good monks who began to instruct and exhort him, he was already showing that he abhorred and detested his crime, as witnessed by his tears and his repentance [322].
>
> God releases those whom Satan enchains. God returns those whom this Evil Spirit enlists in his ranks and brands with a mark. Thus those who escape from the mouth of this wolf seem to have had one foot in Hell and to have escaped. And even though such examples cannot be considered in court to exempt a witch or a werewolf from their punishment, they serve nevertheless to refute the opinion that young people cannot change and leave this form of life.
>
> The court decided that this boy had to be removed from the sight of these villages, where he had committed such acts, for two reasons: one, so that there would be no fear in the future, and two, to restore to its God-fearing state a mind that was so deranged and abused [323–24].

The official sentence of the court, which was "pronounced in 'red robe'" on September 6, 1603 read as follows:

> The court dismissed and dismisses still the appeals and, for the case resulting from the trial, condemned and condemns Jean Grenier to be locked up for the rest of his life in one of the city's monasteries. He is to serve this monastery for the rest of his life. He is forbidden and prohibited from ever leaving there under penalty by hanging or strangling. Regarding Pierre Grenier, his father, named Pierre du Tilhaire, the court ordered him to be more thoroughly investigated later in the month. Yet the court released them after they made customary guarantees in lieu of bail. Jean Grenier was condemned to pay costs to the Baron de la Roche with a tax to be announced later. And the other fines are to be fixed at the end of the trial. Decreed in Bordeaux, 6 September 1603 [326].

And so the court, in consideration of Jean Grenier's age and mental state, did not execute this werewolf, offering him instead some measure of clemency and hope for redemption. But Jean's story does not end there, for Pierre de Lancre visited him at the monastery in 1610:

> I found that he was a young man of twenty or twenty-one, of medium height, rather small for his age, with wild-looking eyes that were sunken and black, and completely distraught. His eyes gave the impression that he was ashamed of his misfortune, which he seemed to understand somewhat; he did not dare look anyone straight in the eye.
>
> He seemed a bit dazed — not that he did not understand what he heard or failed to do promptly what the good fathers asked of him. Rather he was hardly devout, and he did not seem to understand easily even simple things that only seemed commonsensical. Having always tended the flocks, he never saw anything of the world until he came to the monastery, which he rarely left.
>
> He had very long and bright teeth that were wider than normal, protruding somewhat and rotten and half black from being used to lash out at animals and people. His fingernails were also quite long and some were completely black from the base to the tip, even that of the thumb of the left hand, which the Devil prevented him from trimming. With regard to those that were so black, one could say that they were half worn down and more broken than the others, and less normal, because he used them more than he used those on his feet. This clearly shows that he was indeed a werewolf, and that he used his hands both for running and for grabbing children and dogs by the throat.
>
> He cleverly confessed to me that he had been a werewolf and that while in this condition he had roamed the fields following the commands of the Lord of the Forest. This he confessed freely to everyone and denied it to no one, believing that he would avoid all criticism and disgrace for this situation by saying that he was no longer a werewolf. In the beginning, when he entered the monastery, he demonstrated a remarkable ability to walk on all fours, and to jump across ditches like four-legged animals do [329–330].
>
> This young man told me that he had an animal skin that the Lord of the Forest had given him.... He also said that his father used this animal skin. And we were told that he did not want to see his father at all. Thus he would go hide in the monastery each time his father came to see him.... We observed that he greatly despised his father, believing that he was responsible for the bad training he received. He believed, moreover, that he was a werewolf, for he had declared that he would use the same wolf's skin as he did. This is why, when he came to some understanding of his affliction, he hated him for it when I made him see it so strongly.
>
> He confessed to me also, in a straightforward manner, that he still wanted to eat the flesh of little children, and that he found the flesh of little girls particularly delicious. I asked him if he would eat it if he had not been prohibited from doing so, and he answered me frankly that yes he would, and more that of girls than that of boys because they are more tender.... He also

> told us that the Lord of the Forest twice came to see him at the beginning of his confinement in the monastery, that he had been afraid, but that he left right away because he made the sign of the cross many times and continued to do so every day so that he would stay away, and he never came again [331–332].

Physically, Jean has barely changed. In his long black nails he still carries the sign of his former obedience to the Devil. His teeth, too, are marked by his crimes. Mentally, he is still described as "dazed." What is even more appalling, seven years after his last murder, Jean still has an appetite for "the flesh of little children," especially that of little girls. Nevertheless, he has resisted temptation; he has committed no new crimes and he has used the sign of the cross — what "the ancient fathers used to call the Christian's arms and helmet" (312) — to chase away the Lord of the Forest. Lancre is thus able to conclude Book 4 and his discussion of werewolves with his statement that "the Devil has only limited power over mankind" (341). As proof, he offers the case of Jean Grenier: "And we see the truth in this, since the poor boy died a good Christian around the beginning of November of 1610, aided by the good monks where he was living" (341).

Although accounts of "real" werewolves dominate the sixteenth-century, the werewolf also appears in folklore, as we have already seen in the anecdotes recounted by Chauvincourt. What is perhaps most unexpected about these folktales is the fact that the werewolves they portray are not at all like the ferocious monsters that we find in the court cases of the same period. Werewolves are not totally absent from literature either, for two editions of a Middle French prose reworking by Pierre Durand of the twelfth-century adventure romance *Guillaume de Palerne* were published in the sixteenth century: Olivier Arnoullet's 1552 edition, *Lhystoire du noble et preulx vaillant cheua/lier Guillaume de Pal/erne & de la belle Me/lior lequel Guillaume de Palerne fut filz du roy de Cecille/& par fortune et merueil/leuse aduenture deuint vacher. Et finable/ment fut empereur de Romme soubz la conduicte dung Loup Garoux filz au roy despaigne;* and Nicolas Bonfons' 1550–1560 edition, *Lhistoire du no/ble preux & vail/lant cheualier Guillaume de Palerne. Et de la belle Melior. Lequel Guillau/me de Palerne fut filz du roy de Cecille. Et par fortune & mer/ueilleuse auenture devint Vacher. Et finablement fut Empe/reur de Rome souz la conduicte dun Loupgarouxs filz au Roye Despagne. XV F.*[72] There are two surviving copies of the Arnoullet edition: one at the Bibliothèque d'Arsenal and one at the British Museum, and there are three surviving copies of the Bonfons edition: one at the Bibliothèque Bodléianne Douce, one at the Harvard University Library, and one at the British Museum. As John Manolis has observed, "Le fait que nous avons deux exemplaires de l'édition d'Arnoullet et trois de l'édition de Bonfons, semble indiquer que ce roman jouit d'une certaine popularité au XVIe siècle"[73] (16), "The fact that we have two copies of Arnoullet's edition and three of Bonfons' edition seems to indicate that this romance enjoyed a certain popularity in the sixteenth century." It is also worth noting that during the sixteenth century a prose version of the fourteenth-century *William of Palerne* was published by Wynkyn de Worde[74] and that *Guillaume* was also translated into Irish sometime between 1520 and 1600.[75]

The sixteenth- and seventeenth-century derivatives of the medieval *Guillaume de Palerne* are merely prose translations of the verse romance. Indeed, the basic facts of the werewolf's story have not been changed. Alphonse is still the victim of his wicked stepmother and he is still a Spanish prince who is still acting out of unselfish motives to help Guillaume. We do learn that he is seven years old at the time of his original transformation and Pierre Durand, the translator,[76] recounts the werewolf's history immediately after relating the story of the kidnapping instead of waiting until later. Durand also adds the detail that Alphonse was hiding in the shrubbery when he overheard Guillaume's uncle and nursemaids discussing their plans to poison the boy and his father, thus indicating how the werewolf learned of the plot. In the prologue to the prose romance, Durand states that he received a copy of the Old French romance from a friend and decided to translate it into "langage moderne françois" (21), "modern French," because its language was not intelligible or easy to read for most people. For that reason, the romance was "en grant danger d'estre perdue" (21), "in great danger of being lost." Durand also states that he removed from the original text only those passages that seemed "absurdes et moins que raisonnables" (22), "absurd and less than rational." This statement is particularly significant as it serves as evidence of at least one sixteenth-century man's attitude toward werewolves. Since Durand retained the entire story of the werewolf, he clearly did not find these passages absurd or irrational.

Alphonse is perhaps the most striking example, if not the only example, of a literary werewolf in the sixteenth century. But Alphonse is from another time. As the last heir to the twelfth-century literary werewolves, he is the exact opposite of the "real" werewolves that are portrayed in the pages of sixteenth-century court documents and theoretical treatises. He has no real place in the sixteenth century and he can only survive in the imagination. When the idealized werewolf steps out of the pages of a medieval story book into a sixteenth-century world torn apart by religious wars and famine, the courtly hero returns to the beginning and transforms himself once again back into the ferocious and brutal monster of antiquity.

Chapter Nine

Explanations or "Que cele beste senefie"[1]

In the latter part of the twelfth century many conditions come together to generate what Bynum calls the "werewolf renaissance of the twelfth century" (94). As we have seen, this revival of interest culminates in the creation of the chivalrous werewolf, a radical departure from the traditional portrayal of the bloodthirsty werewolf that will find its apotheosis in the character of Alphonse in *Guillaume de Palerne.* Among those circumstances influencing the writers of the werewolf narratives we can include the twelfth century's fascination with the constancy and changeability of identity, the Church's doctrine of metamorphosis as an illusion, as well as its insistence on the rational nature of human beings, the appropriation of the marvelous in courtly romance, the usefulness of the werewolf as an ironic metaphor to warn against facile interpretation, and finally the cultural trauma resulting from an incident of cannibalism during the First Crusade. None of these factors can be totally ruled out, for how are we to enter the minds of those long-ago authors and determine their intentions? All we can do is examine the evidence that they leave behind in their texts. But we must also take into account the cultural context in which they wrote these texts.

The first of these factors is the changing attitude toward the individual in the second half of the twelfth century. Evidence of this first appears in the Cistercian's new stress on knowing yourself, with the idea that one comes closer to God through self-knowledge.[2] Guibert of Nogent connects this knowledge to the ability to discern someone's intentions:

> It is hardly surprising if we make mistakes in narrating the actions of other people, when we cannot express in words even our own thoughts and deeds; in fact, we can hardly sort them out in our own minds. It is useless to talk about intentions, which, as we know, are often so concealed as scarcely to be discernible to the understanding of the inner man.[3]

In the twelfth century the Church, especially the School of Laon, considers intention a critical element for the determination of sin. According to Abelard, "sin lay solely in the intention..."and "in consent to sinful desire."[4] True knowledge of oneself is therefore extremely important, as it is not enough to know that what you did was wrong; to be declared a sinner you must know that you intended to do wrong. Individuals are also encouraged to express their feelings, needs, and desires. Saint Bernard's sermons bear testimony to this, as do Abelard's lyric poetry *Laments.*[5] Individual confession begins to replace public confession; by 1215, the Church requires everyone to make individual confessions at least once a year. A new interest appears in psychology, which frequently manifests itself in monologues about love in courtly romances.[6] At the same time, autobiographies start to be written and portraits and sculptures become more and more personalized. As Norman Cantor points out, there is an obvious shift in emphasis from communal identity to individual identity:

> The values of the second half of the twelfth century were based on a radical philosophy very different from the traditional social thinking of the early Middle Ages, which was founded on the concept of the community. Theoretically, devotion and service to the City of God (in its earthly manifestation, the Church) was regarded as the highest fulfillment of the individual; in practical terms, however, devotion to the family was the dominant ideal. In the twelfth century, on the contrary, the fulfillment of the individual required him to serve himself, to do what made him happiest and follow his own ambitions. The community was transitory, and often an obstacle to his personal quest [225–6].[7]

We find a reflection of this attitude in Arthurian romances when the hero sets off on an adventure quest, not to serve his lord, but to establish his reputation and acquire a name, an identity, for himself. In *Guillaume de Palerne*, on the other hand, Alphonse fulfills himself and establishes his excellence by voluntarily risking his life to protect Guillaume. He thus confirms his heroic identity.

This new stress on the importance of the individual, and along with it individual identity, is accompanied by a growing interest in change. As Bynum observes in her study, *Metamorphosis and Identity*, change is "the other side of identity" since it is that which demarcates the boundaries of an individual's identity (19). Bynum posits two different kinds of change, evolution-change, or "an unfolding of an essence or core forever present" (20), and replacement-change, in which "an entity is replaced by something completely different" (25). Writers of the first half of the twelfth century focus on the first kind of change, the evolution-change, and present their characters with an unchanging essence that reveals itself through their behavior. Although

Guillaume de Palerne is a late-twelfth century romance, we also see this type of change in the depiction of its protagonists. Guillaume and Alphonse are who they always have been; their core identity is revealed through their courtly comportment and their heroic deeds. In the latter part of the twelfth century, however, writers become more interested in replacement-change; texts dealing with metamorphosis, werewolves, fairies and other marvelous creatures start to appear. According to Bynum, this new focus can be explained by social circumstances in which real change, replacing one thing for another, becomes more possible for people. For example, knights give up their inheritance in order to study theology, men leave their farms to go on Crusade, and younger sons are left to seek their own fortune because of the patrilineal nature of inheritance (26–7). But along with such radical changes in the real world come fear and anxiety. Because of this, the texts that are produced at this time demonstrate a strong resistance to the very changes that they are exploring.[8] Bynum thus notes that "[t]he point of Gerald's discussion of the werewolves of Ulster was not only to titillate his readers with the possibility of wolf-humans but also to contain the possibility within theoretical discussion that denied it to be true metamorphosis" (27). Although, as Bynum suggests, the literary werewolf tales that we examined are not "contain[ed] within theoretical discussion" (27), in each case their author demonstrates that the werewolf has retained his human reasoning, therefore his true identity, although it may be hidden much of the time. In keeping with Christian doctrine, the metamorphosis is only an illusion, but it is one over which the beast has little or no control. Nevertheless, the illusion is frightening enough to terrify most witnesses. Perhaps more significant — even more than the truth or illusory nature of these metamorphoses — is the fact that the constancy and changeability of identity becomes visible in all of these tales, including in Gerald's account. In *Guillaume de Palerne*, for example, we see Alphonse undergo the physical transformation inflicted on him by his stepmother Brande, yet we also see that his core identity never changes; it remains constant. Similarly, Guillaume experiences many radical changes in his social condition throughout the romance but his nobility — his core identity — never changes and always reveals itself.[9]

The Church's doctrine of metamorphosis as an illusion, and especially its insistence on the rational nature of human beings, also contributes to the creation of the chivalrous werewolf in the twelfth century. All the literary werewolf narratives of this period conform to the doctrine established by Augustine. In *Bisclavret*, the king notes that the beast "ad sen d'hume" (154), "has the intelligence of a man." Although in *Melion,* King Arthur only observes that the werewolf is "privés" (411), "tame," the narrator has already declared that "sens e memoire d'ome avoit" (218), "he had the intelligence and memory of a man." In *Arthur and Gorlagon*, when King Gargol sees the werewolf for the first time, he tells his men that "he had detected some signs of human understanding in him" (242). Finally, in *Guillaume de Palerne*, the eponymous hero detects Alphonse's "raison et sens" (4378), "reasoning and intelligence," and states that he knows that Alphonse is not really a wolf (4380). For the Church, retention of rationality is essential, for choice — intention — is what makes possible sin and, of course, salvation. Both are reserved for mankind. Acting without understanding is merely the behavior of the animal kingdom. As we have seen, in each narrative the werewolf's courtly behavior supports these observations and, pointing to the illusory nature of his appearance, reveals there is really a man trapped inside this ferocious looking, but chivalrous, beast.

The appropriation of the marvelous in courtly romance is another factor that influences the werewolf renaissance and the creation of a new image for the beast. According to Jacques Le Goff, "in the twelfth and thirteenth centuries the marvelous suddenly makes an appearance in high culture" (29). This coincides, of course, with the sudden appearance of literary accounts of werewolves that depict the beast as a noble victim. Le Goff attributes this emergence of the marvelous to the desire of knights who want a literature of their own that will serve their own interests against those of the upper nobility (29). He adds that by this time "[t]he marvelous had become less threatening, and the Church felt that it could tame it or turn it to advantage" (29). A chivalrous werewolf who retains his humanity throughout his metamorphosis consequently benefits both knighthood and the Church. In his study, *The Art of Medieval French Romance*, Douglas Kelly offers a meticulous analysis of the marvelous as a component of romance.[10] In it Kelly distinguishes between two "levels of coherence" in the romance: the *matiere*, or mythic subject of the narrative, and the *san*, or the author's attitude toward his subject (146). He further notes that "[w]hen romance *matiere* undergoes amplification, it also yields the wondrous, the marvelous, the mythic in the story, and not just the commentary derived from the *san*" (148). Thus there exists an essential link between the marvelous and romance. Indeed, Kelly defines romance as "a record of marvel and the adventure or adventures it generates" (189). Marvels include not only the supernatural, but also anything that is out of the ordinary or unexpected. Of course the werewolves are marvelous simply because they are man-beasts. The adventures that Bisclavret, Melion, Gorlagon, and Alphonse experience while in their lupine form also allow them to demonstrate just how extraordinary — just how marvelous — they are. In addition, marvels are expected to possess secret meanings. According to Kelly, "the marvelous provides the mystery and singularity fundamental to romance adventure" (154). In all of the werewolf tales, those who observe the beast's courtly behavior marvel at it. In the shorter tales, the werewolf's violence causes them to marvel anew, thus arousing their curiosity and generating a mystery that they feel compelled to solve. In *Guillaume de Palerne,* the eponymous hero marvels at Alphonse's chivalrous behavior; mystified by it, Guillaume immediately instigates an investigation into the werewolf's identity. But this particular mystery is never ours to solve; it is for the people living in the worlds created by these authors. As privileged readers of the text, we already know the werewolf's identities and circumstances; indeed, we have known them from the very beginning. The marvel will not dissipate for us until we have understood it, until we have solved our own mystery, the significance of the chivalrous werewolf in the narrative.

The usefulness of the werewolf as an ironic metaphor to warn against facile interpretation also contributes to its new image as a chivalrous hero. Plato (427–347 B.C.) was perhaps the first to use the werewolf as a metaphor. In the following dialogue from *Republic,* Socrates is speaking to Adeimantus:

> "What is the beginning of the transformation from leader of the people to tyrant? Isn't it clear that it happens when the leader begins to behave like the man in the story told about the temple of the Lycean Zeus in Arcadia?"
>
> "What story is that?"
>
> "That anyone who tastes the one piece of human innards that's chopped up with those of other sacrificial victims must inevitably become a wolf. Haven't you heard that story?"
>
> "I have."
>
> "Then doesn't the same happen with a leader of the people who dominates a docile mob and doesn't restrain himself from spilling kindred blood? He brings someone to trial on false charges and murders him (as tyrants so often do), and, by thus blotting out a human life, his impious tongue and lips taste kindred citizen blood. He banishes some, kills others, and drops hints to the people about the cancellation of debts and the redistribution of land. And because of these things, isn't a man like that inevitably fated either to be killed by his enemies or to be transformed from a man into a wolf by becoming a tyrant?" [*Republic* 8.565d].

Plato thus compares the leader who rules like a tyrant to a man who became a werewolf after eating human flesh. We find a similar notion in the Bible, where the bad leaders of Israel are compared to wolves: "Her princes in the midst thereof are like wolves ravening the prey, to shed blood, and to destroy souls, to get dishonest gain."[11] The Christian philosopher Anicius Manlius Severinius Boethius (c. A.D. 480–524), who has been called the "last of the Roman philosophers and the first of the scholastic theologians"[12] reiterates this comparison on two occasions:

> But since virtue alone can exalt us above men, wickedness must needs cast those under the desert of men, which it hast bereaved of that condition.

> Wherefore thou canst not account him a man whom thou seest transformed by vices. Is the violent extorter of other men's goods carried away with his covetous desire? Thou mayest liken him to a wolf [319; 4.Prose.3].
>
> So that he who, leaving virtue, ceaseth to be a man, since he cannot be partaker of the divine condition, is turned into a beast [321; 4.Prose.3]

Boethius thus equates vice with the agent that transforms man into a beast; without virtue, he has no hope for salvation. There is no magic at work here; it is simply a question of choice. Similarly, Dubost suggests that the werewolf motif in medieval literature functions as a metaphoric initiation rite into the exclusive world of the aristocracy:

> Dans la littérature médiévale, le motif de la lycanthropie entre dans le jeu du "miroir des princes." Il est alors soustrait au champ fantastique comme a celui des grandes terreurs mythiques, pour servir de support à une réflexion sur la nature de l'être aristocratique afin d'en illustrer l'excellence. La permanence d'une nature incorruptible et infrangible à travers les avatars les plus dégradants ou les plus avilissants, comme le passage par l'animalité, et malgré l'action pernicieuse des agents du mal (la femme), tel est, semble-t-il, le véritable enjeu moral et social des histoires médiévales de loups-garous [565].
>
> In medieval literature, the motif of lycanthropy goes along with the "mirror for princes." Thus it is removed from the realm of fantasy and from that of the great mythical terrors to serve as a foundation for reflecting about the nature of aristocracy in order to illustrate its excellence. An incorruptible and inviolable nature that endures through the most degrading or most demeaning misadventures, such as becoming an animal, and in spite of the pernicious action of agents of evil (the woman), this seems to be the true moral and social issue of the medieval stories of werewolves.

For Alphonse and the other werewolves, their metamorphosis, as well as the hardships that they must endure because of it, allows them to demonstrate their worth. The poet uses the enormous changes in their appearance after their transformation to accentuate that part of their nature that remains consistent, their nobility. The behavior of the villains in each narrative contrasts with and makes the werewolf's nobility even more apparent. Although frequently obscured by shifting illusions, careful interpretation will always discern the hidden truth. As Plato and Boethius would say, Bisclavret, Melion, Gorlagon, and Alphonse are not the real werewolves in these narratives; the real werewolves are those who seek to harm them.

Finally, the cultural trauma resulting from an incident of cannibalism during the First Crusade plays an important role in this new interest in werewolves in the twelfth century and the dramatic change in their portrayal. The connection between werewolves and cannibals is an old one, going back to some of the first recorded stories. In our examination of Ovid's myth of

Lycaon, we saw that he is transformed into a wolf because he offered human flesh to Zeus.[13] Pliny also recounts the legend of the Arcadian werewolves, who recover their human forms if they abstain from eating human flesh for nine years while in their lupine forms.[14] But these, of course, are just myths. In December 1098, however, after the siege of Ma'arra an-Numan in northern Syria, Christian crusaders ate the flesh of Saracens who had died in the attack.[15] The incident is described by three different chroniclers, who, according to Geraldine Heng, "are immediately driven to defend the cannibalism by invoking extreme famine as exigent explanation" (22).[16] Sometime between 1130 and 1139, Geoffrey of Monmouth wrote his *Historia Regum Britannie* (*History of the Kings of Britain*). This text is especially noteworthy because in it King Arthur makes his first literary appearance. Furthermore, according to Heng, there is a direct link between this narrative and the cannibalism incident at Ma'arra an-Numan in 1098. Heng argues that "[r]omance ... is the name of a developing narrational modality and apparatus in Geoffrey's text that coalesces from the cultural matrix at hand to effect specific forms of cultural rescue" (18). In other words, romance provides a safe medium to deal with the horrific and the taboo. Thus we learn in Geoffrey's *Historia* about Helena, who has been kidnapped by a hideous giant cannibal and taken to Mont Saint-Michel. Frightened to death, she dies before Arthur can rescue her, but her elderly nurse, who has been raped over and over again by the giant, is saved by the king, who then slays the cannibal. As Heng notes:

> [T]he record of the Middle Ages suggests that the charge of cannibalism is one of those instrumentally useful technologies of definition by which the malignant otherness of cultural enemies and outcasts can be established and periodically renewed. Witches, Jews, savages, Orientals, and pagans are conceivable as — indeed, must be — cannibals; but in the twelfth-century medieval imaginary, the Christian European subject cannot, and must not [28–29].

Geoffrey makes his cannibal a hideous giant and has his hero King Arthur slay the cannibal. In so doing, he metaphorically resolves the problem. But the issue of cannibalism remains. Although Bynum does not connect it to the incident at Ma'arra an-Numan, she tells us that at this time people were concerned that receiving the Eucharist was an act of cannibalism.[17] Leslie Dunton-Downer makes a similar observation, but ties it directly to the literary representation of the werewolf:

> The transformation of the literary werewolf in terms of reevaluations of humanness must also be understood in the context of twelfth-century preoccupations with the Eucharistic rite and the important debates regarding the nature of the host. These debates included the problems of Christ's dual nature (human and divine), the host's dual nature (as bread and body of

> Christ) and the difficult nature of its reception (did one masticate Christ's body cannibalistically, or was it a representation of Christ's body that one ingested?). In dealing with the werewolf as a dual creature, a man who appears to be an animal, the secular *Bisclavret* invites its audience to reflect on and redefine itself in relation to sacred models of the miraculous [212].

We have already seen a more direct connection between the Eucharist and werewolves in our study. Scholars criticize Gerald of Wales' account of the Ossory werewolves for its juxtaposition of lycanthropy and the mystery of transubstantiation, while in the tale itself, the priest is forced to defend the fact that he gave communion to the female werewolf.[18] But there is something more pertinent to our study that must be considered. If Heng is correct, then it is very possible, indeed, it is very likely, that the figure of the werewolf is also used to deal with the cultural trauma of cannibalism. The werewolf had already been established as a cannibal, or at the very least a potential cannibal, in Ovid's *Metamorphoses*. Marie de France begins her *lai* telling how the "garvalf," "werewolf," "devours men" (11), but she never refers to Bisclavret as a "garvalf." When his wife asks him what he does when he disappears for three days every week, Bisclavret tells her that he lives "off prey and plunder" (66). He never says that he "devours men." Although the traditional werewolf depicted at the beginning of Marie's *lai* is a cannibal, Bisclavret is not. As for Melion, although the depiction of this werewolf is very violent—we are told that he "killed and strangled many" (255) cows and oxen and that he "killed men and women" (277)—the only thing he is ever shown eating is the piece of meat from the stag that he killed for his wife (251). Like Melion, Gorlagon is also portrayed in a violent manner, slaughtering animals and people and "greedy for bloodshed" (241). He too is never depicted eating anything. In spite of these facts, it is very possible to read all three and totally miss the fact that these werewolves are not presented as cannibals. Our attention is directed elsewhere. In *Guillaume de Palerne,* however, the *leitmotif* of the *goule baee*, the werewolf's gaping mouth, constantly highlights the fact that this wolf's mouth is empty.[19] The *leitmotif* also points to a contradiction: although Alphonse's mouth is frequently depicted "gaping open," he is never shown eating or even biting any living creature. Thus, his empty gaping mouth signifies the absence of cannibalized flesh. Furthermore, this werewolf is portrayed not just as a chivalrous werewolf, but as the embodiment of the Christian concept of selfless service to others. If the giant in Geoffrey of Monmouth's *Historia* allows cannibalism to be displaced into romance where it can be safely discussed, the werewolf in *Guillaume de Palerne* goes one step further and accomplishes something that Geoffrey's giant does not; it entirely erases the notion of cannibalism and redeems the image of the Christian knight.

Each of the literary medieval werewolf tales challenges us to discover "[q]ue cele beste senefie," "what this beast signifies"—what the message is that lies hidden beneath the beast's illusory appearance. Thus like the werewolves, the tales are also much more than they seem. They are not just stories about werewolves. In the Prologue to her *lais*, Marie herself speaks of the need to "gloser la lettre / [e] de lur sen le surplus mettre" (15–16), "comment on the text / and add their own knowledge to it." In the prologue to *Guillaume de Palerne*, the poet talks of "sens celé" (11), "hidden wisdom," but in a romance of 9,667 verses, he reveals Alphonse's identity almost immediately in verse 281. Indeed, Guillaume actually asks "[q]ue cele beste signifie" (7270), "what this beast signifies." Finally, the fact that the author of each narrative emphasizes the werewolf's residual humanity, which reveals itself in spite of his bestial appearance and varying levels of brutality and docility, alerts us to the need to search for the real significance of these tales. As we have seen, each tale is used to teach a different lesson.[20] The werewolf is just a device to get our attention; he is just a messenger. And with him in the tale, we end up with a pretty good story.

Like the twelfth century, the sixteenth century also experiences a werewolf renaissance, for in the sixteenth century we find a sudden increase, indeed a veritable explosion, of texts dealing with werewolves. Unlike the twelfth century, however, the werewolf depicted in these sixteenth-century texts is not at all the chivalrous hero of the twelfth-century renaissance, but rather the traditional ferocious werewolf of antiquity. Furthermore, unlike his twelfth-century counterpart, this new werewolf is not a noble prince or knight; instead, the creature is now a coarse peasant. The most striking difference, however, is the fact that these sixteenth-century werewolves are not presented as literary inventions but as historical reality. But were there really werewolves in the sixteenth century? We will never know for sure. We can say with utmost confidence that there were real wolves at this time attacking and eating people. We can also say that there were real people committing atrocious crimes and that at least one incident involved cannibalism. In addition, we know that people were taught that it was heresy not to believe in the reality of witches and werewolves. Just as we saw with the "werewolf renaissance of the twelfth century," many conditions—albeit different ones—come together to generate the sixteenth-century werewolf renaissance. Included among them are certainly the persecution of witches, the wars of religion, economic conditions in France, and a renewed focus on the Eucharist.

The first factor influencing the revival of the traditional werewolf is the persecution of witches in the sixteenth century. As we have seen, in *Malleus maleficarum* (*The Witches Hammer*), Heinrich Kramer states that anyone who does not believe that witches are real and that they have the ability to fly and transform themselves is committing heresy. His assertion that witches can transform themselves links the practice of sorcery with werewolves. His treatise not only made belief in werewolves permissible, but also made this belief mandatory for those Christians who did not want to be accused of blasphemy and heresy. The *Malleus* had a profound and widespread influence on beliefs and behavior over the next hundred years as Europe was caught up in a frantic witch hunt. Among the thousands put on trial for sorcery were a handful of men and women, primarily in France, who confessed to being werewolves. Kramer's text, whose message was reiterated by others throughout the sixteenth century, played a significant role in creating the psychological climate in which people believed they had transformed themselves into wolves and the witnesses of their crimes felt duty-bound as good Christians to corroborate the testimony of these "werewolves."

The series of religious wars ripping France apart in the sixteenth century also contribute to this new renaissance of the werewolf. Although this era in France is best known for its rebirth of culture, so well known, in fact, that the century itself is more frequently referred to as "the" Renaissance, eight different wars broke out between the Catholics and the Huguenots in the thirty-eight years from 1562 until the end of the century. Bertier de Sauvigny points out that "[s]i les historiens ont généralement compté huit guerres successives, c'est que les hostilités se trouvèrent arrêtées ou ralenties par autant de trêves ou traités, presque aussitôt violés. En fait, la lutte fut pratiquement continue pendant plus de trente ans" (160). "If historians have generally counted eight successive wars, it is because hostilities were stopped or slowed down by just as many truces or treaties, which were almost immediately broken. In fact, fighting was virtually continuous for more than thirty years." According to Max P. Holt, France was the "only state in sixteenth-century Europe to experience such a violent and protracted series of civil wars" because of its proximity to Geneva, the site of Calvin's exile, and because "royal religious policy in France vacillated and changed throughout the second half of the sixteenth century" (191, 192). One of the most notorious events that occurred during the wars was the Massacre of St. Bartholomew, which began in Paris on August 24, 1572, filling the Seine with blood from the bodies that were thrown into it, and then spread over the next two months to twelve different cities throughout France. During the three bloody days of the Paris massacre, some two thousand Protestants were killed; approximately three thousand more were killed in the massacres that took place in the provinces over the next two month (Holt, 94). Almost all the murders shared a common characteristic:

> Viewed by Catholics as threats to the social and political order, Huguenots not only had to be exterminated — that is, killed — they also had to be humiliated, dishonoured, and shamed as the inhuman beasts they were perceived

> to be. The victims had to be dehumanized — slaughtered like animals — since they had violated all the sacred laws of humanity in Catholic culture. Moreover, death was followed by purification of the places the Huguenots had profaned. Many Protestant houses were burned, invoking the traditional purification by fire of all heretics. Many victims were also thrown into the Seine, invoking the purification by water of Catholic baptism. In fact, upon closer inspection the grisly deaths of hundreds of Protestants in Paris on St Bartholomew's night and after reveal distinct patterns of what Professor Natalie Davis has called the "rites of violence".... The provincial cities experienced the same ritualistic murders, the same mutilation of corpses, and the same treatment of pregnant women as in the capital; they each experienced their own version of the Parisian "rites of violence" [Holt, 87, 93].

Although the first Protestants were murdered by the king's men, the majority were killed by "members of the lower classes" who felt that they were "acting on behalf of the king and with the full support of God's divine will" (Holt, 93). In the conclusion to his study, Holt reminds us that although the "ruling elites" were certainly in control, "the feelings, behaviour, and actions of the popular classes were not only significant, but in some cases they were crucial to the story of the civil wars" (191). Indeed, in addition to the eight religious wars, there were also numerous peasant revolts, including several in southwestern France in 1594. The peasants who participated in these revolts called the "nobility *croquants*, saying they only wished to chew up the people. But the nobles turned this nickname of *croquants* against the rebels, on whom it stuck."[21] Jean Grenier, whose case was the last one that we studied, was from this region. His father, Pierre Grenier, was commonly called "le croquant."[22] Is this just a coincidence or is there a cause and effect relationship between the religious wars and the werewolf cases? Witnessing and participating in unspeakable atrocities certainly had to have horrendous consequences on the mental well-being of everyone involved. In addition, the loss in life was tremendous during the religious wars. According to a pamphlet published in 1581, "the civil wars had resulted in the death of 765,200 French men and women as a result of the wars: 8,760 clergymen, 32,950 nobles from both religions, 36,300 civilian male commoners, 1,235 civilian female commoners, 656,000 French troops, and 32,600 foreign troops."[23] All these deaths added to the general societal malaise.

Economic conditions were another major contributing factor to the sixteenth century renaissance of the werewolf. Although the economy was healthy and living conditions were good during the first part of the century, the wars coincided with economic problems and harvest failures:

> The unrestrained population growth since the end of the Hundred Years' War had by then already approached the ceiling of the available arable land and food supply. Prices of all goods, but especially foodstuffs, were already

> running significantly ahead of wages, with the inevitable decline in living standards for many. Moreover, the 1580s and 1590s — which coincided with the wars of the League — also witnessed the most severe and closely spaced series of harvest failures and food shortages in the entire sixteenth century. This resulted in widespread famine and economic distress not only in France, but in much of Europe. All of these economic forces, both the positive and the negative, were independent of the civil wars and would have occurred whether the Wars of Religion had broken out in 1562 or not. So, any attempt to distinguish the effects of war from these economic changes is bound to be problematic [Holt, 194–95].

Mortality rates, wheat prices, and the cost of living were all at their highest in the last two decades of the sixteenth century.[24] These increases coincided, more or less, with the surge in texts regarding werewolves. Although the religious wars and the economic troubles had devastating consequences for everyone, the lower classes — those who were least educated and most likely to believe what others might not — tended to suffer the most.[25] In addition, they had already been told that as good Christians they must believe in witches and werewolves. In Claude Prieur's *Dialogue de la Lycanthropie*, we saw Scipion lamenting the miseries of the times, with bad weather, illnesses, and neighbors fighting wars against one another.[26] Agrippa d'Aubigné, a Huguenot and the squire of Henri de Navarre, the future Henri IV, describes some of the effects of the wars of religion in *Misères,* the first book of his epic poem *Les Tragiques*[27]:

> Les Rois, qui sont du peuple et les Rois et les peres,
> Du troupeau domesticq sont les loups sanguinaires;
> Ils sont l'ire allumee et les verges de Dieu,
> 200 La crainte des vivans: ils succedent au lieu
> Des heritiers des morts; ravisseurs de pucelles,
> Adulteres, souillans les couches des plus belles
> Des maris assommez ou bannis pour leur bien,
> Ils courent sans repos, et quand ils n'ont plus rien
> 205 Pour fouler l'avarice, ils cerchent autre sorte
> Qui contente l'esprit d'une ordure plus forte.
> Les vieillards enrichis tremblent le long du jour;
> Les femmes, les maris, privez de leur amour,
> Par l'espais de la nuict se mettent â la fuite,
> 210 Les meurtriers souldoyez s'eschauffent a la suite;
> L'homme est en proye à l'homme, un loup à son pareil;
> Le pere estrangle au lict le fils, et le cercueil
> Preparé par le fils sollicite le pere;
> Le frere avant le temps herite de son frere [197–214].

> The kings, who are both the kings and the fathers of the people,
> Are the blood-thirsty wolves of the household flock;

They are the wrath of God that has been aroused and his whipping sticks,
200 The fear of those alive: they inherit instead
Of the legitimate heirs of the dead; abductors of maidens,
Adulterers, sullying the beds of the most beautiful [wives of]
Husbands killed or banished for their possessions,
They run without resting, and when they no longer have anything
205 To satisfy their greed, they look for another way
That will content their mind with filth that is stronger.
The elderly who have grown rich tremble all day long;
Wives, husbands, deprived of their love,
In the depth of the night make their escape,
210 The hired murderers work themselves up about following them;
Man is a prey to man, like a wolf to his fellow man;
The father strangles his son in his bed, and the coffin
Prepared by the son beckons to the father;
Before his time the brother inherits from his brother.

In this passage dominated by fear and the destruction of the family and, indeed, of society itself, we see the same idea that evil transforms men into wolves — the kings are the "blood-thirsty wolves of the household flock" and man is "like a wolf to his fellow man" — that we have already seen in the writings of Plato and Boethius, as well as in the Biblical passage cited earlier. In the following passage, D'Aubigné continues to develop the idea of man's "transformation":

Car pour *monstrer* comment en la destruction
L'homme n'est plus un homme, il prend refection
Des herbes, de charongne et viandes non-prestes,
Ravissant les repas apprestez pour les bestes;
315 La racine douteuse est prise sans danger,
Bonne, si on la peut amollir et manger;
Le conseil de la faim apprend aux dents par force
A piller des forests et la robbe et l'escorce.
La terre sans façon a honte de se voir,
320 Cerche encore des mains et n'en peut plus avoir.
Tout logis est exil: les villages champestres,
Sans portes et planchers, sans meubles et fenestres,
Font une mine affreuse, ainsi que le corps mort
Monstre, en *monstrant* les os, que quelqu'un lui fait tort.
325 Les loups et les renards et les bestes sauvages
Tienent place d'humains, possedent les villages,
Si bien qu'en mesme lieu, où en paix on eut soin
De reserrer le pain, on y cueille le foin [311–28].

For in order to show how in the destruction
Man is no longer a man, he takes refreshment
From the grasses, from cadavers and raw meats,

Stealing the meals prepared for the beasts;
315 The questionnable root is eaten without danger,
Good, if it can be softened and eaten;
The counsel of hunger forcibly teaches the teeth
To pillage from the forests both the husk and the bark.
Without labour the earth is ashamed to see itself,
320 It searches again for workers but can no longer have any.
All dwellings are places of exile: the country villages,
Without doors and floors, without furniture and windows,
Give a frightful appearance, just as the dead body
Shows, by displaying its bones, that someone has harmed it.
325 The wolves and the foxes and the savage beasts
Take the place of humans, possess the villages,
So well that in the same place, where in peace they took care
To conserve bread, [now] hay is gathered.

Although it is lost in the English translation, D'Aubigné reinforces the bestiality—the monstrous character—of man by using the verb "monstrer" "to show" three times, which in its Middle French spelling has not yet lost the "s." He is thus able to engage in a play on words as he reminds his readers that this man who eats the "meals prepared for the beasts" is now a "monstre" "monster." Man has undergone a transformation. In a later passage, D'Aubigné depicts an appalling scene that reveals the ultimate horror of the effects of this war:

La mere du berceau son cher enfant deslie;
L'enfant qu'on desbandoit autres-fois pour sa vie
Se desveloppe ici par les barbares doigts
Qui s'en vont destacher de nature les loix.
505 La mere deffaisant, pitoyable et farouche,
Les liens de pitié avec ceux de sa couche,
Les entrailles d'amour, les filets de son flanc,
Les intestins bruslans par les tressauts du sang,
Le sens, l'humanité, le cœur esmeu qui tremble,
510 Tout cela se destord et se desmesle ensemble.
L'enfant, qui pense encor'aller tirer en vain
Les peaux de la mammelle, a les yeux sur la main....
515 Cette main s'employait pour la vie autres-fois;
Maintenant à la mort elle employe ses doits,
La mort qui d'un costé se presente, effroyable,
La faim de l'autre bout bourrelle impitoyable.
La mere ayant long-temps combatu dans son cœur
520 Le feu de la pitié, de la faim la fureur,
Convoite dans son sein la creature aimee
Et dict à son enfant (moins mere qu'affamee):
«Rends miserable, rends le corps que je t'ay faict;

Ton sang retournera où tu as pris le laict,
525 Au sein qui t'allaictoit r'entre contre nature;
Ce sein qui t'a nourri sera ta sepulture.»
La main tremble en tirant le funeste couteau,
Quand, pour sacrifier de son ventre l'agneau,
Des poulces ell' estreind la gorge, qui gazouille
530 Quelques mots sans accents, croyant qu'on la chatouille:
Sur l'effroyable coup le cœur se refroidit.
Deux fois le fer eschappe à la main qui roidit.
Tout est troublé, confus, en l'ame qui se trouve
N'avoir plus rien de mere, et avoir tout de louve.
535 De sa levre ternie il sort des feux ardens,
Elle n'appreste plus les levres, mais les dents,
Et des baizers changés en avides morsures.
La faim acheve tout de trois rudes blessures,
Elle ouvre le passage au sang et aux esprits;
540 L'enfant change visage et ses ris en ses cris;
Il pousse trois fumeaux, et n'ayant plus de mere,
Mourant, cerche des yeux les yeux de sa meurtriere [501–42].

The mother unties her dear child from its cradle;
The child that was released at other times for his life
Is being unwrapped here by barbaric fingers
That are detaching themselves from the laws of nature.
505 The mother undoing, pitiful and wild,
The bonds of pity with those of the child she gave birth to,
Womb of love, little baby from her flanks,
Her intestines burning from the surging of her blood,
Her mind, her humanity, her agitated heart which is trembling,
510 All these are untwisting and disentangling from each other.
The infant, who thinks she is again going to pull in vain
The skin of the breast, has her eyes on the hand...
515 This hand that was used for life at other times;
Now she is using her fingers for death,
On one side death presents itself, frightening,
On the other end is hunger, the executioner without pity.
The mother, having fought for a long time in her heart
520 The fire of pity, the rage of hunger,
Covets in her breast the beloved creature
And says to her child (less a mother than someone who is starving):
"Surrender miserable creature, surrender the body that I made for you;
Your blood will return where you took milk,
525 To the breast which nursed you it will reenter against nature;
This breast which fed you will be your sepulture."
Her hand trembles while drawing the deadly knife,
When, in order to sacrifice the lamb from her womb,
With her thumbs she seizes the infant's throat, which babbles

530 A few words without accents, believing that she is being tickled:
With the horrifying cut the heart is becoming cold.
Twice the blade escapes from the hand that is stiffening.
Everything is troubled, confused, in the soul that discovers
It no longer has any qualities of a mother, and has all those of a wolf.
535 Flaming fires come out from her lifeless lips,
She no longer prepares her lips, but readies her teeth instead,
And her kisses are changed into greedy bites.
Hunger completes three crude wounds,
It opens the passage for the blood and the spirit;
540 The infant transforms its face and its laugh into screams;
It lets outs three breaths of air, and no longer having a mother,
Dying, searches with its eyes for the eyes of its murderess.

Like the men who transform themselves into werewolves, this mother has transformed herself into the murderer of her own child. Worse yet, she has become a cannibal as she feeds on the flesh of her child. Some might say that what is portrayed here is just the product of an overactive imagination, the ravings of a madman, or perhaps the propaganda of a Huguenot seeking to advance his cause, if it were not for the following account related by the English ambassador to France in 1586:

> Here have been with the King two deputies, one from Xaintonge and the other of Périgord, who, upon their knees have humbly desired the King to make a peace and to have pity upon his poor people, whose want was such as they were forced to eat bread made of ardoise and of nut-shells, which they brought and showed to the King. They told him also that the famine was so great as a woman in Périgord had already eaten two of her children and the like had been done in Xaintonge... Many thousand there [are] already dead for hunger, and, in that extremity ... that they feed upon grass ... like horses and die with grass in their mouths.[28]

Thus because of the wars and because of economic conditions and resulting famine, the poor, who have nothing to protect them when they have already lost the very little that they had, are "like horses" and have nothing to eat but grass. Some of them are even reduced to eating their own children. The majority, of course, would die before they would ever descend to such bestial behavior and as a result "many thousand" die from hunger. As we have seen, in *Dialogue de la Lycanthropie* Claude Prieur writes of the extraordinary boldness of the wolves that he, or rather Proteron, encountered in the Périgord region in 1587. Prieur attributes this boldness to the fact that all the livestock had been killed in the war and that wolves had now acquired a taste for human flesh. Starving humans who resort to cannibalism and starving wolves thus combine to create the model for a new werewolf for the sixteenth-century.

Finally, a renewed focus on the Eucharist also heavily influences the sixteenth century werewolf renaissance. On October 18, 1534, a manifesto, which was written by Antoine Marcourt, a Protestant, against the Catholic mass was posted all over France so that Catholics would see them on their way to mass that morning. One was even posted on the door of François Premier's bedchamber. The manifesto stated that the Catholic Church's pretense at repeating Christ's sacrifice in the mass is blasphemous, since his original sacrifice was perfect, that Communion is just symbolic since the body of Christ is in heaven with God, not present in the bread and wine, and that the doctrine of transubstantiation contradicts Holy Scripture. The last paragraph of Marcourt's manifesto is of particular interest to our study:

> By this [mass] the poor people are like ewes or miserable sheep, kept and maintained by these bewitching wolves [Catholic priests], then eaten, gnawed, and devoured. Is there anyone who would not say or think that this is larceny and debauchery? By this mass they have seized, destroyed, and swallowed up everything; they have disinherited kings, princes, nobles, merchants, and everyone else imaginable either dead or alive. Because of it, they live without any duties or responsibility to anyone or anything, even to the need to study. What more do you want? Do not be amazed then that they defend it with such force. They kill, burn, destroy, and murder as brigands all those who contradict them, for now all they have left is force. Truth is lacking in them, but it menaces them, follows them, and chases them; and in the end truth will find them out. By it they shall be destroyed.[29]

Comparing Catholic priests to wolves that bewitched their parishioners and then proceeded to devour them, Marcourt's manifesto had profound consequences. Even though the "Affaire des placards" 'Affair of the Placards' did not directly cause the Wars of Religion, it did initiate the persecution of Protestants, some of whom were tried as heretics and burned at the stake. In addition, Jean Calvin, one of the leaders of French Protestantism, was forced to leave France and go into exile in Switzerland. Marcourt's comparison also place's the Protestant attitude toward the Holy Eucharist, or at the very least one sixteenth-century man's attitude toward the Holy Eucharist, on the same level — that is, metaphorically — with sorcery and lycanthropy. For Marcourt, priests are witches, they are wolves, thus werewolves, and they are cannibals.

In 1572, Michel de Montaigne began to write his *Essais*, which were first published in 1580.[30] In one of his essays, "Des cannibales" Montaigne writes about the discovery of "cet autre monde qui a esté descouvert en nostre siecle, en l'endroit où Vilegaignon print terre" (I.31.203a), "this other world that was discovered in our century, in the place where Vilegaignon landed [on the coast of Brazil]." Montaigne begins his discussion of this new world by redefining the word "sauvage, "savage, wild":

> [I]l n'y a rien de barbare et de sauvage en cette nation, à ce qu'on m'en a rapporté, sinon que chacun appelle barbarie ce qui n'est pas de son usage....

> Ils sont sauvages, de mesmes que nous appellons sauvages les fruicts que nature, de soy et de son progrez ordinaire, a produicts ... [I.31.205.a].
>
> There is nothing barbaric or savage about this nation, as far as what has been reported to me about it, except that everyone calls barbarism what they are not used to.... They are savages [wild] in the same way that we call wild [savage] the fruits that nature, by itself and its ordinary progress, has produced....

Throughout the rest of his essay, Montaigne idealizes the "savages" of this new world. Eventually, however, he reveals that one of their customs includes eating their prisoners of war:

> Apres avoir long temps bien traité leurs prisonniers, et de toutes les commoditez dont ils se peuvent aviser, celuy qui en est le maistre, faict une grande assemblée de ses cognoissans: il attache une corde à l'un des bras du prisonnier, [C] par le bout de laquelle il le tient, esloigné de quelques pas, de peur d'en estre offencé, [A] et donne au plus cher de ses amis l'autre bras à tenir de mesme; et eux deux, en presence de toute l'assemblée, l'assomment à coups d'espée. Cela faict, ils le rotissent et en mangent en commun et en envoient des lopins à ceux de leurs amis qui sont absens. Ce n'est pas, comme on pense, pour s'en nourrir, ainsi que faisoient anciennement les Scythes: c'est pour representer une extreme vengeance [I.31.209.a,c].
>
> After having treated their prisoners well for a long time, and all the comforts they might think of, the one who is the prisoner's owner calls a great assembly of his acquaintances: he attaches a cord to one of the prisoner's arms, [C] and holds on to the end of it, a few steps away, for fear of being attacked, [A] and gives to the dearest of his friends the other arm to hold in the same way; and the two of them, in the presence of the whole assembly, kill him with a sword. That done, they roast him and eat him in common and send pieces of him to those of their friends who are absent. This is not done, as one thinks, for nourishment, as the Scythes formerly did it: it is done as a display of utmost vengeance.

These new world cannibals with their ritual displays of vengeance are not at all like the werewolf cannibals that we have seen, nor do they resemble the mother depicted by D'Aubigné in *Les Tragiques*. As Montaigne notes, more barbaric acts have occurred in France:

> Je pense qu'il y a plus de barbarie à manger un homme vivant qu'à le manger mort, à deschirer, par tourmens et par geénes, un corps encore plein de sentiment, le faire rostir par le menu, le faire mordre et meurtrir aux chiens et aux pourceaux (comme nous l'avons, non seulement leu, mais veu de fresche memoire, non entre des ennemis anciens, mais entre des voisins et concitoyens, et, qui pis est, sous pretexte de pieté et de religion), que de le rostir et manger apres qu'il est trespassé [I.31.209.a].
>
> I think that there is more barbarism in eating a man who is still alive than in eating a man that is dead, to tear to pieces, by means of physical agony

> and torture, a body still endowed with all its senses, to roast him bit by bit, to have a man bitten and killed by dogs and swine (as we have, not only read, but seen in recent memory, not between old enemies, but between neighbors and fellow citizens, and, what is worse, under the pretext of piety and religion), than to roast him and eat him after he has died.

According to Montaigne, then, the cannibalism that occurs in the new world is preferable, less barbaric, than the atrocities that have been committed during the wars of religion in France. Montaigne thus uses his essay, and more specifically this comparison between the cannibals of Brazil and his fellow citizens and fellow Catholics, to offer a biting criticism of what has been occurring in France in the name of religion. Indeed, Montaigne declares almost immediately, "Nous les pouvons donq bien appeller barbares, eu esgard aux regles de la raison, mais non eu esgard à nous, qui les surpassons en toute sorte de barbarie." (I.31.210a) 'We can therefore truly call them barbaric, with regard to the rules of reason, but not with regard to us, who surpass them in all kinds of barbarity.' After discussing at length the true nature of valor and honor, Montaigne returns to his discussion of the cannibals and their prisoners:

> J'ay une chanson faicte par un prisonnier, où il y a ce traict: qu'ils viennent hardiment trétous et s'assemblent pour disner de luy: car ils mangeront quant et quant leurs peres et leurs ayeux, qui ont servy d'aliment et de nourriture à son corps. Ces muscles, dit-il, cette cher et ces veines, ce sont les votres, pauvres fols que vous estes; vous ne recognoissez pas que la substance des membres de vos ancestres s'y tient encore: savourez les bien, vous y trouverez le goust de vostre propre chair. Invention qui ne sent aucunement la barbarie. Ceux qui les peignent mourans, et qui representent cette action quand on les assomme, ils peignent le prisonnier crachant au visage de ceux qui le tuent et leur faisant la mouë. De vray, ils ne cessent jusques au dernier souspir de les braver et deffier de parole et de contenance [I.31.212.a].
>
> I have a song made by a prisoner, where there is this taunt: let them all boldly come and assemble to dine on him: for they will eat at the same time their fathers and their forefathers, who served as food and nourishment for his body. These muscles, he said, this flesh and these veins, are yours, poor fools that you are; you do not recognize that the substance of your ancestors' limbs is still there: savor them well, you will find the taste of your own flesh there. That's an invention which does not seem at all barbaric. Those who paint them dying, and who portray the action when they are killed, paint the prisoner making faces and spitting at those who are killing him. In truth, until their last breath they do not stop challenging and defying them with their words and attitude.

As George Hoffman has so convincingly argued in his article "Anatomy of the Mass: Montaigne's 'Cannibals,'" the prisoner's challenge recalls the

Catholic Eucharist, in which the priest consecrates the bread and wine, saying, "Take, eat. For this is my body, which is broken for you, and divided for the remission of sins.... Drink ye all of it. For this is my blood of the new testament which is shed for you and for many, and distributed among you for the remission of sins."[31] According to Hoffman, Montaigne's essay appears to be "a ludic inversion of the High Mass, a transposition of eucharistic [sic] rites onto cannibalistic ritual to radically defamiliarize the paradoxical sacrifice of god, rather than to god, that lies at the heart of Christian belief" (212). It is, of course, not sacrifice of god, but rather *self*-sacrifice of god that "lies at the heart of Christian belief." Although this is a small distinction, it is an important one. For the ritual of the Catholic mass, in which sixteenth-century Protestants saw Catholics re-enacting Christ's sacrifice, breaking his body, and eating it in the form of the Host, was a major factor in the dissension between Protestants and Catholics. For the Protestants it was an act of blasphemy. For the Catholics it was an act that brought them in union not only with God but also with each other because the Church required that they be in a state of grace — that they first confess their sins and restore their relationships with their family, friends, and neighbors — before they could be considered eligible to receive the body and blood of Christ. Protestant pamphlets also accused the Catholics of theophagy: since Catholics believed in the real presence of Christ in the consecrated bread and wine, then they were in effect eating Christ — they were eating God — when they consumed the bread and wine. Protestants, on the other hand, believed only in the symbolic presence of Christ in the Lord's Supper.[32] At the end of his essay, Montaigne writes of three Brazilians who visited Rouen when Charles IX, the king of France, was visiting the city. According to Montaigne, when asked their opinion about what they had seen, they gave three answers, but he could only remember two: that they were surprised that so many adults were obeying a king who was no more than a child and that they were surprised that all the poor people they had seen were not rebelling against the wealthy (I.31.213–14.a). Hoffman proposes that the third opinion that Montaigne "forgot" might have been the Brazilians' surprise, after attending mass with Charles IX, that Catholics eat their god (209). Because of this, Hoffman suggests that "[t]he three natives' omitted views on Christianity, Montaigne's explicit condemnation of his coreligionists' ferocity, and popular Protestant opinion converge in the implication that the true cannibals might be France's Catholics" (210). Of course we cannot say with one hundred per cent confidence what Montaigne forgot any more than we can determine what he was trying to imply in his essay. Nevertheless, what does emerge from a careful reading of "Des cannibales" is the fact that the Eucharist, cannibalism, and the Wars of Religion are inextricably linked and cannot be separated from one another.

The werewolves of the twelfth-century renaissance are nobles who protect others or wage war in order to avenge themselves while in their lupine form. The werewolves of the sixteenth-century renaissance, however, are peasants who attack and eat other human beings while in their lupine form. There is nothing noble about their actions, but, without excusing these actions, it could be argued that everything they do is done to ensure their survival. The twelfth-century werewolf is an idealized werewolf, whereas the sixteenth-century werewolf is a "real" werewolf that reflects the harshness of the peasant world and the reality and turbulence of the times. The differences between these two werewolves are not so surprising, then, especially when the difference in social classes and the violence and economic conditions of the times that the wars of religion created and/or exacerbated are all taken into account. Unlike the twelfth-century werewolves, there is no happy ending or redemption for the werewolves of the sixteenth century. Recognized for the monsters that they are, most of them meet their fate by being burned as witches. But by deflecting attention away from the other cannibalistic violence — as well as away from the other kinds of violence — that occurs during the wars of religion, these werewolves perform, in some small way, a cultural rescue of the sixteenth century. For when most people think of sixteenth-century France, they think of the Renaissance; they do not think of all the blood that was spilled in the last forty years of that century. Though unlike the werewolves of the twelfth century, these new, "reborn" werewolves do not erase the issue of cannibalism, but instead firmly engrave themselves and their horrific acts in cultural memory. This is the enduring legacy that they leave to their heirs, whom we will meet in nineteenth-century Gothic horror stories, twentieth- and twenty-first century Hollywood horror films, twenty-first century adult erotica, and even in Jean Pierre Gaultier's fashion show for his autumn-winter 2008-2009 line, in which he dressed one of his models as a female werewolf returning from her cannibal meal. But the heroic werewolf has his own legacy, too, as any fan of Harry Potter certainly knows. Indeed, today there is a werewolf for everyone and anyone, to suit any taste. And so it seems that werewolves, as a cultural product, have been and always will be a reflection of their time.

Notes

Introduction

1. "Thonne moton tha hyrdas beon swydhe wacore and geornlice clypigende, the widh thonne theodsceadhan folce sceolan scyldan, thaet syndon biscopas and maessepreostas, the godcunde heorda bewarian and bewarian sceolan, mid wislican laran, thaet se wodreca werewulf to swidhe ne lyte ne to fela ne abite of godcundse heorde." "Therefore must be the shepherds be very watchful and diligently crying out, who have to shield the people against the spoiler; such are bishops and mass-priests, who are to preserve and defend their spiritual flocks with wise instructions, that the madly audacious were-wolf do not too widely devastate, nor bite too many of the spiritual flock." Anglo-Saxon text and English translation quoted by Summers (4) from *Ancient Laws and Institutes of England,* ed. B. Thorpe, 1840, pp. 160–1.

2. All translations are mine, unless indicated otherwise.

Chapter One

1. For further information, see *Epic of Gilgamesh*, xi–xvi, 171–218; and *Gilgamesh*, vii–ix, 3–42.

2. *Gilgamesh* 152; Tablet VI, Column ii, vv. 58–63.

3. Virgil, p. 63.

4. Zeus is the supreme god of the Greek pantheon. Jove, who was also known as Jupiter, is the Roman equivalent and is the name actually used by Ovid.

5. There are at least two other versions of the myth: 1) According to Pausanias, a Greek writer of the second century, Lycaon was transformed into a wolf after sacrificing a baby to Zeus (351; VIII, ii, 3); 2) Apollodorus, the second-century Greek mythographer, writes that Lycaon's fifty sons, not Lycaon himself, attempted to deceive Zeus by serving him the flesh of a boy that they had killed. Instead of being transformed into werewolves, they were struck dead by a thunderbolt (Apollodorus, 167). For a discussion of the different versions, see Eckels 55–58.

6. In the second century, Apuleius also describes metamorphosis into a beast, but from his own point of view as he is transformed into an ass. See Apuleius 53; III.24.

7. Petronius ix–xlvi.

8. See Petronius, sec. 61–62.

9. See Suard, "'Bisclauret' et les contes du loup-garou"; Ménard, "Les Histoires de loup-garou"; Smith.

10. Pausanias tells a similar story about an Arcadian boxer named Damarchus who was a wolf for nine years, not ten, but declares that he does not believe "what romancers say about him" (49; VI, viii, 2).

11. Summers offers a brief review of scholarship prior to 1933 regarding belief in werewolves in Arcadia (134–143). See also Douglas 54–66.

12. For a discussion of beliefs about the wolf in Greece, see Eckels 21–31.

13. In 1937 Richard Eckels also classified werewolves in four groups, according to whether they were voluntary or involuntary werewolves and whether their ability to transform themselves was acquired or congenital. Classifying Petronius' werewolf as voluntary / congenital, he failed to notice, however, that a condition one is born with is hardly a matter of choice (41–44).

14. François Suard provides a lengthy comparison of various motifs in werewolf literature, legend, and folktales, as well as a psychoanalytic interpretation of Marie de France's *Bisclavret*. He is primarily interested in the rituals involved in each metamorphosis, however ("'Bisclavret' et les contes du loup-garou").

15. According to Joseph Pappa, "critics have tended to use humanity as a 'catch-phase' for anything that is culturally sanctioned as 'good' (reason, chivalry, society, culture), while shunting the unsanctioned behavior or characteristics (bestial, ravenous appetitive sexuality, sadistic violence) onto the werewolf body" (119). In this study, however, humanity is not used in this way, but is used to refer to *any* and *all* behaviors and characteristics of a human being, without attaching any value judgments to them.

Chapter Two

1. All citations from *On the Soul* are from Tertullian, *Apologetic Works.*

2. "Introduction" to Augustine, *The City of God*, xi.

3. Elsewhere in *The City of God*, we learn that Augustine is referring to the Roman writer and "heathen," Marcus Varro. See especially 185–6, 187, 858.

4. See Chapter One for a discussion of the Arcadian legend and the story of "Daemenetus."

5. For a discussion of the clerical condemnation of superstition and folk culture in the Middle Ages, see Schmitt 14–24.

6. Medieval theologians did not, of course, invent this idea, but found it in the Bible: "And God said, Let us make man in our image, after our likeness" (Bible, King James Version, Gen. 1. 26). "For a man indeed ought not to cover his head, forasmuch as he is the image and glory of God" (Bible, King James Version, 1 Cor. 11.7).

7. See Maertens 193–194 and McGinn 318–319 for further discussion.

8. For additional reading on this subject, see Barkan 97–98; Delcourt, 24–25; Salisbury, 1–11; and Kratz.

9. Augustine notes, however, that Diomedes' men were not transformed into birds, but that birds were merely substituted for his men, just as a deer was substituted for Iphigenia, Agamemnon's daughter.

10. See Harf-Lancner, "La Métamorphose illusoire" and "De la Métamorphose au moyen âge," Kratz, and Dubost 543–550 for their discussions and summaries of clerical texts on werewolves.

11. The provenance of the *Canon Episcopi* has not been established. Regino attributed it to the Council of Anquira, but no one has been able to substantiate this. According to Paul Fournier, Regino himself may be the author of the penitential. Jeffrey Russell believes, however, that it was a Carolingian capitulary. See Lea, I.180, and Russell 76.

12. Translation provided in Lea, I.179.

13. Translation provided in Lea, I.179–80.

14. Translation and Latin text provided in Kratz, 63.

15. See R.M. Thomson's Introduction to William of Malmesbury's *Gesta Regum Anglorum*, xliv.

16. "18 And when Simon saw that through laying on of the apostles' hands the Holy Ghost was given, he offered them money, 19 Saying, Give me also this power, that on whomsoever I lay hands, he may receive the Holy Ghost. 20 But Peter said unto him, Thy money perish with thee, because thou hast thought that the gift of God may be purchased with money. 21 Thou hast neither part nor lot in this matter: for thy heart is not right in the sight of God" (Bible, King James Version, Acts 8. 18–21).

17. The entire *De Universo* has not been translated into English. For the original Latin, see Guillaume d'Auvergne, *Opera Omnia*, (1043; II, 3, 13). This particular passage was translated from Latin into French by Laurence Harf-Lancer and is found in "La Métamorphose illusoire" 214–215.

18. Exod. 7.11–12, 8.7.

19. Job 1.13–19.

20. See Barkan for references for further reading 95–103.

Chapter Three

1. Brecknockshire, which is also known as Breconshire or the County of Brecon, is, like Pembrokeshire, one of the 13 historic counties of Wales.

2. All citations will be from *The Historical Works of Giraldus Cambrensis*, ed. Thomas Wright, trans. Thomas Forester (London: Bell, 1913) 79–84, rpt. in Otten, 57–61.

3. The viaticum is the Eucharist given to a dying person or someone in danger of dying.

4. Noting that he is unaware of any synod meeting in Meath in 1185 or of a dossier on this subject ever being sent to Rome, Don Carey also suggests that Gerald fabricated these details to make his account more believable (49).

5. In *Guillaume de Palerne*, bearskins and deerskins are utilized by the eponymous hero and his sweetheart Melior in order to escape from Rome and evade their pursuers. These disguises are perhaps intertextual allusions to the wolf skin motif in Gerald of Wales' anecdote.

6. Similarly, Francis Dubost declares that the "la réalité de la métamorphose est ici neutralisée," "'the reality of metamorphosis is neutralized here," in Gerald's account, although he says that this is because the curse is attributed to di-

vine decree (939, n. 49). John Carey, on the other hand, notes that he is "tempted to conjecture that [the use of the wolf skin motif] here may be a piece of conscious symbolism on Gerald's part, reflecting his view that beneath their savage exterior the Irish were fundamentally good" (64).

7. For further reading on the Volsung saga and Norse shapeshifters, see Smith (22–29), and Davidson.

8. See Chapter One.

9. According to Boivin, Gerald's juxtaposition of these two examples borders on heresy (58–9).

10. Denyse Delcourt has made a similar observation about the relationship between the two: "Elle [L'Église] arrive à la [la métamorphose] dénier en utilisant, mais renversé, le même ensemble conceptuel qui a servi à avancer la théorie de la transubstantiation" (25), "It [The Church] manages to deny it [metamorphosis] by using the same set of concepts, only inverted, that were used to advance the theory of transubstantiation."

11. A *miroir des princes* is a moral guide written to educate a prince about politics, morality, and courtly behavior.

12. For further reading, see Carey, 52–53.

13. An English translation of the poem is quoted in Carey, 53.

14. According to Carey, two versions of *De Ingantaib Érenn (On the Wonders of Ireland)* exist, "attested in the Book of Ballymote and in Dublin, Trinity College, MS 1336 (formerly H.3.17)" (54). It is the latter that Carey quotes and it is that one that we will be considering here.

15. An English translation of the text is provided in Summers, 206–207.

16. See also Claude Lecouteux for his work on the double.

17. See Chapter One.

18. For further reading on the kings of Ossory, see Carey 57–58.

19. See Chapter Two.

20. For further reading on Melusine, see Harf-Lancner, *Les Fées au moyen âge* and Lecouteux, *Mélusine et le Chevalier au cygne*.

21. For further reading, see the bibliography provided by Summers (129, n.90).

22. The motif of the werewolf running with its mouth gaping open is fully developed in *Guillaume de Palerne and* will be discussed at length in Chapter Seven.

23. For further reading, see Lecouteux, *Witches, Werewolves, and Fairies*, 113–116.

24. See Chapter Four.

Chapter Four

1. For a full discussion, see Rychner, Introduction to his edition of *Les Lais de Marie de France*, viii–xii; Burgess, Introduction to Ewert's edition of *Marie de France Lais*, vii–viii; Hoepffner, 54–55; and Ménard, *Les Lais de Marie de France*, 19–24.

2. For a discussion of attempts to identify Marie, see Burgess, Introduction to Ewert's edition of *Marie de France Lais*, viii–ix; Hoepffner, 48–53; and Ménard, *Les Lais de Marie de France*, 14–19, 28–31.

3. Quoted by Burgess in his introduction to Alfred Ewert's edition of *Marie de France Lais*, v.

4. The manuscript, Harley 978, is at the British Library.

5. Burgess, Introduction to Alfred Ewert's edition of *Marie de France Lais*, v.

6. All citations from *Bisclavret* are from Jean Rychner's edition of *Les Lais de Marie de France*, unless otherwise noted. All translations are mine, unless otherwise noted, and are intended to be as literal as possible in order that they might serve as an aid to reading the original.

7. For a brief overview, see Burgess, *The Lais of Marie de France*, 9. For further reading on the etymology of the term *bisclavret*, see Bailey, Chotzen, Loth, and Sayers.

8. See Chapter Three.

9. See Chapter One.

10. According to Hoepffner, Marie probably found her inspiration for this scene in the biblical story of Samson and Delilah (146).

11. From this moment on in Marie's *lai*, the knight is referred to only as Bisclavret.

12. See Chapter One.

13. See Chapter One.

14. *Les Lais de Marie de France*, 175.

15. "Les Histoires de loup-garou," 220–221.

16. See, for example, *Yonec*, *Guigemar*, and *Le Laustic*.

17. Amanda Hopkins argues, however, that the rewriting of *Bisclavret* as *Biclarel* in the fourteenth-century Old French *Roman de Renart le Contrefait* did produce a misogynous tale. See her study "*Bisclavret* to *Biclarel* Via *Melion* and *Bisclaret*: The Development of a Misogynous *Lai*."

18. Faure has also noted that there is a transfer in affection; the sentiment that formerly existed between husband and wife now binds vassal and king (351).

19. I fail to see any indication in the *lai* of pride or ambition on the part of the wife prior to her betrayal; I would say rather that she made her husband and lover "prey" to her fear.

20. In blaming the wife for Bisclavret's dual nature, Rothschild fails to take into account the fact that he was a werewolf before his wife was

aware of his duality and before she refused to give him the tenderness and understanding he needed.

21. There is nothing in the *lai* to suggest that Bisclavret is afraid of his duality, although there is evidence to suggest he is ashamed of it. Furthermore, there is nothing in the *lai* to suggest that he hasn't *always* controlled his "beast with his human ... understanding and good sense."

22. Benkov has also commented on the wife's hidden identity (34).

23. Hoepffner has also pointed out this similarity (150). M. Faure (350) and Judith Rothschild (137, fn. 118) have also compared Bisclavret's wife to Eve. In her footnote, Rothschild asks "Why should Marie tell us (in 309) that it was the wife who had children (and not the couple)?" I would suggest that the answer to her question is perhaps that it is due to the fact that in the Middle Ages paternity was always unclear, whereas maternity was never in doubt. For this reason, nephews enjoyed a high status. Roland, the nephew of Charlemagne in *La Chanson de Roland* is a good example.

24. Hopkins notes that in *Bisclarel,* the Old Norse translation of Marie de France's *Bisclavret*, Bisclarel tears off his wife's clothes instead of biting off her nose (318).

25. See Burgess, *Lais de Marie de France*, 104; Rothschild, 135, fn 115; Freeman, 296–7; and Benkov, 35–36.

Chapter Five

1. All citations will be from Prudence Mary O'Hara Tobin's edition of *Melion* in *Les Lais anonymes des XIIe et XIIIe siècles.* Unless otherwise indicate, all translations are mine and are intended to be as literal as possible in order that they might serve as an aid to reading the original.

2. See Micha's edition of *Lais féeriques des XIIe et XIIIe siècles* (259, fn. 2), which is a bilingual Old French/Modern French edition of the *Lais anonymes* and is based on Tobin's critical edition.

3. See Micha's edition of *Lais féeriques des XIIe et XIIIe siècles* (259, fn. 2).

4. *Guigemar* (58) in Rychner's edition of *Les Lais de Marie de France.*

5. Bogaert, 91.

6. *Les Fées au moyen âge*, 225.

7. "Les Histoires de loup-garou au moyen-âge," 222.

8. "Metamorphosis and Return in the Lays of *Bisclavret* and *Melion*," n. pag.

9. "Breton Lais," 120. See also Wace's *Roman du Brut*, vv. 9669–9698.

Chapter Six

1. George Kittredge's edition of the text in Latin, *Arthur and Gorlagon: Versions of the Werewolf's Tale*, offers the major study of the tradition. All citations from Kittredge's study will use pagination from original printing. All citations of the tale in English will be from "*Arthur and Gorlagon*," trans. by Frank A. Milne, notes by Alfred Nutt, *Folklore* 15 (1904): 40–67, rpt. in Otten, 234–55. Citations from the translation will use Otten's pagination. According to Kittredge, *Arthur and Gorlagon's* source is Old Irish. John Carey (41–43), Kemp Malone, and A. Haggerty Krappe disagree and believe that an Oriental source is more likely. Loomis also suggests the possibility of a Breton story as its source ("Latin Romances," 478).

2. According to A. Haggerty Krappe (213) and R.E. Bennett (71), Arthur's queen sends him on this quest. Although Arthur is certainly motivated by her comments, there is nothing in the tale to indicate that the quest was imposed on him by his wife.

3. For examples, see Otten, 240, 242, 243, 244, 246, 247, 248, 249. Gorlagon also makes the same comment before beginning his tale (237).

4. Again, see Otten, 240, 242, 243, 244, 246, 247, 248, 249, as well as 237.

5. Gervase of Tilbury relates the story of the werewolf Chaucevaire. Although he does not "narrate" his story, the werewolf provides information about his experiences, which are recorded by Gervase in the third person. See Chapter Three. In *Guillaume de Palerne*, Alphonse narrates some of his experiences as a werewolf after he recovers his human form. See Chapter Seven.

6. See the discussion of Gervase de Tilbury's account of Raimbaud de Pouget in Chapter Three.

7. *Canis* relates the story of a pet — usually a dog — that kills an animal in order to save the life of a baby while the child's father is away. When the father returns home, seeing the blood and the signs of the attack, he kills his pet because he believes that it has killed his son. It is only after killing his faithful pet that he finds the boy safe. On *Canis*, see Schmitt, *The Holy Greyhound*; and Speer, "Specularity in a Formulaic Frame Romance." The motif is also discussed briefly by Kittredge in *Arthur and Gorlagon: Versions of the Werewolf's Tale*, 74–75; and by Malone, 434–438.

8. This is a possible flaw in the story, as Kittredge observes (185). There is no way that Arthur could have known about the sapling, unless the queen or her new husband had told others about it. On the other hand, Gorlagon's sub-

jects also could not have known that he had been transformed into a wolf by his wife unless she or her new husband had told someone.

9. According to Malone (422–423), the source for this motif can be found in various versions of the Oriental tale known as *Rose and Cypress*. Studies of *Arthur and Gorlagon* have dealt almost exclusively with attempting to determine its origin(s).

10. According to Kittredge (200–205) the names of all three brothers mean "werewolf," thus demonstrating that they were "originally three separate manifestations of one and the same person" (205). Loomis refers to Kittredge's etymologies as questionable, however ("Latin Romances," 477). Furthermore, it is not plausible that all three brothers could have been different manifestations of the same person, since their appearance in the tale is not merely sequential. Someone helped Gorlagon; if Gargol and Gorlagon are "one and the same person," then who came to the werewolf's aid?

11. Bacou's assertion is somewhat problematic, since the wife in *Melion* has no lover.

12. See Chapter Four.

13. See Chapter Five.

Chapter Seven

1. "Introduction," *Guillaume de Palerne: An English Translation of the 12th Century French Verse Romance*, 4.

2. All Old French (Picard) citations from *Guillaume de Palerne* are from Alexandre Micha's edition, unless otherwise noted. All English translations are mine and are taken from *Guillaume de Palerne: An English Translation of the 12th Century French Verse Romance*, unless otherwise noted, and are intended to be as literal as possible in order that they might serve as an aid to reading the original.

3. "Introduction," *Guillaume de Palerne: An English Translation of the 12th Century French Verse Romance*, 3.

4. The plot of *Guillaume de Palerne* is as follows: Guillaume is a young prince of Sicily who is kidnapped by a werewolf at the age of four and then brought up by a cowherd. Nathaniel, the Emperor of Rome, finds him in the forest and gives him as page to his daughter Melior. Guillaume and Melior eventually fall in love and flee Rome, disguised in bearskins. The werewolf then reappears in the romance and leads them to Palermo, where Guillaume helps Queen Felise defeat the Spanish armies besieging the city. The werewolf is recognized by the King of Spain as his long-lost son Alphonse. After his stepmother is forced to help him recover his human form, Alphonse reveals Guillaume's identity as Felise's son. Guillaume marries Melior and is crowned king of Apulia and Sicily. Alphonse marries Guillaume's sister Florence and after his father's death takes his place as king of Spain. Later, after the death of Nathaniel, Guillaume becomes the new emperor of Rome.

5. Although Charles Dunn refers to Kittredge's contention, he does not offer an opinion (86, 117).

6. "Les Histoires de loup-garou au moyen-âge," 222. Ménard is not alone. Other critics have commented on the similarities between the tales and *Guillaume de Palerne*. Gaston Paris indicates that the story of the werewolf in *Guillaume de Palerne* is probably based on *Bisclavret* and *Melion* (§67). Although Kittredge points out some resemblances (vv. 7207 ff., 7629 ff., 7731 ff., 7759ff.), he is reluctant to draw a conclusion: "There may or may not be a some connection between *Guillaume de Palerne* and *The Werewolf's Tale*" (36). According to Irene McKeehan, *Guillaume de Palerne* combines the story of the Fair Unknown, the Wolf's Fosterling, the Werewolf's Tale, and allusions to contemporary events (789). Finally, in her edition of *Les Lais anonymes des XIIe et XIIIe siècles*, Tobin notes two similarities between *Guillaume de Palerne* and *Melion*: the werewolf submits to the king inside the king's lodging as opposed to the forest, and the transformation of the wolf into a man occurs under similar conditions in a room with the help of someone else and a magic ring (72). As has been already pointed out, however, it is also very possible that *Guillaume de Palerne* influenced *Melion*, rather than *Melion* influencing *Guillaume de Palerne*. See Chapter Five.

7. See Chapters Four, Five and Six.

8. *Guillaume de Palerne* is not the only werewolf narrative in which the werewolf is transformed by his stepmother. As Alan Bruford points out, "there are two quite distinct œcotypes of the [werewolf's] tale. One is the Irish type which he [Kittredge] studies, where the werewolf is enchanted, as in *Arthur and Gorlagon*, by his faithless wife. The other includes all the Scottish folk versions, and in it the enchantress is the werewolf's stepmother. The wicked stepmother is, of course a commonplace of international folk-tale." (158).

9. Although the poet does not reveal the age of Alphonse at the time of his metamorphosis, he must be more than a year old, since his stepbrother Brandin had already been born. The poet does note, however, that during the two years after the werewolf's arrival in Apulia "Molt devint fiers et fors et grans" (332), "He grew very fierce, strong, and big." This comment suggests that Alphonse is transformed into a young wolf, perhaps even a wolf pup, rather than an adult wolf, to reflect his actual age.

10. Chaucevaire, the French werewolf described by Gervase of Tilbury, explains that a wolf runs with its mouth gaping open because it is so difficult to unlock its jaw. See Chapter Three.

11. For the queen's reaction, see vv. 125–64.

12. The poet first alludes to his source, an ancient story, in verse 20. This allusion to a written source adds authority to his narrative.

13. See Chapter Six.

14. "Introduction" to *Guillaume de Palerne: Roman du XIIIe siècle*, 31.

15. "Introduction" to *Guillaume de Palerne: Roman du XIIIe siècle*, 31.

16. McKeehan offers another intriguing possibility: because of resemblances between *Guillaume de Palerne* and contemporary history, its original audience may have been preoccupied with determining the exact identity of the people to whom the author was alluding with his fictitious characters. See McKeehan's article, "*Guillaume de Palerne*: A Medieval 'Best Seller,'" and "Introduction," *Guillaume de Palerne: An English Translation of the 12th Century French Verse Romance*, 6.

17. Core identity is one of the terms that I developed as part of my dissertation on *Guillaume de Palerne*. I use it to refer to those qualities or characteristics that distinguish the individual from all others. More specifically, it is the individual's fundamental character and as such does not change but remains consistent. See *Metamorphosis and Identity: The Individual in Society in* Guillaume de Palerne, 10–13.

18. See Chapter Two.

19. All citations will be from Mario Roque's edition of Chrétien de Troyes' *Erec et Énide*. All translations are mine, unless otherwise noted, and are intended to be as literal as possible in order that they might serve as an aid to reading the original.

20. See "Glossaire," 248, of Roque's edition of *Erec et Énide*.

21. Burgess, *Contribution*, 50–51.

22. Both Michelant and Micha print this verse without the comma.

23. See, for example, vv. 1916–20, 2753–64 in Ewart's edition of Béroul's *Roman de Tristan*.

24. Literally, he would put himself in a hazardous situation, "en aventure."

25. In Melior's dream, Alphonse also arrives "goule baee" (4016), "his mouth gaping open."

26. For other references to the werewolf's great effort and suffering, see vv. 3869–76, 4080–85, 4135–40.

27. The Strait of Messina, which separates Sicily from mainland Italy, is three kilometers wide at its narrowest point.

28. Even though Guillaume risks his life in the battles against the duke of Saxony and the Spanish army, the narrator never says that Guillaume put his life *en aventure*. Furthermore, both battles are preceded by a speech in which Guillaume reminds the other noblemen of their vassalic duty to fight and serve (1972–84, 5596–5619). The poet thus emphasizes the obligatory character of Guillaume's behavior, whereas he highlights the voluntary nature of the werewolf's conduct.

29. The poet uses a variation of the phrase *goule baee* when Alphonse attempts to attack Brande immediately after his metamorphosis: "Seure li cort geule estendue" (315), "Toward her he runs, his mouth stretched open."

30. "La Métamorphose illusoire," 215.

31. Caroline Walker Bynum notes that "in *Guillaume de Palerne*, a witty werewolf teaches naive lovers to survive and triumph by employing animal disguises" (95). Although Alphonse does provide the stag and doe, whose skins Guillaume and Melior will use to replace the bearskins that they left in the grotto in Benevento, Bynum's comment is a bit of a stretch and inaccurate. The idea for the original bearskin disguises comes from Alixandrine, Melior's cousin and confidante, not from the werewolf (vv. 3011–27). Indeed, the werewolf reappears in the romance only after the two lovers escape from the palace in their bearskin disguises (vv. 3244–49). The werewolf leads the lovers from Rome to Palermo and provides for their needs, but there is no evidence in the text that he ever teaches them anything.

32. For *Bisclavret*, see Chapter Four. For *Arthur and Gorlagon*, see Chapter Six. In *Melion*, Arthur says that the werewolf is tame. See Chapter Five.

33. This passage echoes one from *Le Chevalier au lion* in which Chrétien de Troyes describes the actions of the lion rescued by Yvain (vv. 3388–94).

34. A halberd is a long spear with a wide axe-like head and a spike; a falchion is a large single-sided sword with a curved cutting edge.

35. See Chapter Four.

36. The only other events that could remotely be considered violent are the kidnappings of Guillaume and the provost's son. In addition, the werewolf also kills the stag and the doe in order to procure new disguises for Guillaume and Melior. There is no evidence in the romance of the werewolf killing any animals for his own food; even the skinned bodies of the stag and doe are left behind (v. 4393).

37. *Bisclavret*, v. 288; *Melion*, v. 542.

38. See Chapter Four.

39. See Chapter One.

40. The werewolf was in Apulia for two years before kidnapping Guillaume (vv. 328–31). Guillaume lived with the cowherd and his wife for seven years (v. 359). Guillaume was at the

emperor's court in Rome for three years before he became a knight and before he and Melior fell in love (v. 807).

41. "An Historical Study of the Werwolf in Literature," 19, 26–27. Davidson notes that Norse folklore shows the same connection between outlaws and wolves (152).

42. See Milin, who provides citations from numerous annals and chronicles describing wolf attacks, 23–24.

Chapter Eight

1. An English translation of *Summis desiderantes affectibus* can be found in Montague Summers' translation of Kramer's *Malleus Maleficarum*, 29–32.

2. For centuries, it was thought that Heinrich Kramer — who called himself "Institoris"— and Jakob Sprenger were co-authors of the *Malleus Maleficarum*. According to P.G. Maxwell-Stuart, however, "[i]t is now generally accepted that Jakob Sprenger was not the co-author of the *Malleus*" (*The Malleus Maleficarum*, trans. P.G. Maxwell-Stuart, 30).

3. Kramer, 33. In P. G. Maxwell-Stuart's edition and translation of *The Malleus Maleficarum* this sentence is translated as follows: Is it so much part of orthodox Catholic [doctrine] to maintain that workers of harmful magic do exist that stubbornly maintaining the opposite is in every respect and in all circumstances heretical?" (41). Although Maxwell-Stuart's translation is perhaps more comprehensible to the modern reader, his edition is not a complete translation of the original but includes paraphrases of some passages for brevity's sake. For that reason, unless otherwise indicated, all citations from the *Malleus Maleficarum* will be from Summer's translation.

4. See Anglo's analysis of the *Malleus Maleficarum* in "Evident Authority."

5. All translations in this chapter are mine unless otherwise indicated.

6. Kramer, 33.

7. Kramer, 33–34. In P.G. Maxwell-Stuart's edition and translation of *The Malleus Maleficarum*, the last two sentences are translated as follows: "Therefore it appears they cannot bring about any real change in bodies at all, so that one must trace back this sort of change to some hidden cause" (43).

8. Part I. Question 10, Kramer and Sprenger's *Malleus Maleficarum*, 151–160. See also "Can witches use the art of trickery and deception to change people into animal shape?" Part I Question 10, P.G. Maxwell-Stuart's edition and translation of *The Malleus Maleficarum*, 88–91.

9. In *Guillaume de Palerne*, the werewolf Alphonse exhibits this same behavior and skill, although he never eats or harms the children (Guillaume and the provost's son) that he "snatches." See Chapter Seven.

10. See Chapter 2 for the full story recounted in the thirteenth century by William of Paris, who was also known as Guillaume d'Auvergne.

11. See Chapter Eight.

12. All quotations and citations will be from Mora and Kohl's edition and John Shea's translation: *Witches, Devils, and Doctors in the Renaissance: Johann Weyer, De praestigiis daemonum.*

13. The translation of the French text in this citation is as follows: "who have the power and the particular gift of chasing out the devils."

14. For an explanation of the four humors, see Douglas, 8–9.

15. Bourgot's and Verdung's confession is much too long to include here. For full details, see Weyer, 511–514.

16. As Douglas points out, Weyer got this idea from Giovanni Battista Della Porta, who published *Natural Magic or Natural Miracles* in 1560 (272). In Book Three, Chapter 17, Weyer cites a passage from Della Porta's book dealing with the ointments used by a witch and the hallucinations involving night flight and traveling to the otherworld that she experienced afterward while asleep (225–226). To my knowledge, however, Della Porta did not expand this link between ointments and hallucinations to include delusions regarding werewolf transformations.

17. Quoted by Summers (76) from Bodin, *De la démonomanie des sorciers*, n.p.

18. For a full discussion of the *Canon Episcopi*, see Chapter Two.

19. Quoted by Summers (76) from Bodin, *De la démonomanie des sorciers*, n.p.

20. Quoted by Milin (123) from Bodin, *De la démonomanie des sorciers*, 106–107.

21. Extracts from Pierre des Hayes (Paris, 1574) edition of "L'arret du 18 janvier 1574 contre Gilles Garnier" can be found in Milin, 125–126. An English translation of the Sens edition is available in Summers, 226–228. Both documents follow very closely what is found in Bodin's account, adding only a few details here and there.

22. Quoted by Milin (123–124) from Bodin, *De la démonomanie des sorciers*, 106–107.

23. Quoted by Milin (124) from Bodin, *De la démonomanie des sorciers, 106–107.*

24. See Chapter Three.

25. See Chapter Three.

26. See Chapter One.

27. Book V, 92–102. Reprinted in Otten, 115–126.

28. See Chapter Two.

29. According to Mack P. Holt, there was one last war of religion in France that began in 1610 and continued until 1629 (173–79).

30. Summers presents this portion of the account in the following manner: "that only half an hour before a huge wolf had snatched up a little girl who was playing at the door of her hut," although there is nothing in the text to indicate that the little girl had been playing (Summers, 95).

31. To this account, Summers adds the following: "Their teeth gleamed sharp and white; their red tongues hung from their hot panting jaws; their eyes glinted horribly; and the grey fur bristled as they ran. It seemed as though it were a hunt of demons who passed in headlong course" (Summers, 96). This sensational description does not appear in Prieur's text.

32. The manuscript is indistinct here; more specifically the second consonant could be either an "s"— which resembles an elongated "f" in this manuscript — or an "l." Thus, the word could be "failoit," but "faisoit" makes more sense in the context of the sentence and within the larger context of the paragraph.

33. The alternate translation, if the word were "failoit," would be "almost," in which case "eat" would be "eating" ("who was almost eating human flesh"). See previous endnote regarding manuscript.

34. *Escus*, or "crowns," were an ancient form of money.

35. A lamia was a female vampire or a monster with the body of a serpent and the head and breasts of a woman. Like the vampire, this monster also sucked the blood of humans, particularly that of children.

36. The ellipses in this passage are due to an ink blot, or possibly thumb print, which obscures some of the words on four lines on one page of my copy of the text.

37. Prieur may also have intended "rabies" here, as "rage" translates either as "rage" (anger) or as "rabies."

38. Because of the ellipses in the original, it is impossible to provide a coherent translation of a major portion of one sentence, from "trop bien" to the next sentence, which begins with "Mais." The words in italics are from Summers' representation of the text (97).

39. In this last sentence, James is most likely alluding to the devil with the phrase "the author of all lyes." I have not, however, been able to determine the meaning of the phrase that precedes it: "but as to their hauing and hyding of their hard & schellie sloughes, I take that to be but eiked, by vncertaine report." It appears that James might be attributing some blame as well to the devil, but without knowing the meaning of the phrase cited, I can only speculate.

40. Quoted by Milin (103) from Chauvincourt, *Discours de la lycanthropie*, 15.

41. See Chapter Five for a full discussion of *Melion*.

42. See Chapter Seven.

43. Quoted in Milin (103–104) from Chauvincourt, *Discours de la lycanthropie*, 16.

44. Livonia is a region that includes southern Latvia and northern Estonia.

45. Milin never explains this comment but merely quotes the passage from Chauvincourt's treatise.

46. Quoted in Milin (122) from Chauvincourt, *Discours de la lycanthropie*, 21.

47. According to Gerhild Scholz Williams, *L'Incrédulité et mescreance des sortilèges* is "a résumé and extension" of his first two witch tracts, *Tableau de l'inconstance de toutes choses* and *Tableau de l'inconstance des mauvais anges et demons*. See Introduction to Pierre de Lancre's *On the Inconstancy of Witches*, xxviii.

48. Translated in Summers (230) from Lancre, *L'Incrédulité et mécréance du sortilège*, 785 sqq.

49. Quoted in Douglas (156–157) from Lancre, *L'Incrédulité et mécréance des sortilèges*, n.p.

50. Quoted by Milin (126–124) from Chauvincourt, *Discours de la lycantropie*, 18–20.

51. A harquebuse is a matchlock gun.

52. Quoted by Milin (127) from Chauvincourt, *Discours de la lycantropie*, 18–20.

53. Quoted by Milin (139) from Chauvincourt, *Discours de la lycantropie*, n.p.

54. The Conciergerie, which is the medieval part of the Palais de Justice on the Île de la Cité in Paris, was used as a prison beginning in the fourteenth century.

55. Quoted by Milin (136) from Chauvincourt, *Discours de la lycantropie*, 18–19.

56. Quoted by Milin (136) from the *Journal de Pierre de L'Estoile*, 1598.

57. Quoted by Milin (127, 159–60) from Chauvincourt, *Discours de la lycantropie*, 20.

58. E. Allen Ashwin translated *Discours des Sorciers* as An *Examen of Witches*. All English quotations will be from Ashwin's 1929 translation of Bouget's treatise, unless otherwise noted.

59. See Douglas, 158. Douglas indicates that Boguet made this claim "in his later writings" but he does not cite a source and lists no other work by Boguet other than his *Discours des sorciers*.

60. For full information on *Bisclavret*, see Chapter Four.

61. See Chapter Two.

62. Augustine referred to the entity that actually committed the deeds — the illusion that appeared to be a werewolf— as the phantasm. See Chapter Two.

63. Boguet gives several other examples of cannibalism. See 152–153.

64. All citations from Lancre's work will be from Harriet Stone and Gerhild Scholz Williams' translation, *On the Inconstancy of Witches: Pierre de Lancre's Tableau de l'inconstance des mauvais anges et demons (1612).*

65. At the beginning of Book 4, Lancre states that he decided *not* to provide the "actual texts of the appellate courts" word-for-word, "omitting and changing nothing" (268) because they were spoken, not written, and recorded by a transcriber as Lord Daffis, the first president of the court of the Parlement of Bordeaux, spoke and could therefore be incorrect (268). In addition, documents were missing. On the very next page, however, he notes that he is presenting the "principal and most important parts of this case that will clarify what he [Lord Daffis] said about it, taken word for word from the trial, just as it is recorded in the documents of the court of the *Parlement* of Bordeaux, without adding anything to it or omitting anything" (268). Given these contradictions, it is difficult to know how much, if at all, Lancre has changed Daffis' words. When citing from Lancre's text, I will follow the convention of referring to Lancre, rather than Daffis, keeping in mind that Daffis may indeed be the person who made these statements.

66. See Chapter One for a discussion of the werewolf in *Satyricon* and the Arcadian werewolves. See Chapter Four for Bisclavret and Chapter Five for Melion.

67. See Chapter Seven.

68. See Chapter Three.

69. See Chapter Seven.

70. The term "werewolfery," which is not my own, but was used by Montague Summers (232), is particularly appropriate and inclusive for referring to all the crimes and behaviors that a werewolf might engage in.

71. At least there is no evidence of this kind of testimony in the court report as it is conveyed to us via Lancre's treatise.

72. Two additional editions were published in the seventeenth century: Louiys Coste's 1620 edition, *L'Histoire dv noble prevx et vaillant chevalier Gvillaume de Palerne et de la belle Melior. Leqvel Gvillaume de Palerne fut fils du Roy de Cecille. Et par fortune & merueilleuse aduenture deuint vacher. Et finablement fut empereur de Rome sous la conduicte d'vn Loupgarou fils au Roy d'Espaigne. XIIII F.*; and the widow Coste's 1634 edition, *L'histoire dv noble, prevx et vaillant chevalier Guillaume de Palerne & de la belle Melior. Lequel Guillaume de Palerne fut fils du Roy de Cecille. Et par fortune & merveilleuse adventure deuint vacher. Et finalement fut Empereur de Rome sous la conduite d'vn Loupgarou fils du Roy d'Espaigne. XIIII F.* The titles of all four editions may be translated loosely as "*The Story of the noble, courageous and valiant knight Guillaume de Palerne and of the beautiful Melior. This Guillaume de Palerne was the son of the king of Sicily and through fortune and marvelous adventure became a cowherd. Led by a werewolf who was the son of the king of Spain, Guillaume finally became Emperor of Rome.*"

73. See Introduction to Manolis' edition of *Guillaume de Palerne: Les Versions en Prose*, 16.

74. Only a fragment remains of this version. See O'Rahilly's Introduction to *Eachtra Uilliam: An Irish Version of William of Palerne*, x.

75. *Eachtra Uilliam: An Irish Version of William of Palerne.*

76. The translator is identified only by means of an acrostic at the end of the romance.

Chapter Nine

1. "What this beast signifies," *Guillaume de Palerne*, v. 7270.

2. See Morris, 65–66.

3. Quoted in Morris, 66.

4. Abelard wrote about intention and sin in *Ethics: or, Know Yourself.* See Morris, 75.

5. For further information on this subject, see Morris, 67–70.

6. As Morris points out, Alexander and Soredamors engage in such monologues in Chrétien de Troyes' *Cligés* (76). We see something similar with Guillaume and Melior in *Guillaume de Palerne.*

7. On the new interest on the individual and individual identity, see Cantor 203–48 and Morris 64–95.

8. See Bynum, 27–29.

9. For further reading on the constancy and changeability of identity in *Guillaume de Palerne*, see Sconduto, *Metamorphosis and Identity*, especially 103–268, 308–332.

10. See Kelly, 146–204. For additional reading, see Jacques Le Goff's essay "The Marvelous in the Medieval West" in *The Medieval Imagination*, 27–44.

11. *Holy Bible, King James Version*, Ezek. 22:27.

12. The Consolation of Philosophy, x.

13. See Chapter One.

14. See Chapter One.

15. The First Crusade began in 1096 and ended in 1102.

16. For quotations from Fulcher of Chartre's *Historia Hierosolymitana* (*History of the Expedition to Jerusalem*) the anonymous *Gesta Fancorum et Aliorum Hierosolimitanorum* (*Deeds of the Franks and other pilgrims to Jerusalem*) and Raymond d'Aguilier's *Historia Francorum Qui Ceperunt Iherusalem* (*History of the Franks who captured Jerusalem*) regarding the cannibalism at Ma'arra an–Numan in December 1098, see

Heng, 22–23. Heng also discusses other possible incidences of crusader cannibalism in Antioch in June 1098 (23–25).

17. For readings on this concern, see Bynum, fn. 119, 244–45.

18. See Chapter Three.

19. See Chapter Seven for a complete analysis of the motif of the *goule baee.*

20. See Chapters Four, Five, Six, and Seven. Jeffrey Cohen offers another possible function of the werewolf motif when he suggests that the werewolf in *Topographia Hibernica* serves as a metaphor for the Irish people: "when the episode is taken as it rather starkly stands in the text's first version, unadorned and uninterpreted, it is difficult not to see in the bodies of the Irish werewolves the flesh of Irish race.... The Irish inside their wolfskins are not very different from the treacherous, plunder-driven Irish inside their human forms. Their lycanthropy only makes visible in their bodies what they already are, and perhaps that is why we never learn why the villagers should have earned a saint's curse" (86–87).

21. See Potter, 234.

22. See Lancre, 271.

23. Holt quotes this passage from Nicolas Froumenteau's *Le secret des finances de France ... pour ouvrir les moyens legitimes et necessaires de payer les dettes du Roy, descharger ses sujets des subsides imposez depuis trente un ans et recouvrer tous les deniers prins a Sa Maiesté* ([Paris], 1581), part iii, 377–80. According to Holt, Nicolas Froumentau is a fictitious name that the author, a "financial officer who worked in the royal treasury," used to protect his identity (195).

24. See Holt (196, 197,199) for the data for representative cities.

25. For information on how the religious wars affected the life of ordinary people, see Max P. Holt's *The French Wars of Religion, 1562–1629.*

26. See Chapter Eight.

27. D'Aubigné began writing *Les Tragiques* in 1577 and completed the first version in 1589, although he did not publish the work until 1616.

28. Holt is quoting this from an essay by Mark Greengrass, "The Later Wars of Religion in the French Midi," in Peter Clark, ed., *The European Crisis of the 1590s: Essays in Comparative History* (London, 1985), 117.

29. Quoted in Holt (19) from Gabrielle Berthoud, *Antoine Maracourt, réformateur et pamphlétaire: du 'Livres des marchands' aux placards de 1534* (Geneva, 1973), 287–9.

30. All citations will be from the Villey-Saulnier edition. All translations are mine.

31. "Divine Liturgy of St. Mark," *The Catholic Encyclopedia.*

32. See Holt for quotations from some of these pamphlets (210).

Bibliography

Primary Sources

Ambrose. "On His Brother Satyrus." In *Funeral Orations by Saint Gregory Nazianzen and Saint Ambrose.* Trans. Leo P. McCauley, John J. Sullivan, Martin R.P. McGuire and Roy J. Deferrari. Fathers of the Church 22. Washington, D.C.: Fathers of the Church, 1953.

Apollodorus. *Gods and Heroes of the Greeks: The Library of Apollodorus.* Trans. Michael Simpson. Amherst: University of Massachusetts Press, 1976.

Apuleius. *The Golden Ass.* Trans. P.G. Walsh. Oxford's World Classics. Oxford, England: Oxford University Press, 1994.

"*Arthur and Gorlagon.*" Trans. Frank A. Milne. Notes Alfred Nutt. *Folk-Lore* 15 (1904): 40–67. Rpt. in Otten 234–255.

Arthur and Gorlagon: Versions of the Werewolf's Tale. Ed. G[eorge] L[yman]. Kittredge. [Harvard] *Studies and Notes in Philology and Literature* 8 (1903): 149–275. Rpt. New York: Haskell House, 1966.

Augustine, Saint. *The City of God.* Trans. Marcus Dods. Intro. Thomas Merton. New York: Modern Library, 1950.

Béroul. *The Romances of Tristran by Béroul: A Poem of the Twelfth Century.* Ed. A[lfred] Ewert. 2 vols. Oxford: Blackwell and Mott, 1939, 1970.

Bodin, Jean. *De la démonomanie des sorciers.* Paris: n.p., 1587.

Boethius. *The Theological Tractates.* Trans. H.F. Stewart, E.K. Rand. *The Consolation of Philosophy.* Trans. I.T. Rev. H.F. Stewart. Loeb Classical Library. 1918. Cambridge: Harvard University Press, 1962.

Boguet, Henry. *An Examen of Witches Drawn from various trials of many in this sect in the district of Saint Oyan de Joux commonly known as Saint Claude in the county of Burgundy including the procedure necessary to a judge in trials for witchcraft...by Henry Boguet, chief Judge in the said county.* Ed. Montague Summers. Trans. E. Allen Ashwin. 1929. New York: Barnes & Noble, 1971.

Chauvincourt, Beauvoys de. *Discours de la lycantropie* [sic] *ou de la transmutation des hommes en loups.* Paris: n.p., 1599.

Chrétien de Troyes. *Erec et Énide.* Ed. Mario Roques. Classiques Français du Moyen Âge 80. Paris: Champion, 1952.

D'Aubigné, Agrippa. *Les Tragiques.* 1616. Paris: Garnier-Flammarion, 1968.

Eachtra Uilliam: An Irish Version of William of Palerne. Ed. and trans. Cecile O'Rahilly. Dublin, Ireland: Dublin Institute for Advanced Studies, 1949.

The Epic of Gilgamesh: A New Translation, Analogues, Criticism. Trans. and ed. Benjamin

Foster. "The Sumerian Gilgamesh Poems." Trans. Douglas Frayne. "The Hittite Gilgamesh." Trans. Gary Beckman. New York: Norton, 2001.
Gervase of Tilbury. *Otia Imperialia: Recreation for an Emperor.* Ed. and trans. S.E. Banks and J.W. Binns. Oxford Medieval Texts. Oxford, England: Clarendon Press, 2002.
Gilgamesh: Translated from the Sîn-Leqi-Unninnī Version. Trans. John Gardner, John Maier, and Richard A. Henshaw. New York: Vintage, 1985.
Guillaume d'Auvergne. *Opera Omnia.* Paris: 1674. Vol. I. Frankfurt: Minerva, 1963.
Guillaume de Palerne. Ed. H[enri] Michelant. Société des Anciens Textes Français 5. Paris: Firmin-Didot, 1876.
Guillaume de Palerne: The Ancient English Romance of William the Werwolf. Ed. Frederick Madden. 1832. New York: Burt Franklin, 1970.
Guillaume de Palerne: An English Translation of the 12th Century French Verse Romance. Trans. and ed. by Leslie A. Sconduto. Jefferson, NC: McFarland, 2004.
Guillaume de Palerne: Roman du XIIIe siècle. Ed. Alexandre Micha. Textes Littéraires Français. Genève: Droz, 1990.
Guillaume de Palerne: Les Versions en Prose. Ed. John C. Manolis. Diss. Florida State University, 1976.
The Holy Bible Containing the Old and New Testaments; Commonly Known as the Authorized (King James) Version. Philadelphia: National Bible Press, 1958.
James I. *Daemonologie, 1597 [by] King Kames the First; Newes from Scotland, declaring the damnable life and death of Doctor Fian, a notable sorcerer who was burned at Edenbrough in Ianuary last, 1591.* Ed. G. B. Harrison. Elizabethan and Jacobean Quartos. 1922–1926. New York: Barnes & Noble, 1966.
The King's Mirror. (*Speculum Regale — Konungs Skuggsjá:*); Translated from the Old Norwegian. Trans. Laurence Marcellus Larson. Scandinavian Monographs 3. New York: American-Scandinavian Foundation; London: Oxford University Press, 1917.
Kramer, Heinrich, and James Sprenger. *Malleus Maleficarum.* Trans. Montague Summer. 1928. London: Arrow, 1971.
Les Lais anonymes des XIIe et XIIIe siècles: Édition critique de quelques lais bretons. Ed. Prudence Mary O'Hara Tobin. Publications Romanes et Françaises 143. Genève: Droz, 1976.
Lais fëeriques des XIIe et XIIIe siècles. Trans. Alexandre Micha. Le Moyen Âge. Paris: Flammarion, 1992.
Lancre, Pierre de. *L'Incrédulité et mécréance des sortilèges.* Paris: n.p., 1622.
_____. *On the Inconstancy of Witches: Pierre de Lancre's Tableau de l'inconstance des mauvais anges et demons (1612).* Gen. Ed. Gerhild Scholz Williams. Assoc. Ed. Michaela Giesenkirchen and John Morris. Trans. Harriet Stone and Gerhild Scholz Williams. Medieval and Renaissance Texts and Studies 307. Tempe, AZ: Arizona Center for Medieval and Renaissance Studies–Brepols, 2006.
The Malleus Maleficarum. Ed. and trans. P.G. Maxwell-Stuart. Manchester, England: Manchester University Press, 2007.
Marie de France. *Les Lais de Marie de France.* Ed. Jean Rychner. Classiques Français du Moyen Âge 93. Paris: Champion, 1966.
_____. *Lais de Marie de France.* Ed. Karl Warnke. Trans. Laurence Harf-Lancner. Lettres Gothiques. Paris: Libraire Générale Française, 1990.
_____. *Marie de France Lais.* Ed. Alfred Ewert. 1944. London: Bristol Classic, 1995.
Montaigne, Michel de. *Les Essais.* Ed. Pierre Villey and V[erdun]-L[ouis] Saulnier. Paris : Presses Universitaires de France, 1965.
Ovid (Publius Ovidius Naso). *The Metamorphoses.* Trans. Horace Gregory. New York: Mentor-NAL, 1960.
Pausanias. *Description of Greece.* Trans. W.H.S. Jones. 1933. Cambridge: Harvard University Press, 1960.

Petronius. Trans. Michael Heseltine. Rev. E. H. Warmington. Seneca. *Apocolocyntosis*. Trans. W. H. D. Rouse. Loeb Classical Library 15. 1913. Cambridge: Harvard University Press, 1969.

Plato. *Complete Works*. Ed. John M. Cooper. Indianapolis: Hackett, 1997.

Pliny. *Natural History; With an English Translation in Ten Volumes*. Vol. III Libri VIII–XI. Trans. R. Rackham. Loeb Classical Library. 1940. Cambridge, MA: Harvard University Press, 1947.

Prieur, Claude de Laval. *Dialogue de la Lycanthropie, ou transformation d'hommes en loups, vulgairement dit loups-garous, et si telle se peut faire*. Louvain, 1596.

The Romance of William of Palerne (Otherwise Known as the Romance of "William and the Werwolf"). Ed. Walter Skeat. Early English Text Society, Extra Series 1. 1867. London: Kegan Paul, Trench, Trubner, & Co., 1890.

Scot, Reginald. *The Discoverie of Witchcraft*. 1584. Arundel: Centaur, 1964. Booke V, 92–102 : Rpt. in Otten 115–126.

Tertullian. *Tertullian: Apologetical Works and Minucius Felix Octavius*. Fathers of the Church 10. New York: Fathers of the Church, 1950.

Thomas Aquinas, Saint. *Summa Theologica: Complete English Edition in Five Volumes*. Trans. Fathers of the English Dominican Province. Vol. 1[a] QQ. 1–119. 1911. Westminster, MD: Christian Classics, 1981.

Virgil. *Virgil / with an English Translation by H. Rushton Fairclough*. Vol. 1. Loeb Classical Library. Rev. ed. Cambridge, MA: Harvard University Press, 1947.

Wace. *Wace's* Roman de Brut*: A History of the British; Text and Translation*. Ed. and Trans. Judith Weiss. Exeter Medieval English Texts and Studies. 1999. Exeter, England: University of Exeter Press, 2002.

Weyer, Johann. *Witches, Devils, and Doctors in the Renaissance: Johann Weyer, De praestigiis daemonum*. Gen. ed. George Mora. Assoc. ed. Benjamin Kohl. Trans. John Shea. Medieval & Renaissance Texts & Studies 73. Binghamton, NY: Center for Medieval and Early Renaissance Studies, 1991.

William of Malmesbury. *Gesta Regum Anglorum: The History of the English Kings*. Ed. and Trans. R.A.B. Mynors. Completed by R.M. Thomson and M. Winterbottom. Oxford Medieval Texts. 2 vols. Oxford, England: Clarendon Press, 1998.

William of Palerne: an alliterative romance. Ed. G. H. V. Bunt. Groningen, Netherlands: Bouma's Boekhuis, 1985.

Secondary Sources

Anglo, Sydney, ed. *The Damned Art: Essays in the Literature of Witchcraft*. London: Routledge & Kegan Paul, 1977.

_____. "Evident Authority and Authoritative Evidence: The *Malleus Maleficarum*." Anglo, *The Damned Art: Essays in the Literature of Witchcraft*, 1–31.

_____. "Reginald Scot's *Discoverie of Witchcraft:* Scepticism and Sadduceeism." Anglo, *The Damned Art: Essays in the Literature of Witchcraft*, 106–39.

Bacou, Mihaela. "De quelques loups-garous." Harf-Lancner, *Métamorphose et bestiaire* 29–50.

Bailey, H[oward] W. "*Bisclavret* in Marie de France." *Cambridge Medieval Celtic Studies* 1 (1981): 95–97.

Barkan, Leonard. *The Gods Made Flesh: Metamorphosis and the Pursuit of Paganism*. New Haven, CT: Yale University Press, 1986.

Baxter, Christopher. "Johann Weyer's *De Praestigiis Daemonum:* Unsystematic Psychopathology." Anglo, *The Damned Art: Essays in the Literature of Witchcraft*, 53–75.

Benkov, Edith Joyce. "The Naked Beast: Clothing and Humanity in *Bisclavret.*" *Chimères* 19 (1988): 27–43.

Bennett, R.E. "*Arthur and Gorlagon*, the Dutch *Lancelot*, and St. Kentigern." *Speculum* 13 (1938): 68–75.

Bertier de Sauvigny, G[uillaume] de. *Histoire de France*. Paris: Flammarion, 1999.

Bloch, Marc. *Feudal Society*. Trans. L.A. Manyon. 2 vols. Chicago: University of Chicago Press, 1961.

Bogaert, J., and J. Passeron. *Moyen-Âge*. Les Lettres Françaises. Paris: Éditions Magnard, 1954.

Boivin, Jeanne-Marie. "Le Prêtre et les loups-garous: Un Épisode de la *Topographia Hibernica* de Giraud de Barri." Harf-Lancner, *Métamorphose et bestiaire* 51–69.

Bruford, Alan. *Gaelic Folk-Tales and Mediæval Romances: A Study of the Early Modern Irish 'Romantic Tales' and Their Oral Derivatives*. Dublin, Ireland: Folklore of Ireland Society, 1969.

Burgess, Glyn Sheridan. *Contribution à l'étude du vocabulaire pré-courtois*. Publications Romanes et Françaises 10. Genève: Droz, 1970.

_____. *The Lais of Marie de France: Text and Context*. Athens: University of Georgia Press, 1987.

Bynum, Caroline Walker. *Metamorphosis and Identity*. New York: Zone, 2001.

Cantor, Norman F. *The Meaning of the Middle Ages*. Boston: Allyn and Bacon, 1973.

Carey, John. "Werewolves in Medieval Ireland." Cambrian Medieval Celtic Studies 44 (2002): 37–72.

Chotzen, Th. M. "*Bisclavret.*" *Études Celtiques* 2 (1937): 33–44.

Clark, Stuart. "King James's *Daemonologie:* Witchcraft and Kingship." Anglo, *The Damned Art: Essays in the Literature of Witchcraft*, 156–181.

Cohen, Jeffrey Jerome. *Hybridity, Identity and Monstrosity in Medieval Britian: On Difficult Middles*. The New Middle Ages. New York: Palgrave Macmillan, 2006.

Davidson, H. R. Ellis. "Shape-changing in the Old Norse Sagas." Harf-Lancner, *Métamorphose et bestiaire* 142–160.

Delcourt, Denyse. *L'Éthique du changement dans le roman français du XIIe siècle*. Histoire des idées et critique littéraire 276. Genève: Droz, 1990.

"Divine Liturgy of St. Mark." *The Catholic Encyclopedia*. Ed. Kevin Knight. 2007. 18 March 2008 <http://www.newadvent.org/fathers/0718.htm>.

Douglas, Adam. *The Beast Within: A History of the Werewolf*. New York: Avon, 1992.

Dubost, Francis. *Aspects fantastiques de la littérature narrative médiévale XIIeme–XIIIeme siècles): L'Autre, l'ailleurs, l'autrefois*. 2 vols. Paris: Champion, 1991.

Dunn, Charles W. *The Foundling and the Werwolf: A Literary-Historical Study of* Guillaume de Palerne. University of Toronto Department of English Studies and Texts 8. Toronto: University of Toronto Press, 1960.

Dunton-Downer, Leslie. "Wolf Man." Cohen, Jeffrey Jerome and Bonnie Wheeler, eds. *Becoming Male in the Middle Ages*. New York: Garland, 2000.

Eckels, Richard Preston. "Greek Wolf-Lore." Diss. University of Pennsylvania, 1937.

Faure, M. "Le *Bisclavret* de Marie de France, une histoire suspecte de loup-garou." *Revues des Langues Romances* 83 (1978): 345–56.

Freeman, Michelle A. "Dual Natures and Subverted Glosses: Marie de France's 'Bisclavret.'" *Romance Notes* 25 (1985): 288–301.

Friedman, Lionel J. "Occulta cordis." *Romance Philology* 11 (1957): 103–119.

Grimes, E. Margaret, ed. *The Lays of Desiré, Graelent and Melion: Edition of the Texts with an Introduction*. Diss. Columbia University, 1928.

Harf-Lancner, Laurence. "De la métamorphose au moyen âge." Harf-Lancner, *Metamorphose et bestiaire* 3–25.

_____. *Les Fées au moyen âge: Morgane et Mélusine; La naissance des fées*. Nouvelle Bibliothèque du Moyen Âge 8. Genève: Slatkine, 1984.

_____, ed. *Métamorphose et bestiaire fantastique au moyen âge*. Collection de l'École Normale Supérieure de Jeunes Filles 28. Paris: École Normale Supérieure de Jeunes Filles, 1985.

_____. "La Métamorphose illusoire: des théories chrétiennes de la métamorphose aux images médiévales du loup-garou." *Annales Économies Sociétés Civilisations* 40 (1985): 208–226.

Heng, Geraldine. *Empire of Magic: Medieval Romance and the Politics of Cultural Fantasy*. New York: Columbia University Press, 2003.

Hoepffner, Ernest. "The Breton Lais." Loomis, *Arthurian Literature* 112–121.

_____. *Les Lais de Marie de France*. Paris: Librairie A.-G. Nizet, 1971.

Hoffman, George. "Anatomy of the Mass: Montaigne's 'Cannibals.'" *PLMA* 117 (2002): 207–221.

Holt, Mack P. *The French Wars of Religion, 1562–1629*. Cambridge, MA: Cambridge University Press, 1995.

Holmyn, Robyn A. "Metamorphosis and Return in the Lays of *Bisclavret and Melion*." *South Carolina Modern Language Review* 4 (2005): n. pag.

Hopkins, Amanda. "*Bisclavret* to *Biclarel* Via *Melion* and *Bisclaret*: The Development of a Misogynous *Lai*." *The Court Reconvenes: Courtly Literature Across the Disciplines; Selected Papers from the Ninth Triennial Congress of the International Courtly Literature Society, University of British Columbia 25–31 July 1998*. Ed. Barbara K. Altmann and Carleton W. Carroll. Cambidge: D.S. Brewer, 2003.

Kelly, Douglas. *The Art of Medieval French Romance*. Madison: University of Wisconsin Press, 1992.

Krappe, A. Haggerty. "*Arthur and Gorlagon*." *Speculum* 8 (1933): 209–222.

Kratz, Dennis M. "Fictus Lupus: The Werewolf in Christian Thought." *Classical Folia: Studies in the Christian Perpetuation of the Classics* 30 (1976): 57–80.

Lea, Henry Charles. *Materials Toward a History of Witchcraft*. 3 vols. Philadelphia: University of Pennsylvania Press, 1939. New York: Thomas Yoseloff, 1957.

Lecouteux, Claude. *Mélusine et le Chevalier au cygne*. Paris: Imago, 1997.

_____. *Witches, Werewolves, and Fairies*: Shapeshifters and Astral Doublers in the Middle Ages. Trans. Clare Frock. Rochester, VT: Inner Traditions, 2003. Trans. of *Fées, sorcières et loups-garous au Moyen Age: Histoire du double*. Paris: Imago, 2001.

Le Goff, Jacques. *The Medieval Imagination*. Trans. Arthur Goldhammer. Chicago: University of Chicago Press, 1988.

Loomis, Roger Sherman, ed. *Arthurian Literature in the Middle Ages: A Collaborative History*. Oxford, England: Oxford University Press, 1959.

_____. "The Latin Romances." Loomis, *Arthurian Literature* 472–479.

Loth, J[oseph]. "*Le Lai du Bisclavret*: le sens de ce nom et son importance." *Revue Celtique* 44 (1927): 300–307.

Maertens, Guido. "Augustine's Image of Man." *Images of Man in Ancient and Medieval Thought: Studia Gerardo Verbeke ab amicis et collegis dicata*. Symbolae Facultatis Litterarum et Philosophiae Lovaniensis Ser. A Vol. 1. Eds. F. Bosser, et al. Leuven, Belgium: Leuven University Press, 1976. 175–198.

Malone, Kemp. *Rose and Cypress*. *PMLA* 43 (1928): 397–446.

McGinn, Bernard. "The Human Person as Image of God: II. Western Christianity." *Christian Spirituality: Origins to the Twelfth Century*. Eds. Bernard McGinn and John Meyendorff. New York: Crossroad, 1985. 312–330.

McKeehan, Irene Pettit. "*Guillaume de Palerne*: A Medieval 'Best Seller.'" *PMLA* 41 (1926): 785–810.

Ménard, Philippe. "Les Histoires de loup-garou au moyen âge." *Symposium in honorem prof. M. de Riquer*. Barcelona: Universitat de Barcelona Quaderns Crema, 1984. 209–38.

_____. *Les Lais de Marie de France: Contes d'amour et d'aventure du moyen âge.* Littératures Modernes. Paris: Presses Universitaires de France, 1979.

Milin, Gaël. *Les Chiens de Dieu: La représentation du loup-garou en Occident Xie–XIXe siècles.* Centre de Recherche Bretonne et Celtique: Cahiers de Bretagne Occidentale 13. Brest: Université de Bretagne Occidentale, 1993.

Morris, Colin. *The Discovery of the Individual 1050–1200.* 1972. Medieval Academy Reprints for Teaching 19. Toronto: University of Toronto Press, 1987.

Otten, Charlotte F., ed. *A Lycanthropy Reader: Werewolves in Western Culture: Medical Cases, Diagnoses, Descriptions; Trial Records, Historical Accounts, Sightings; Philosophical and Theological Approaches to Metamorphosis; Critical Essays on Lycanthropy; Myths and Legends; Allegory.* Syracuse, NY: Syracuse University Press, 1986.

Pappa, Joseph. "The Bewildering Bounded/Bounding *Bisclavret*, or Lycanthropy, Lieges, and a Lotta Leeway in Marie de France." *Crossings; A Counter-Disciplinary Journal* 4 (2000): 117–43.

Paris, Gaston. *La Littérature française au moyen âge (XIe–XIVe siècle).* 1888. Bibliothèque de Littérature. Paris: Hachette, 1905.

Potter, David, ed. and trans. *The French Wars of Religion: Selected Documents.* New York: St. Martin's, 1997.

Quénet, Sophie. "Mises en récit d'une métamorphose: Le Loup-garou." *Le Merveilleux et la magie dans la littérature.* Ed. Gérard Chandès. CERMEIL 2. Amersterdam, Netherlands: Rodopi, 1992. 137–63.

Rothschild, Judith. *Narrative Technique in the* Lais *of Marie de France: Themes and Variations; Vol. I.* North Carolina Studies in the Romance Languages and Literatures 139. Chapel Hill: University of North Carolina Press, 1974.

Russell, Jeffrey Burton. *Witchcraft in the Middle Ages.* Ithaca, NY: Cornell University Press, 1972.

Salisbury, Joyce E. *The Beast Within: Animals in the Middle Ages.* New York: Routledge, 1994.

Sayers, William. "*Bisclavret* in Marie de France: A Reply." *Cambridge Medieval Celtic Studies* 4 (1982): 77–82.

Schmitt, Jean-Claude. *The Holy Greyhound: Guinefort, Healer of Children Since the Thirteenth Century.* Trans. Martin Thom. Cambridge Studies in Oral and Literate Culture 6. Cambridge, England: Cambridge University Press; Paris: Éditions de la Maison des Sciences de l'Homme, 1983.

Sconduto, Leslie A. *Metamorphosis and Identity: The Individual in Society in* Guillaume de Palerne. Diss. Rutgers University, 1995.

Smith, Kirby Flower. "An Historical Study of the Werwolf in Literature." *PMLA* 9 (1894): 1–42.

Speer, Mary B. "Specularity in a Formulaic Frame Romance: 'The Faithful Greyhound' and the *Roman des Sept Sages.*" *Literary Aspects of Courtly Culture: Selected Papers from the Seventh Triennial Congress of the International Courtly Literature Society,...27 July–1 August 1992.* Eds. Donald Maddox and Sara Sturm-Maddox. [Bury St.-Edmonds]: Boydell and Brewer, 1994. 231–240.

Suard, François. "'Bisclauret' et les contes du loup-garou: Essai d'interprétation." *Marche Romane* 30 (1980): 267–76.

Summers, Montague. *Werewolf.* 1933. Whitefish, MT: Kessinger, 2003.

Viarre, Simone. *L'image et la pensée dans les* Metamorphoses *d'Ovide.* Publications de la Faculté des Lettres et Sciences Humaines de Paris, Séries Recherches, Tome 22. Paris: Presses Universitaires de France, 1964.

"Werewolf." Def. 1. *The Oxford English Dictionary.* 2nd ed. Oxford, England: Oxford University Press, 1989.

Williams, David. *Deformed Discourse: The Function of the Monster in Mediaeval Thought and Literature.* Montreal: McGill-Queen's University Press, 1996.

Index

Abelard 181, 209
Actaeon 7, 8, 44, 78, 92
Aesop's Fables 39
Affair of the Placards 196, 210
Akkadian 7
Alphonse 4, 64, 90–126, 130, 135, 157, 171, 179, 180, 181, 182, 183, 184, 185, 187, 188, 204, 205, 206, 207
Ambrose, Saint 2, 16, 17
Angers 160, 161, 162
Anglo, Sydney 127, 128, 130, 139, 207
animal skins (bear, deer, wolf) 27, 28, 29, 31, 103, 114, 120, 123, 144, 151, 169, 170, 171, 172, 175, 177, 202, 203, 205, 206, 210
Apollas 12
Apollodorus 201
Apuleius 17, 150, 201
Arcadia and the Arcadian werewolves 9, 12, 17, 42, 122, 132, 171, 184, 186, 201, 202, 209
Arnoullet, Olivier 178, 179
Arthur, King 57, 58, 59, 60, 65, 68, 70, 71, 72, 73, 74, 75, 76–89, 182, 186, 204, 206
Arthur and Gorlagon 3, 5, 76–89, 91, 92, 96, 104, 114, 115, 120, 123, 183, 204, 205, 206
Augustine, Saint 2, 17–19, 20, 21, 22, 23, 24, 25, 28, 30, 35, 36, 45, 52, 75, 76, 128, 129, 146, 152, 167, 173, 174, 182, 202, 208
Augustus, Emperor 9
Auvergne, wolves of 148–149

Bacou, Mihaela 87, 88, 89, 205
Barkan, Leonard 9, 10, 18, 25, 202
Baxter, Christopher 131
Benkov, Edith 55, 124, 125, 204
Bernard, Saint 181
Béroul 106, 206
Bisclavret and the *lai* of *Bisclavret* 3, 5, 13, 37, 39–56, 57, 58, 62, 63, 64, 65, 66, 70, 71, 72, 73, 74, 76, 78, 80, 81, 82, 83, 86, 88, 91, 92, 111, 114, 115, 116, 118, 120, 122, 124, 166, 171, 182, 183, 185, 187, 201, 203, 204, 205, 206, 208, 209
Bloch, Marc 45
Bocquet, Jacques 165, 168
Bodin, Jean 4, 134–138, 139, 140, 150, 155, 158, 164, 207
Boethius, Anicius Manlius Severinius 184, 185, 192
Boguet, Henri 5, 163–169, 208
Boivin, Jeanne-Marie 28, 31, 203
Bonfons, Nicolas 178, 179
Bourgot, Pierre 132–134, 137–138, 168, 170, 171, 207
Brande, Queen 91, 97, 98, 99, 119, 120, 121, 122, 123, 125, 182, 206
Bruckner, Matilda Tomaryn 53, 55
Burchard of Worms 3, 20, 21
Burgess, Glyn 101, 203, 204, 206
Bynum, Caroline Walker 1, 31, 68, 123, 180, 181, 182, 186, 206, 209, 210

Cain 54
Calogrenant 102
Canis 83; 204
cannibal and cannibalism 5, 9, 10, 12, 113, 137, 138, 144, 149, 150, 151, 153, 160, 161, 168, 169, 170, 172, 175, 180, 185, 186, 187, 188, 195, 196, 197, 198, 199, 200, 208, 209
Canon Episcopi 19–20, 128, 129, 135, 173, 202, 207
Cantor, Norman 181, 209
Carey, John 28, 32, 33, 34, 202, 203, 204
Charles IX 199
Chaucevaire 37, 38, 42, 204, 205
Chauvincourt, Beauvoys de 5, 156–163, 178, 208
Chrétien de Troyes 101, 102, 206, 209
Circe 16, 17, 167
City of God 17, 23, 24, 30, 181, 202
Clark, Stuart 153
clothes motif 3, 11, 12, 13, 37, 42, 43, 44, 45, 48, 51, 52, 62, 63, 64, 73, 75, 122, 123, 170, 171, 204
Cnut, King 1

Cohen, Jeffrey 210
Constantinople 133, 134
Corrector 20, 21, 23
Coutras 169, 174
Croquant, Pierre (Pierre Grainier or Pierre Grenier) 170, 171, 172, 176

Daemenetus 12, 202
Daemonologie 5, 153–156
Daffis, Lord 172, 209
Damarchus 201
D'Aubigné, Agrippa 191–195, 197, 210
De hominibus qui se vertunt in lupos (Men Who Change Themselves Into Wolves) 34
De Ingantaib Érenn (On the Wonders of Ireland) 33, 34, 35, 203
De la démonomanie des sorciers (Demonomania of Witches) 4–5, 135, 139, 155, 158, 207
De Mirabilibus Hibernie (On the Marvels of Ireland) 33
De Praestigiis Daemonum (Witches, Devils, and Doctors) 4, 131, 155, 207
De Universo 22, 202
Decretum Libri XX 20
Delcourt, Denyse 203
Dialogue de la Lycanthropie (Dialogue of Lycanthropy) 5, 141–153, 191, 195
Diana 7, 20, 44
Discours de la lycantropie (Treatise on Lycanthropy) 5, 156–163, 208
Discours des sorciers (An Examen of Witches) 5, 163–169, 208
Discoverie of Witchcraft 5, 139–141
disguise 28, 31, 32, 92, 101, 103, 111, 114, 123, 125, 144, 151, 153, 171, 202, 205, 206
Douglas, Adam 9, 12, 79, 131, 164, 165, 166, 201, 207, 208
Dubost, Francis 13, 22, 29, 37, 63, 65, 123, 185, 202
Dunn, Charles 100, 101, 205
Dunton-Downer, Leslie 186
Durand, Pierre 178, 179

Eckels, Richard Preston 201
Edict of Nantes 142
Embron, King 92, 94, 99, 109, 110, 112
Erec et Énide 101, 206
Espurgatoire seint Patriz (The Purgatory of Saint Patrick) 39
Eucharist 5, 18, 29, 30, 32, 186, 187, 188, 195, 196, 199, 202

fairy 64, 65, 102
Fauchet, Claude 39
Faure, M. 203, 204
Felise, Queen 92, 93, 95, 99, 101, 104, 113, 115, 116, 125, 205
First Crusade 5, 180, 185
Franche-Comté 130
Freeman, Michelle 43, 53, 204

Gaboriaut, Jeanne 169
Gaillard, Clauda 165, 168
Gargol 77, 81, 85, 87, 115, 183, 205
Garnier, Gilles 135–137, 166, 207
Gaultier, Jean-Pierre 200
Geoffrey of Monmouth 186, 187
Gerald of Wales 3, 26–32, 33, 34, 171, 182, 187, 202, 203
Gervase of Tilbury 3, 35–38, 42, 138, 158, 204, 205
Gesta regum Anglorum 21, 202
Gilgamesh, Epic of 1, 7, 8, 44, 78, 201
Golden Ass 17
Gorlagon 77–89, 91, 92, 99, 111, 124, 183, 185, 187, 204, 205
goule baee (mouth gaping open) 37, 92, 93, 98, 99, 107, 112–114, 119, 202, 205–206
Grainier, Pierre (le croquant or Pierre Croquant or Pierre Grenier) 170, 171, 172, 176
Grenier, Jean 169–178, 190
Grenier, Pierre 170, 171, 172, 176
Grimes, E. Margaret 63
Guibert of Nogent 180
Guigemar 39, 59, 203, 204
Guillaume and *Guillaume de Palerne* 4, 5, 32, 64, 67, 90–126, 130, 157, 171, 178, 179, 180, 181, 182, 183, 184, 187, 188, 202, 203, 204, 205, 206, 207, 209
Guillaume d'Auvergne (William of Paris) 3, 22, 23, 202, 207
Guinevere 76

Harf-Lancner, Laurence 38, 64, 65, 114, 202, 203
Heng, Geraldine 186, 187, 209
Henri IV 142, 169, 191
Herodotus 132
Historia Britonum (History of the British) 34
Historia Naturalis (Natural History) 12, 15
Historia Regum Britannie (History of the Kings of Britain) 186, 187
Hoepffner, Ernest 53, 54, 55, 68, 203, 204
Hoffman, George 198, 199
Holman, Robyn 68
Holt, Max P. 189, 190, 191, 207, 210
homage ceremony 45, 46, 50, 81, 115–119, 121, 132
Hopkins, Amanda 203, 204

Innocent VIII, Pope 127
Incrédulité et mécréance des sortilèges (Incredulity and Skepticism of Magic Spells) 160, 208
Irish werewolves 3, 26–35
Ishtar 7, 8, 13, 44, 92

James I of England, VI of Scotland 5, 153–156, 208
Jamguillaume, Clauda 165, 168
Jamprost, Clauda 165, 168

Kelly, Douglas 183, 209
Kittredge, George 77, 91, 204, 205
Konungs Skuggsjá (King's Mirror) 3, 32, 33, 34, 35
Kramer, Heinrich 4, 127–130, 139, 153, 154, 156, 188, 189, 207
Kratz, Dennis 38, 202

Lancelot 76
Lancre, Pierre de 5, 160, 161, 162, 169–178, 208, 209, 210
Lassie 84
Laustic 203
Lecouteux, Claude 203
Le Goff, Jacques 183, 209
L'Estoile, Pierre de 162–163, 208
Lord of the Forest 170, 171, 174, 177, 178
Loth, Joseph 40, 203
Lot's wife 30, 31, 139, 140, 141, 167
Lycaon, King 2, 9, 10, 12, 13, 37, 132, 166, 186, 201

Ma'arra an-Numan 186, 209
Malleus maleficarum (The Hammer of Witches) 4, 127–130, 139, 154, 188, 189, 207
Malone, Kemp 76, 79, 204
Manolis, John 178–179, 209
Marcourt, Antoine 196
Marie de France 39–56, 57, 59, 65, 66, 67, 70, 73, 79, 81, 85, 99, 116, 123, 187, 188, 201, 203, 204
Massacre of St. Bartholomew 189, 190
McKeehan, Irene 205, 206
Meath 26, 27, 202
medical explanations for lycanthropy 131, 134, 141, 167, 173
melancholy 131, 156
Melion and the *Lai de Melion* 3, 5, 57–75, 76, 78, 79, 80, 81, 82, 85, 88, 91, 92, 95, 96, 99, 104, 111, 114, 115, 120, 122, 123, 124, 157, 158, 171, 182, 183, 185, 187, 203, 204, 205, 206, 208, 209
Melior 101, 103, 104, 105, 106, 107, 110–115, 157, 171, 178, 202, 205, 206, 209
Melusine 36, 203
Melusinian tales 64–65
Ménard, Philippe 4, 13, 14, 29, 44, 45, 47, 64, 68, 91, 123, 201, 203, 205
Mesopotamia 7
Messina, Strait of 93, 109, 110, 111, 206
Micha, Alexandre 58, 59, 100, 101, 204, 205, 206
Michel de Montaigne 196–199
Milin, Gaël 128, 157, 158, 159, 169, 207, 208
miroir des princes (mirror for princes) 32, 125, 126, 203
Moeris 2, 8, 9, 13
moon 35, 36, 37, 149, 171, 175
Morganian tales 64–65, 102
Morris, Colin 209

Natalis 26, 32, 33, 34
Nebuchadnezzar (also Nabuchodonosor) 18, 36, 141, 156, 166, 167
Nero 10, 11, 143, 144, 151
Neuri 132
Niceros 12, 37, 138, 158

ointment 97, 120, 132, 134, 137, 160, 171, 207
Olaus Magnus 157, 158
Olympic Victors 12
On the Soul 15
Ossory werewolves 3, 26–32, 33, 34, 171, 187, 203
Otia Imperialia (Recreation for an Emperor) 3, 35, 38, 42, 138
Otten, Charlotte 27, 124, 202, 204, 207
Ovid 2, 8, 9, 10, 12, 37, 44, 78, 132, 146, 152, 166, 185, 201

Padua 138, 158
Paget, Thievenne 165, 168
Pappa, Joseph 202
Parlement of Bordeaux 169, 172, 173, 209
Parlement of Paris 162, 163
Patrick, Saint 32, 33, 34, 39
Paulus Aegineta 131
Pausanias 201
Perigord, wolves of 147–148, 195
Petronius 2, 10, 11, 12, 37, 42, 44, 138, 158, 171, 201
phantasm 19, 20, 23, 24, 25, 208
Philip Augustus, King 90
Plato 184, 185, 192
Pliny the Elder 2, 12, 15, 122, 186
Poirier, Marguerite 169, 170, 172, 173
Poligny (werewolves of) 132–134, 137–138, 166, 171
Potter, David 210
Potter, Harry 200
Praestantius 19
Prieur, Claude 5, 141–153, 155, 191, 195, 208

Quénet, Sophie 56, 63

Raimbaud de Pouget 36, 38, 80, 138, 158, 204
Regino 3, 19, 202
Republic 184
ring 3, 62, 63, 64, 65, 73, 74, 75, 121, 122, 157, 166
Roman du Brut 68, 204
Roques, Mario 101
Rothschild, Judith 53, 203, 204
Roulet, Jacques 159–163, 171
Rudel, Jaufré 61
Rychner, Jean 203

Satyricon 11, 37, 44, 138, 158, 171, 209
Sauvigny, Bertier de 189
Schmitt, Jean-Claude 202, 204

Scot, Reginald 5, 139–141, 154, 155, 156, 173
Simon Magus 21, 22, 25
Sin-leqe-unninni 7
Smith, Kirby 13, 44, 124, 201, 203
Speer, Mary 204
Sprenger, Jakob 127, 207
Suard, François 53, 201
submission motif 4, 45, 71, 73, 81, 91, 92, 115–119
Summa Theologica 23
Summers, Montague 21, 156, 201, 203, 207, 208, 209
sympathetic injury or wound 11, 34, 138, 166

Tableau de l'inconstance des mauvais anges et demons (On the Inconstancy of Witches) 5, 169–178, 208, 209
Tertullian 2, 15–16, 202
Third Crusade 90
Thomas Aquinas, Saint 3, 23–25, 128, 129
Tilhaire, Pierre du 170, 171, 172, 176
Tobin, Prudence 64, 65, 204, 205
Topographia Hibernica (Topography of Ireland) 3, 26, 32, 92, 210
Torleil 77, 87
Les Tragiques 191–195, 197, 210
transubstantiation 18, 31, 32, 187, 203
Trimalchio 11, 138

Verdung, Michel 132–134, 137–138, 170, 171, 207
versipellis (Latin) 1
Viarre, Simone 10
Virgil 2, 8–9, 201
Volsung Saga 28, 171, 203
vrykolakas (Greek) 1

Wace 68, 204
wars of religion 5, 131, 142, 188, 189–190, 191, 196, 198, 199, 200, 210
water into wine 30, 31
Werewolf's Tale 3, 4, 91, 204, 205
Weyer, Johann 4, 131–134, 141, 154, 155, 156, 167, 173, 207
William of Malmesbury 3, 21, 22, 202
William of Palerne 179, 209
William of Paris (Guillaume d'Auvergne) 3, 22, 23, 202, 207
witches, magic and sorcery 4, 5, 8, 9, 13, 17, 18, 22, 24, 25, 63, 73, 78, 92, 97, 98, 120, 121, 122, 124, 127, 130, 131, 132, 135, 139, 141, 153, 157, 161, 164, 165, 166, 167, 168, 169, 171, 174, 175, 176, 186, 188–189, 191, 196, 200

Yolande, Countess 90
Yonec 203
Yvain 102

Zeus 2, 9, 10, 12, 184, 186, 201